WHAT OTHERS ARE SAYING ABOUT THIS BOOK

"A rich and rewarding book."   —BETH GOEHRING, *The Literary Guild*

"*Mojo Triangle* is the seminal nexus of psychology, history, and aesthetics. It crystallizes the essence of Ernie K-Doe's quote, 'I'm not sure, but I'm almost positive, that all music came from New Orleans.' Black Top Records' CD entitled Neville-Ization is perhaps the best example of "The Gumbo That Keeps on Giving." Ditto for Otis Redding's original version of "Respect" that encapsulates the Memphis sound in "Great Balls of Fire." Dickerson's notion of genetic and cultural history is supported by Jung's psychological archetype. The fruits of natural expression are indeed country, blues, jazz, and rock 'n' roll."   —GREG GORMANOUS, PH.D.
Psychologist and Professor of Psychology
Louisiana State University at Alexandria

"In the search for a unified-field theory of American popular music, few journalists come as well equipped as James L. Dickerson. Blessed with the scene-setting panache of a natural storyteller, an eye for the telling detail, and the audacity to reach for the big picture, Dickerson has walked back out of the jungle bearing this remarkable, pioneering compendium. The "mojo triangle" of his title is what you get when you play connect-the-dots with Memphis, Nashville, and New Orleans: A multicultural musical stew, four kinds of holy ground, and—not incidentally—a land bisected by the Natchez Trace, ancient footpath of an Indian tribe whose vital antebellum contributions to black and white musical traditions are merely one of this book's many revelations. Again and again Dickerson dredges up forgotten or suppressed histories and teases out connections that other historians of southern music have missed. I learned a great deal from this book."   —ADAM GUSSOW, author
Mister Satan's Apprentice: A Blues Memoir and
Seems Like Murder Here: Southern Violence and the Blues Tradition

"*Mojo Triangle* asserts that while America's popular music may be worldwide in scope, it's all still being created in that mystical cauldron of the South. Mojo Triangle doesn't miss a single ingredient in analyzing the recipe—or the cooks. It dissects important and previously obscured elements as diverse as genetics and the influence of Native American culture on blues and rock 'n' roll."
—BROWN BURNETT, editor,
BlueSpeak Magazine

"*Mojo Triangle* is a very good book. Author Jim Dickerson, a southerner himself, has written a great, in-depth history of the area and its musical background…all aimed at the birthplace of American music. He hit it right on the button."
—SCOTTY MOORE,
Guitarist and Elvis' first manager

MOJO
TRIANGLE

Birthplace of Country, Blues, Jazz and Rock 'n' Roll

James L. Dickerson

SCHIRMER TRADE BOOKS

New York / London / Paris / Sydney / Tokyo / Berlin / Copenhagen / Madrid

Schirmer Trade Books
A Division of Music Sales Corporation, New York

Exclusive Distributors:
Music Sales Corporation
257 Park Avenue South, New York, NY 10010 USA

Music Sales Limited
8/9 Frith Street, London W1D 3JB England

Music Sales Pty. Limited
120 Rothschild Street, Rosebery, Sydney, NSW 2018, Australia

Order No. SCH10141
International Standard Book Number: 0-8256-7301-1

Printed in the United States of America
by Quebecor World

Cover Design: Adrian Cross

Library of Congress Cataloging-in-Publication Data

Dickerson, James.
  Mojo triangle : birthplace of country, blues, jazz and rock 'n' roll / by James L. Dickerson.
    p. cm.
  Includes bibliographical references and index.
  ISBN 0-8256-7301-1 (hardcover : alk. paper)
  1. Popular music—Mississippi River—History and criticism. 2. Mississippi River—History. I. Title.

ML3477.D53 2005
781.63'0976—dc22
                                      2004016821

To my college roommate, Billy Bobbs, an Ole Miss Deke
who kept the music of Bobby "Blue" Bland,
Mose Allison, and Jimmy Reed wafting through Kincannon Hall.

CONTENTS

Chapter One Natchez Under the Hill
The Cradle of American Music   *1*

Chapter Two The Apocalyptic Furies
Earthquakes, Pestilence, Floods, War, Night Terrors   *21*

Chapter Three The Natchez Trace
Spiritual Aorta of the American Experience   *51*

Chapter Four Mississippi Delta
Highway 61 Revisited   *83*

Chapter Five Memphis
Great Balls of Fire   *115*

Chapter Six New Orleans
A Gumbo That Keeps on Giving   *157*

Chapter Seven Muscle Shoals
When a Man Loves a Woman   *181*

Chapter Eight Nashville
Workin' On the Next Big Thing   *207*

Postscript   *230*

Endnotes   *232*

Bibliography   *237*

Index   *241*

ACKNOWLEDGEMENTS

I would like to thank the following individuals for their help with this book, which from conception to completion, was about twenty years in the making: Allie and Mattie, for their help during the hectic days while the book morphed from thought to computer screen (the book could not have been written without them); Marty Stuart, with whom I've shared conversations about music for twenty years; Jimmy Johnson and David Hood; the late Johnny Cash and the late Waylon Jennings, both of whom allowed me into the studio while they made records; Amanda Williams at the Mississippi Band of Choctaw Indians (MBCI) Archives; the late Stevie Ray Vaughan, who always made time to talk about the blues; Dave Edmunds; the late Carl Perkins, who, with a straight face, told me I had rhythm after I substituted for Jerry Lee Lewis in Carl's video; the late Sam Phillips; Chips Moman, one of the most creative and loyal people I know; Scotty Moore, who, besides being the most important guitarist that ever tuned a Gibson, is a great friend; the late Chet Atkins; the incomparable Jerry Lee Lewis; the late Roy Orbison; Rick Blackburn, Joe Galante, and Pam Lewis; Jack Clement, who, after fifty years in the music business, hasn't lost his sense of humor; the late Estelle Axton, Jim Stewart, Bobby Manuel, Rufus Thomas, Booker T. Jones, Steve Cropper, Duck Dunn, and Don Nix; the staff at the Flowood Public Library; the staff at the Mississippi Valley Collection at the University of Memphis; the staff at the Jean and Alexander Heard Library at the Vanderbilt University Library; my agent for this project, Bob Diforio; and my editor at Schirmer Trade Books, Andrea Rotondo, who believed in the book.

ABOUT THE AUTHOR

The author of 18 non-fiction books and over 2,000 magazine and newspaper articles, James L. Dickerson has been the dominant voice in the South for 25 years on matters related to popular culture and music.

Born and raised at the intersection of Highways 61 and 82, the heralded blues "cross-roads" of the Mississippi Delta, Dickerson attended the University of Mississippi, where he played keyboards and sax in a series of well-known Southern college bands, including the Dynamics, the Roadrunners, and the Strokers. After leaving college, Dickerson put his sax and keyboards aside to write for a living. His first magazine article, an interview with singer Bobbie Gentry, was published in 1967.

After becoming a regular contributor to the book pages of the *Baltimore Sun* and the *Toronto Star* in the early 1970s, Dickerson began writing full-time in 1977 when he joined the staff of the Pulitzer Prize-winning *Delta Democrat-Times* in Greenville, Mississippi. In the years that followed, he worked as a reporter, editorial writer, and editor for several newspapers, including the *Greenwood* (Miss.) *Commonwealth,* the *Jackson Daily News* in Jackson, Mississippi, and *The Commercial Appeal,* the largest circulation newspaper in the mid-South.

In 1986 the author left *The Commercial Appeal* to edit and publish a pop-culture magazine, *Nine-O-One Network.* At the time *Nine-O-One Network* magazine suspended publication in 1988, it was sold on newsstands in all fifty states and was the third largest circulation music magazine in the United States. Also, during this time Dickerson served as the executive producer and co-owner of Pulsebeat—Voice of the Heartland, a radio syndication that offered a weekly blues program and a weekly country program to a network of 100 stations that stretched from New York to the Yukon.

For the past several years, Dickerson has worked as a freelance writer, book editor, and photographer. His work has appeared in numerous national and regional magazines, including *Mid-South Magazine, CoverStory, BookPage, Good Housekeeping, Omni, Glamour,* and *Penthouse,* to name a few.

Dickerson, who makes his home in Jackson, Mississippi, is the author of several critically acclaimed music books, including: *Goin' Back to Memphis, That's Alright, Elvis, Dixie Chicks: Down-Home and Backstage, Faith Hill: Piece of My Heart, Colonel Tom Parker: The Curious Life of Elvis Presley's Eccentric Manager, Just for a Thrill: Lil Hardin Armstrong, First Lady of Jazz,* and *The Fabulous Vaughan Brothers: Jimmie and Stevie Ray Vaughan.*

Man and the mighty Mississippi River. (Steve Gardner)

1 ▼ NATCHEZ UNDER THE HILL
The Cradle of American Music

When Christian Schultz stepped off the boat in Natchez Under the Hill in April 1808, he was greeted by an enthusiastic band of Native-American musicians, who performed for new frontier arrivals in the hopes of being compensated with money, whiskey, or provisions. "You would no doubt have been surprised, if you had inspected the band, with their instruments, before the beginning of the performance," he later wrote. "But you would have been satisfied, after hearing the music, that a given quantity of discord may produce harmony. I must certainly do them the justice to say, that I never was more agreeably disappointed in my life, and the harmony produced by such an unpromising collection of instruments and performers, exceeded all my expectations."

Schultz, an American investor who had set out from New York in 1807 to investigate the potential of the Ohio wilderness, had traveled to Natchez by way of the Ohio River, which begins where the Allegheny and Monongahela rivers meet in the city of Pittsburgh, and empties into the Mississippi River at what is now Cairo, Illinois. Traveling down the Mississippi River at that point was a treacherous voyage for a flatboat on a good day, but in the spring, when the winter snows melted and swelled the river with high water and floating debris, it was sometimes akin to a suicide mission.

Music had a soothing effect on the wobbly legged sailors who were invariably elated to set foot on firm soil after being tossed about on a river that could be mirror-smooth on one stretch, only to descend around the next bend into a nightmarish gauntlet of giant whirlpools and floating trees. Those boats that traveled close to the bank had to deal with ambushes by natives who were proficient with arrows and spears. On top of the visual dangers were a host of hidden threats such as poisonous cottonmouth moccasins, occasional alligators, and scavenger catfish that grew as large as a man and lurked beneath the surface, feeding on the river bottom. Most travelers understood that if their flatboat overturned in the churning waters, they had little chance of making it to safety.

Schultz unknowingly had stepped foot on sacred ground, at least in a musical sense. Draw a straight line from New Orleans to Nashville, then over to Memphis and back down to New Orleans following the curves of the Mississippi River, and you have the Mojo Triangle, a geometrical, cultural, and spiritual configuration that represents the geographical birthplace of America's original music—blues, jazz, rock 'n' roll, and country. Without knowing that he was doing so, Schultz tapped into the life force of that music long before those distinct art forms ever existed.

Schultz was especially interested in the musical instruments. "The first and largest was a joint of thick cane, open at both ends, which, when applied to the mouth, and sung or blown through with a strong voice, served as a bass to the whole," he wrote. "The next was also a joint of cane with both ends closed, containing a few small pebbles: This was used by shaking it to the time and motions of the piece. The third was two separate joints of cane, each of which were cracked in several places, and used by suspending the one between the fingers of the left hand, and striking the other upon it with the right, producing a kind of rattling, jarring sound. The fourth was likewise a joint of cane open at one end, having a small slip of cane inserted directly across the aperture. This was held in a perpendicular direction, when by contracting the lips and blowing or singing through the aperture upon the slip, it produced a hollow hissing sound. The fifth was another joint of cane closed at both ends, with a narrow strip out from end to end, over which was extended a strong deer sinew, which being set in vibration by the thumb, produced a dull monotonous sound, something like the lowest string of the African jumbo." He also described a drum that was constructed from a two-gallon tin kettle with a buckskin stretched over the mouth; the instrument was carried under one arm and struck with a stick that was held in the other hand.

It's difficult to know whether the word "band" was first used to describe a group of people living and working together, or whether it was used to describe a group of people playing musical instruments. (The first musical bands are attributed to Frederick the Great of Prussia, who ordered the formation of a military band in 1763.) However, it is possible that the phrase "band of Indians," as used to describe a tribe, evolved from the frequency with which white settlers encountered Native Americans performing with musical instruments.

Schultz was dazzled by the Indian band that he encountered. Contrary to the European tradition, the Natchez and Choctaw bands included a mixture of men and women, along with children of various ages. As he observed, they formed under a tree a short distance from where the boats docked, and then advanced singing short stanzas of "ho, ha—ho, ha—ho, ha—ho, ha—ho, ha." The rhythmic chant, which many years later could be heard supplying the unspoken rhythm beneath the melody of the popular song, "Old Man River," served as a marching cadence for the band.

"When near the boats, the captain or leader advances before with a white or striped silk banner, taking long and solemn strides, and then halting a moment for the rest to come up," Schultz wrote. "After reaching the boat he stands as still as a post, not moving his eyes, or any of his limbs. The men approach next, and form a circle round him: Then follow the boys—after then, the squaws with the girls in the rear. The music now becomes slow and solemn for about five minutes, when it gradually increases to a brisker motion, during which you will first perceive the captain move his eyes, next his lips, then his head and hands, and at last a very curious and pleasing pantomimical [sic] dance strikes up, which continues for about a quarter of an hour."

Their vocals made a two-part harmony, with the men and boys singing the tenor parts and the women and girls singing the treble parts. "The several instruments were used with such accurate time and motion, and so blended with the vocal music, that it rendered the performance far superior to any thing I had anticipated," Schultz noted. "The burthen of the song was the same throughout, consisting of a single stanza, and, as near as I can remember as follows: Ho, hoa, ho—ho, al, hoa—hoa, ho, ho—ho, hoa, ho!"

By the time Schultz arrived in Natchez Under the Hill, it had existed as a white settlement for ninety-four years. First visited by Spanish conquistador Hernando de Soto, who died in 1542 just north of the city from an infected wound, it was later visited by French explorer La Salle, who made friends with the Natchez before going on to discover what later became known as New Orleans. As a result of that contact, a group of Frenchmen set up a trading post on the river's edge in 1714, to be followed two years later by a French military garrison that built a fortification named Fort Rosalie on the two hundred-foot bluff overlooking the Mississippi River.

Within ten years, enough slaves had been imported from Africa to clear and cultivate more than ten thousand acres around Natchez. As a result, the Natchez, the Native Americans who first inhabited the area, were pushed farther away from the river. Finally, in 1729, the Natchez Indians retaliated by attacking the settlement and killing more than one-third of its seven hundred residents. All of the males were killed, except for one soldier, twenty planters who swam across the river to safety, and a tailor who was allowed to live so that he could alter the clothing left behind by the French. The four hundred women and children who were captured were sold into slavery to other tribes.

The French responded with a counter-attack that practically annihilated the tribe, which already had been reduced by the infectious illnesses that the Europeans brought to the area. The 450 women and children who survived the attack were shipped away and sold into slavery at Santo Domingo. The French held onto the city for another thirty years, at which time it was ceded to the British in the Treaty of Paris. In 1779, the British surrendered the city to a Spanish force, which governed until 1799, when the settlement was admitted to the new American union.

Most of the new residents who came to the wilderness outpost were Irish, Scottish, and British loyalists who wanted to escape from the colonies. The loyalists did not believe in the new government because they still felt an allegiance to the British monarchy. They felt a kinship with the planters because they, too, were opposed to extending individual rights to all Americans. Natchez society represented the conservative side of the classic liberal/conservative political battle over individual rights: Liberals insisted on a Bill of Rights, which would, in effect, make all men equal in the eyes of the law, while the conservatives fought the concept, arguing that some men, by virtue of their wealth and social standing, were more equal than other men.

By the time Schultz arrived in Natchez, the city boasted about three thousand residents. There were two newspapers and several department stores, one of which imported goods directly from England. The streets were not paved, nor did the city have any sidewalks. "The buildings in general are neat, yet I found none within the town that can be considered as elegant," he observed. "The principal hotels are upon a genteel establishment, yet not in a style corresponding to the general character of the place for luxury—but to a Mississippi sailor, who like an alligator may be said to have lived in mud while upon the river, they afford no trifling luxury."

In 1808, Natchez was considered by easterners to be the "remotest corner" of the American frontier. Everyone of that era understood its importance as a cotton-growing region—and everyone recognized its wild, sometimes apocalyptic, spirit—but no one then understood its importance to the evolution of American music. Natchez, in effect, is the time portal through which one must pass to enter the Mojo Triangle.

◆　▲　◆　▲　◆

The Natchez Indians were the youngest of the tribes that inhabited the lower Mississippi River Valley, with a culture that began around 700 A.D., hundreds of years later than the other two major tribes of the region, the Choctaw and the Chickasaw.

All three tribes were descendants of migrants who crossed from Siberia to Alaska, presumably over an ice bridge, more than fifteen thousand years ago. It took nearly five thousand years for them to make their way across North America and then down into the Mississippi Valley. One of the earliest tribes, the Adena, lived in the Ohio Valley around 1000 B.C. They were mound-builders and left behind cone-shaped burial mounds. The Hopewells, who arrived in the valley around 400 B.C. followed. They, too, were mound-builders, though their mounds were larger and were used as repositories for jewelry, headdresses, and copper breastplates, in addition to deceased tribe members. A spiritual people, they walked the forests of Mississippi at the same time, on the far side of the planet, that Jesus Christ walked the streets of Jerusalem. Indeed, there are those who believe that the Hopewells, with their highly developed religious rites, were one of the lost tribes of Israel and were once visited by Jesus and Mary.

That ancient history of the people of the Mississippi Valley pales in comparison to the history of the land itself. Forty-five million years ago, the Mojo Triangle was covered by what is now the Gulf of Mexico. Beneath the surface of the salty water lurked some of the fiercest creatures on the earth, feeding above what are now New Orleans, Natchez, Tupelo, Muscle Shoals, and the Mississippi Delta. Among them were Basilosaurus, a sea serpent with powerful jaws and long, jagged teeth, and a body that grew up to eighty feet in length. When the water receded from the Mojo Triangle, perhaps thirty million years ago, it left behind the remains of Basilosaurus and various whales. Just as the State of Mississippi honored the magnolia as the state flower, it honored Basilosaurus as one of two official state fossils, the other being Zygorhiza, a twenty-foot whale that had had a more benign demeanor.

Like the Hopewells, the Natchez Indians were mound-builders who worshiped the sun god and used music to express their deepest feelings about life. They built a village at Natchez because it was one of the highest points between Memphis and the Gulf of Mexico. Unlike the Choctaw and Chickasaw, the Natchez Indians were ruled by a male monarch called the Great Sun and by a royal family, referred to as Suns, made up of the Great Sun's relatives. Everyone else in the tribe was relegated to a commoner status, without a voice in tribal decisions.

By the time the first white settlers arrived, the Natchez tribe numbered nearly five thousand. They had the most advanced civilization of all the southeastern tribes, and they were skilled craftsmen and farmers. They lived in permanent dwellings, and they built temples that were the focus of their religious life. They believed in a god that built the first man out of clay, and then was so pleased with the result that he breathed life into the clay figure. After the first man was created, he was provided with female companionship— not from a rib taken from his body, but as the result of a sneezing fit that cast a mysterious substance from man's nose. When the substance hit the ground, it grew larger and larger, finally taking the shape of a woman.

Interestingly, after man and woman had lived together for a while, two figures descended from the sun—a male and a female—for the purpose of delivering a set of commandments, beginning with, "Thou shall not kill except in self-defense." They also were instructed not to bear false witness and told to live in monogamous unions of one man, one wife. When the French and the Spanish first arrived on the Natchez bluffs, they were fond of referring to the Natchez Indians as savages, but it is apparent that they lived under a higher moral code than either the French or the Spanish. Were the man and woman who descended from the sun the same individuals known as Jesus and Mary to Christians? Archeological study may yet prove that to be true.

One of the greatest surviving Natchez myths concerns the temple, in which two priests were charged with maintaining an eternal flame. One day, one of the priests left the temple for a short while, leaving the flame with the second priest, who fell asleep and allowed the flame to die. When he awoke and saw that the flame had extinguished, he panicked because the penalty for such negligence was death. Luckily, a passerby happened by with a lit pipe in hand; the priest begged a light from the man, explaining that he wanted to light his pipe but was forbidden to use the eternal flame for such a mundane use. With the man gone, the priest re-lighted the flame with what he knew to be a profane fire, causing the royal family, the Suns, to start dying off in rapid succession. With the death of the ninth Sun, the priest himself became ill, prompting him to send word to God that it was imperative that he meet with him before he died.

When God arrived at the village, the priest told him that he had done a very bad thing. "I am going to die, so it makes no difference to me whether the sickness or a man kills me," he explained. "I know that I am a bad man for having for so long a time concealed, in order to preserve my life, what I am going to tell you. I am the cause of the death of my nation, therefore I merit death, but let me not be eaten by the dogs."

God promised him that if he spoke the truth he would not be put to death, nor would dogs be allowed to eat his bones when he did expire (another way of saying that he would be buried). God assembled the village's old men and encouraged the priest to tell his story. In the end, the old men agreed to allow the priest to live; the problem was solved by sending a runner to the nearest temple to bring back a sacred fire with which to re-light the extinguished flame. Once that was done, the Suns stopped dying and the village returned to normal.

As with other tribes, music was an integral part of the Natchez's social and religious fabric. Little is known about the instruments they used, but we know from the stories passed down that they incorporated music into their myths, creating operas that featured both spoken narrative and musical dialogue. In one instance, the Natchez told the story of a cannibal who decided to trick a large flock of ducks that he found swimming unmolested on a lake. He gathered together a large quantity of hickory bark and dove into the lake, swimming underwater so that he could surface, unseen, in their midst. With only his nose exposed for air, he gathered the ducks, one by one, and tied them to his body with the bark. Thinking that they could not fly, he surfaced a short distance away and started singing:

Agu'shuwe'bangini. Agu'shuwe'bangini.
Ada'gitsa'gitsak a'tsaga' girtsagitsak

His words were a celebration of his capture of the ducks. It seemed to be a great victory until the ducks began asking each other, "What is he singing?"

When they realized that they were tied to his body, they flew into the sky, dragging the cannibal behind them. One by one, the bindings broke away, sending the cannibal back to earth, where he landed in a hollow tree. He remained there for seven days before a woodpecker arrived and began pecking at the bark. He told the woodpecker that if he brought all his friends to the tree he would be very grateful. When the birds arrived they broke out into song:

Tom'shithlho'nho'nogua shu'uhuts gai 'tsii ni 'yi ni dogotilu 'shik

The words of the song explained that they were pecking at a hollow tree in which there was a cannibal. Finally, they pecked open the tree and set the cannibal free. He told them that if they gathered around he would tell them a very strange story. When they got close to him, he grabbed as many as he could and ate them for dinner. Later, he was walking through the forest when he heard someone singing in a low voice:

Tom'shithlhonho'nogua dahaba'li gabi'shgua gabukta

The words meant: "Kill that cannibal and let us eat him." He followed the singing until he reached a bush that contained a redbird's nest, in which sat a number of little ones with their feathers just starting out. He gobbled them up, nest and all, and shouted to the forest: "Sing on—sing on, again!"

The Natchez's music would probably not be of much importance to the development of the Mojo Triangle were it not for the fact that they were the first tribe to hold African Americans as slaves. Long before African Americans were ever assimilated into white society, they were assimilated into Natchez society, which meant that they were exposed to the instruments and musical styles employed by the Indians.

Most of the African Americans who arrived in Natchez came from Virginia and the Carolinas, or directly from West Africa, where they were stripped of all their possessions and herded onto slave ships for the voyage across the Atlantic. Whatever musical instruments they possessed were left behind, but that did not mean that they were without music, for one of the shippers' common requirements was that the slaves be taken to the deck on a regular basis so that they could sing and dance and uplift their spirits. On those occasions, the slaves used tin plates and buckets for noisemakers and drums as they sang and danced.

Thomas Jefferson was among the first to document the differences he perceived between African Americans and Native Americans. In his writings, he claimed that Indians were superior to slaves in imagination and artistic skill, but he gave the edge to the slaves when it came to musical talent. "In music they are more generally gifted than the whites, with accurate ears for tune and time, and they have been found capable of imagining a small catch," he wrote in *Notes on Virginia*. "Whether they will be equal to the composition of a more extensive run of melody, or of complicated harmony, is yet to be proved." The only instrument that Jefferson mentioned in his notes on slave music was the "banjar," a four-string instrument that later was developed into the banjo. He didn't describe the instrument in detail, but it is consistent with four-string instruments that slaves subsequently made from gourds.

◆ ▲ ◆ ▲ ◆

Three months before Christian Schultz's arrival in Natchez, the United States government prohibited the importation of slaves. Planters were not allowed to bring new slaves into the country to work their plantations, but they could keep the slaves that they already owned. The planters compensated by encouraging their existing slaves to breed at every opportunity. Slaves were rewarded for promiscuity that led to new workers, for only in that way could planters expect to have a continuing supply of slaves.

If the first Native American tribe that the slaves encountered upon their arrival in Mississippi was the Natchez, the Native Americans who had the greatest impact on them, long term, was the Choctaw, a tribe that originally lived northeast of Natchez. Together with the Chickasaw, a tribe that lived in northern Mississippi, the Choctaw were the dominant aboriginal population in the region. With the massacre of the Natchez Indians, they filtered into the city of Natchez, along with a handful of survivors from the Natchez tribe, where they came into contact with the slaves on a regular basis. In his 1808 letters, Schultz identifies the Native Americans in the band that played on the docks as Choctaw and Natchez, but there would have been very few, if any, of the latter.

The Choctaws descended from the same mound-building tribes that evolved from the Hopewells. Indeed, Choctaw legend has it that the tribe was one of four that emerged from Nanih Waiya, a mound located near Philadelphia, Mississippi. The first tribe to emerge from the mound was the Creek; they sunned themselves on the mound until they were dry of the earthy wetness associated with birth, after which they traveled east. The second to emerge were the Cherokees, who then traveled north. The third tribe was the Chickasaw, who followed the Cherokee trail and then settled nearby. The fourth tribe was the Choctaw, which settled on the land surrounding the mound.

Unlike the Natchez Indians, the Choctaw befriended the French invaders when they first entered the region and became important allies, even to the point of allowing the French to be dispersed throughout their villages on those occasions when French food supplies dwindled to starvation levels. Later, when the colonists won their independence, the Choctaws sided with the new American government. They fought on the American side in the War of 1812, and in 1815 they accompanied Andrew Jackson to fight with him in the Battle of New Orleans.

Also, unlike the Natchez, the Choctaw did not covet African American slaves. On those occasions when slaves escaped their masters' plantations, the Choctaw invariably returned them to the plantations, usually in expectation of a reward. Even so, there was considerable social interaction among the Choctaw with both whites and blacks. Whites took Choctaw women as wives, and white planters did nothing to discourage sexual relations between the Choctaw and the slaves because it produced more work hands to send into the cotton fields. Almost always, the sexual aggressors were white males taking female Indian partners, and Choctaw males taking black female partners. Black males were usually punished when they took partners of a different race.

The social interactions enjoyed by whites, Indians, and black slaves were limited. They didn't worship together. They didn't eat together. And they only conducted business together under strict conditions designed to give the whites the upper hand psychologically, if not in fact. The only area that was open to more democratic interaction was music. Whites allowed Indians and slave servants to witness their musical festivities, and, in turn, they were allowed to observe musical events staged by both Indians and slaves. The Indians and the slaves shared a common love of music: It became the universal language that allowed them to communicate with each other, and share each other's hopes and dreams for the future. The interaction became so intense at one point that plantation owners thought it prudent to ban the possession of Indian drums among the slaves, for fear they would use them to signal organized insurgencies.

One of the best chroniclers of Choctaw life in the 1800s was a man of European descent named Horatio Bardwell Cushman, a son of missionaries who lived among the Mississippi Choctaws in the early 1800s. In 1899 he published a book titled *History of the Choctaw, Chickasaw and Natchez Indians,* a loving remembrance that still stands as the major source for information about those three tribes. The only musical instruments that Cushman credited the Choctaw with inventing were the cane flute and a deerskin-covered drum, which was struck by a stick. "Yet the ancient Choctaw," he wrote, "in all his solemn ceremonies, as well as amusements and merry-makings, did not depend so much upon the jarring tones of the diminutive drum as he did upon his own voice, which in concert with the monotonous tones of the drum—to the cultivated and sensitive ear a mere jargon of sound—was to the Indian ear the most exciting music, and soon wrought him to the highest state of excitement."

The Choctaw never developed melody instruments, beyond the flute, because they considered that aspect of music to be a function of the human voice. Instead, they used an assortment of percussive instruments such as the drum, bells, and flattened striking sticks called claves, instruments that comprised a rhythm section capable of keeping the beat going beneath the fluid ramblings of the human voice. Vocally, they chanted and they shouted, and they interwove harmonies into rhythms that often ran counter to the beat laid down by the rhythm instruments. That concept was foreign to Europeans, who preferred melodies that kept time with the beat, or in the case of Africans, melodies that kept time with one of several rhythms that were played simultaneously.

In the early years, American musical development was a two-way street with many side alleys. Native Americans admired the military snare drum used by the French and the Spanish, and they adapted it to their own uses, even though they already had a drum made of cypress knees over which was stretched deerskin or bearskin. Their original drum made a deeper, more resonant sound (later called a tom-tom) than the snare drum, which had a lighter, more immediate sound to it. African slaves admired the steady beat that Native Americans used beneath their melodies, and the way that both Native Americans and the white settlers used harmony to create more complex vocals. Oddly, the white settlers seemed to have little appreciation for the music of either the slaves or the Indians; it would take nearly two hundred years for that cultural lapse to be rectified.

For the most part, whites encouraged their slaves to adapt to European instruments, for it was considered a mark of high status to have a slave that could perform before guests, using instruments such as the fiddle or the French horn. In the 1700s, reports author Gilbert Chase, the *Virginia Gazette* ran an advertisement for "an orderly Negro or mulatto who can play well the violin." Another announcement requested the return of a runaway slave who took his fiddle with him when he left.

Of the three groups—Native Americans, whites and African slaves—the Native Americans were probably the least affected by the music of the other two groups. They borrowed ideas for musical instruments, such as in the creation of the snare drum, but the songs themselves were never altered. That was because they felt that their music was given to them by God, who alone had the ability to compose new music. If the words to a song were forgotten, it could not be rewritten or restructured; it simply disappeared from the tribe's repertory and was not replaced, for to attempt to do so would be to usurp the mound-given authority of God.

◆　▲　◆　▲　◆

With a high, sloping forehead, a stern gaze that was more likely than not to be cast over his shoulder, and a humorless demeanor, Winthrop Sargent was a Massachusetts-born graduate of Harvard University and a decorated soldier in the Continental Army. (Of his service in the Revolutionary War, George Washington once proclaimed that Sargent "...displayed a zeal, integrity and intelligence," qualities that entitled him to have the status of an "officer and a gentleman.") This imposing figure arrived in Natchez in 1798 to become Mississippi's first territorial governor.

Natchez was populated by wealthy plantation owners, riverboat captains and sailors, slaves, Indians, military officers, and a growing community of storekeepers, all of whom reveled in the fact they resided on the "far side" of civilization. At that time, Natchez was the most remote settlement in America, a distinction that kept it at daily risk of succumbing to the machinations of evil-doers intent on slicing off the county's most prosperous wart for use in their own vision of the city's future. Travel to the city from the east was considered an ordeal, not just because of hostile Indians, but because of the uncompromising heat. On his journey to Natchez, Sargent became ill and confined himself to his bed until he could recover from what he called the "ill effects of a vertical sun."

There were two categories of people in Natchez in those days: Those living in the moment and those preparing for the future. Sargent worried about both groups of people. Natchez was a wide-open city, the docks lined with rowdy bars and casinos; there was little law and order, and violence was commonplace on the streets. One of his first letters was to Secretary of War Timothy Pickering, with whom he pleaded for a judge knowledgeable in the law. The only judge in town, he wrote, was "worthy and sensible," but "beyond doubt deficient."

What especially concerned Sargent was the flagrant mixing of the races that he saw taking place. He proposed to remedy that by reducing the number of Choctaw that were permitted to enter the city. "It will be well, I think, to be very sparing of passports for Indians to visit white people, and to confine them to chiefs and men of real consequence amongst the tribes, for the less we mix, the better the prospect of harmony," Sargent wrote. "Horse stealing, robberies, and murders, may in some measure thereby be avoided, and our friendship of course, longer continued."

Sargent's efforts at segregation did not go over very well, especially among the Choctaw—for they had intermarried with whites for decades without protest from white leaders—and life continued pretty much as it always had, with whites, slaves, and Indians mingling and conducting their business as they saw fit, regardless of what the "government" thought about it.

Perhaps because of his military background, Sargent became obsessed with raising a militia to protect the Mississippi territory. To do that, he declared a military draft that required all free men between the ages of sixteen and fifty to be inducted into service. All free men over the age of fifty were advised to arm themselves in the event the governor needed to call them in for emergency service. So that everyone would be acquainted with the existence of the new militia, he ordered that the men assemble and parade on the first Saturday of each month, taking care to fire their rifles and demonstrate the effectiveness of their bayonets.

Sargent had reason to be concerned, but not for the reasons he supposed. The biggest threat, as he saw it, were the thousands of Choctaw and Chickasaw Indians in the territory and the thousands of slaves, which in his eyes were capable of staging a revolt. As an outsider to the area, he had little understanding of either the slave or Indian cultures. He assumed that any conflicts would be based on race. In reality, neither the slaves nor the Choctaw were in any danger of staging a revolt against the white settlers. It was during those years that the Shawnee chief encouraged the Choctaws to join them in a war against the Americans. Choctaw Chief Pushmataha, who believed that his people could live in peace with the whites, rejected the alliance, saying:

> These white Americans buy our skins, our corn, our cotton, our surplus fame, our baskets and other wares . . . They have encouraged and helped us in the production of our crops. They have taken many of our wives into their homes to teach them useful things. They pay them for their work while learning. You all remember well the dreadful epidemic visited upon us last winter. During its darkest hours these neighbors whom we are now urged to attack responded generously to our needs. They doctored our sick. They clothed our suffering. They fed our hungry.

Sargent's misjudgment seemed to be due more to ignorance than to racism. The settlers had formed a separate peace with the Choctaw, treating them as neighbors and not potential adversaries. Pushmataha thought that because he was friends with individual settlers he was also friends with the government—and that was not the case. Sargent worked behind the scenes to destroy the friendships that had been built up over the years by the settlers and the Indians. His efforts to limit socializing between Indians and settlers in Natchez failed because the two parties simply got together outside the city limits. In 1798, in an effort to control socializing in remote areas, he issued a proclamation prohibiting settlers from giving the Choctaw any "whiskey, rum, brandy, or other ardent spirits, upon penalty of being punished with the utmost rigour."

Sargent's term came to an end in 1801, with President Adams' defeat by Thomas Jefferson in the presidential election. Aware that complaints had been made about him, Sargent traveled to Washington to argue his case for reappointment as territorial governor. The new president was not interested. Instead, he appointed twenty-six-year-old William C. C. Claiborne, a member of a prominent Virginia family that had fought on the side of the colonies in the Revolution. Claiborne was a handsome man who wore his close-cropped hair in the style made famous by Napoleon. He was greeted with great enthusiasm when he arrived in Natchez; unlike the stodgy Sargent, he was affable and made an effort to understand the settlers' problems.

Like Sargent, he possessed an almost obsessive fear of both the slaves and the Indians. In a letter to Secretary of State James Madison, he urged him to ask the president to send four hundred muskets and as many rifles to the territory. "Until the militia of the territory are well armed and disciplined, my mind will not be tranquil," he wrote. "Bordering upon the dominions of a foreign power, separated from the nearest state [Tennessee] by a wilderness of six hundred miles in extent—in the neighborhood of numerous savage tribes, and with a population of negroes, nearly equal to the number of whites—there exists no certainty for peace and our best reliance for safety must depend upon a well armed and well trained militia."

In 1802, he gathered together a group of Choctaw Indians at a government house in Natchez to lecture them on their perceived shortcomings:

It is my way to speak straight. Listen then to what I say, and hold fast my talk. The white people have made to me of late, many complaints. Several men in the country have had their cattle and hogs killed. One man in town has had four barrels of flour taken from his door in the night, and another has lost out of his house a deal of meal, and to tell you the truth, all those bad acts are charged upon some of the Indians.

Brothers, I hope none of you present are guilty of these acts. If you are men and warriors, I know you would not take anything that was not your own, but I must tell you that if any thing should be missing in the town or country hereafter, I will have your camps searched, and if I should discover that any of you have acted improperly, you shall be punished according to the white people's laws.

I am going now to give you some good advice. Quit drinking whiskey, for it will make you fools and old women. Return to your own land and make bread for your families ... If you will take this advice, I will give you some provisions to eat on the path, but while you remain in our settlements, you shall not have one ounce of flour from me.

Claiborne remained in his post until 1803, when he learned that President Jefferson had chosen him to travel to New Orleans to receive the Louisiana Purchase from France. After the transfer, he was appointed governor of the Territory of Orleans, where he served until Louisiana was admitted into the union, at which point he was elected the state's first governor.

In his absence, Mississippi became the union's twentieth state in 1817, with Natchez chosen for the capital (later the capital would be moved to Columbia, then to Jackson). With statehood came an influx of white settlers in search of land. The first census, taken in 1817, showed twenty-three thousand black slaves, twenty-five thousand whites, and thirty-five thousand Native Americans. The only land not held by other white settlers was the land occupied by the Choctaw and the Chickasaw.

Incredibly, the Choctaw became the first victims of the Indian Removal Law. Through coercion, they were forced to sign the 1830 Treaty of Dancing Rabbit Creek, which required them to relocate to Oklahoma. Thirteen thousand Choctaw made the 550-mile trek, with four thousand of them dying of hunger and exposure along the way, thus reducing the Indian census figure to twenty-two thousand. Seven thousand refused to move and remained in Mississippi, where they were stripped of tribal status and subjected to state laws, many of which were harsh when it came to administering justice to Native Americans (not until 1945 were the survivors granted special status with the right to a Choctaw Constitution).

An effort was made to strike the same deal with the Chickasaw, who were situated in northern Mississippi and Alabama, but the deal fell apart when a suitable relocation area could not be agreed upon. Instead, the Chickasaw ceded their land to the United States government with an understanding that the land would be sold quickly and the money placed in a special Chickasaw account. Most of them ended up moving to Oklahoma, where they purchased land from the Choctaw.

With a stroke of a pen, the United States government reduced Mississippi's Indian population from thirty-five thousand to about twelve thousand, unceremoniously ripping away the ancient soul of the Mojo Triangle, leaving it to wander for eternity.

◆　▲　◆　▲　◆

With the arrival of statehood and the removal of the Indians, Mississippi became a magnet for those in search of cheap land and get-rich-quick opportunities. New settlers poured in from Pennsylvania, New York, Ohio, Virginia, Maryland, and Massachusetts, most of them of Scottish and Irish descent, a marked contrast to previous years when at least half of the new arrivals were African slaves. The ban on the importation of slaves had a profound influence on African American music, because it began to eliminate the influence of those with a personal remembrance of African music. By the 1830s, there were few, if any, slaves with first-hand knowledge of African music. By that point, their musical tradition was a mixture of African adaptations, based on what slaves had learned from the Choctaw and from the white settlers, who encouraged them to learn the European music that brought them pleasure and comfort.

Natchez became an entertainment mecca, similar to the Las Vegas of today, a stark reminder that America's original music has always had more to do with commerce than with art. Society operated on three levels. At the bottom of the rung were the riverboat captains and sailors, the travelers in search of adventure, the free farm workers, the last remnants of the Choctaw nation, the prostitutes, the gamblers, and the outlaws that traveled to the city from time to time for supplies. The middle rung was composed of shopkeepers, seamstresses, blacksmiths, ministers, gunsmiths, hospital workers (the first hospital was built in 1805), and the teachers (in 1818, the Elizabeth Female Academy opened its doors). At the top rung were the governor and other state officials, judges, bankers, successful entrepreneurs, and, at the very top of this group, the plantation owners, who by the 1830s had amassed considerable fortunes. Their fabulous mansions are still in existence today, open for public visitation.

Natchez had more millionaires, per capita, during that time than any city in the United States, with most of the wealth coming from land speculation and cotton. By the early 1800s, Natchez was exporting up to three million pounds of cotton a year, all of which was harvested by slaves who, on average, could produce thirty-two hundred pounds of cotton for each man, woman, and child sent into the fields. Most of the slaves lived on the plantations scattered out across the countryside, but many lived within the city limits of Natchez, accounting for about one-quarter of the city's population.

Music played an important role in the lives of Natchez's upper crust, but it was viewed more as a social aid than an art form. Bands were hired for social functions so that formally attired men and women could dance and socialize on a grand scale after engaging in sumptuous banquets. The music was always European in origin; the waltz in particular allowed dancers to glide about the floor with a minimum display of emotion, sliding their feet in time to the music, conforming to their own vision of a genteel tradition.

While the fancy dances were taking place high up on the bluffs, something altogether different was happening in Natchez Under the Hill, at river level. Because it was where the common people gathered, no one made any pretense to tradition, genteel or otherwise. Every night of the week, gamblers played cards, prostitutes turned tricks, gunfighters faced off in duels, drinkers drank themselves into alcoholic stupors, and working people danced the hours away, blowing their hard-earned money on the guilty pleasures of the moment.

There were few single women in Natchez in those days. Women were in such great demand throughout the territory that it was rare to see a woman who was not married. Often, the only available women, for whites, were female slaves and Indian maidens. For the most part, the only available white women were prostitutes. That was one reason why the nightlife at Natchez Under the Hill was such a tourist draw. With more than a dozen brothels on the docks, it was possible for men to sleep with a woman early in the evening and then dance with her until late into the night.

The dancing that took place under the hill was a world apart from the action going on in the ballrooms of the mansions high on the bluffs. The music was raw, energetic, sexual, possessed of the character of the wild men and women who brought it down the Natchez Trace from Nashville, and the sailors who brought it upriver from the Caribbean, Spain, France, and Great Britain.

When these people danced, they didn't glide their way across the floor in a waltz; they lifted their legs high and swung their arms, tossing their partners about with abandon. The music itself flowed from guitars brought from Spain, from flutes and drums devised by the Choctaw, and from fiddles imported from Scotland and Ireland. Watching the white "commoners" kick up their heels and move their shoulders in time with the music were the black slaves and Indians who worked in the taverns and cafes, witness to the debauchery and merrymaking; they also were witness to the genteel music up on the hill, but it did nothing for them, at least not in the sense of setting fire to their souls or instilling in them the value of music as a money-maker, for only under the hill was music associated with economic gain. Music was played by people who earned money for their efforts, and it was enjoyed by people who had money to spend: It was the tried-and-true currency of the common man, the one thing that could be counted on to obliterate the pain of daily living on the rowdy edge of the frontier.

Fiddling was the main musical style of that time among lower-class whites, blacks, and Indians. Guitars were available, having come into the city from Spanish ports, but that instrument was slow to find common usage, primarily because no one had yet figured out how to do anything with the guitar, other than to play slow-moving chords that did not lend themselves to dance music. The fiddle, on the other hand, was perfect, for it could grind out up-tempo tunes with the precise urgency required to lift men and women to their feet.

A fiddle tune titled "Natchez Under the Hill," one of the first original songs ever published in America, originated in the dives along the docks. It was a fast-paced tune, obviously written for the high-spirited dances favored by the common man. When it was published in 1834, it was re-titled "Old Zip Coon." The first verse went as follows:

> There once was a man with a double chin
> Who performed with skill on the violin,
> And he played in time and he played in tune,
> But he wouldn't play anything but Old Zip Coon.

The song went on to become a popular minstrel song, though it was later re-titled "Turkey in the Straw," the name by which it is now best known. Its influence can not only be seen in the bluegrass and country styles that were developed a hundred years later—and bloomed commercially in Nashville, the northeastern tip of the Mojo Triangle—but in the music that made its way northward into the Mississippi Delta, which became known as the blues, carried there by slaves who heard "Old Zip Coon" played in the dives in and around Natchez Under the Hill.

Natchez was not only an actual portal for wilderness expansion, it was a symbolic portal for the advancement of America's original music. This "new" music, whether you call it country or blues or jazz or rock 'n' roll, was born of the unique hardships, passions, and remembrances of those who lived and died in the Mojo Triangle.

There is a line of thought that human DNA consists of more than a simple imprint for physical building blocks, such as height, hair, and eye color. Some believe it is also a conduit, through dreams, for the passage of myth, from generation to generation—myth being the essential building block for all creativity, whether expressed as music, literature, or fine art. This line of thought would explain how so much original music and literature could blossom in such a small geographical area.

Richard Wright, a slave descendant born on a plantation just outside Natchez—and the first literary genius to emerge from the Mojo Triangle—well understood the relationship of the land of one's birth to his or her humanity. In his 1940 novel, *Native Son*, he has a character utter during a murder trial: "Men adjust themselves to their land; they create their own laws of being; their notions of right and wrong. A common way of earning a living gives them a common attitude toward life. Even their speech is colored and shaped by what they must undergo."

The same sentiments can be applied to the music and literature that has arisen within the triangle. Music is a joyous celebration of life, when properly executed, but it is also a history of the life that makes the music. The Choctaw felt that music was sacred, a gift to them from God. They didn't play music—they *were* the music. That thought is not too far removed from the thesis of this book: That all original music is the product of the land, and of the myths, experiences, beliefs, and events that shape the people who live on the land. Great music is born of great trauma. Viewed from that perspective, the blues, rock 'n' roll, jazz, and country could not have arisen in any other part of the country by virtue of the fact that those styles of music *are* the Mojo Triangle.

2 THE APOCALYPTIC FURIES
▼ Earthquakes, Pestilence, Floods, War, Night Terrors

In September 1809, when Meriwether Lewis stepped off the boat at Fort Pickering, a Mississippi River outpost that would later become Memphis, Tennessee, he was not himself. He was ill, displaying many of the symptoms of liver disease or malaria. His skin was jaundiced and he was feverish. His legs wobbled when he walked.

Lewis should have turned back to St. Louis, where he resided as governor of the vast Louisiana Territory, but he was on an urgent mission to Washington, D.C., and he could not be persuaded by concerned friends to postpone his trip. He planned to travel by riverboat to New Orleans, then board a ship that would take him up the East Coast. Traveling with him was a Creole servant, who, according to one account, had been rescued by Lewis from the streets and taken into his home. By today's standards, it was the equivalent of taking in a homeless person.

Lewis, who had been greeted with considerable interest upon his arrival, decided to stay at the outpost to rest and treat his illness. The fort's commander, Captain Gilbert Russell, later reported that Lewis had been "deranged" upon his arrival, perhaps a reference to a high fever. Russell had only recently taken over the fort's command from nineteen-year-old Lt. Zachary Taylor, who mysteriously dropped out of sight in the weeks prior to Lewis' arrival. (He later surfaced in Louisville, Kentucky, where he met and courted a young woman named Margaret. He would later be elected America's twelfth president, with Margaret as First Lady.)

Some accounts have Lewis drinking heavily at Fort Pickering. Others point out that was unlikely because he had never been known to be a heavy drinker. Clearly, he was ill, as he himself acknowledged in letters written from the fort—and, clearly, his personal life was in a state of chaos.

In 1809, at the age of thirty-five, Lewis was a national hero and a prominent government official. As leader of the Lewis and Clark expedition that had set out in 1804 to explore the Northwest, he had earned the admiration of the American people and the respect of his close friend President Thomas Jefferson, who had rewarded him for his courage by appointing him governor of the Louisiana Territory.

Lewis' life had begun to unravel earlier in the year, shortly after the inauguration of President James Madison, who made it clear that he wanted to replace Lewis. His expense vouchers were returned unpaid, making it necessary for him to pay the bills out of his own pocket and borrow money from friends. Rumors circulated in Washington that Lewis was using his office to set himself up as an Indian trader once his term expired. Where his relationship with the Jefferson administration had been warm and trusting, his relationship with the Madison administration was marked by insults and hostility.

A few weeks before setting out for Washington, Lewis received a letter from the War Department, scolding him for not getting permission for a five hundred-dollar expenditure. The letter writer warned Lewis that he was rebuking him with the full approval of President Madison. Lewis dashed off a hot-tempered response. America "may reduce me to poverty," he wrote, "but she can never sever my attachment from her."

New administrations don't require good reasons to replace appointees left over from previous administrations—it is a recognized perk of high office—but why was the Madison administration so hell-bent on getting rid of Lewis, a national treasure, a man who had never demonstrated the slightest hint of political ambition or corruption?

The answer may lie not in Lewis' politics, but rather in his personal life. Lewis never married, and there is no record of him ever engaging in a personal relationship with a woman. When his friends tried to introduce him to eligible young women, he always found excuses not to meet them. He obviously preferred the company of other men. Was Lewis homosexual? Was the Madison administration intent on purging Lewis for what it would have considered "moral reasons?" Did the Madison administration see a need to protect itself and the previous administration from a scandal that had the potential to damage the fledging nation's entry into the world community? Scholars have debated Lewis' sexual preference for nearly two hundred years, without resolution.

One can imagine the anger, frustration, and disappointment that whirled through Lewis' thoughts when he arrived at Fort Pickering. He was on a journey that would conclude with the most important battle of his career, but it would be a confrontation that would be fought with words, not firearms, on a battleground where he had little worldly experience. Despite his illness, Lewis was determined to face his accusers. He carried with him a trunk filled with notes and receipts detailing his business transactions as governor, the journals written on his trip to the Northwest, and one hundred dollars in cash, a sizeable amount in those days.

Major John Neelly, a new appointee of the Madison administration, was the Indian agent for the Chickasaw nation. He met Lewis at Fort Pickering. Neelly had bad news for Lewis: Hostilities had broken out with the British, and there were rumors that the British were seizing American ships headed out of New Orleans. There was talk that American passengers were being captured and mistreated. Fearful of capture and the seizure of his journals, Lewis decided to take an overland route to Washington. On September 16, he sent a letter to President Madison, informing him of his change in plans: "Providing my health permits, no time shall be lost in reaching Washington."

After resting for about two weeks at the fort, Lewis, accompanied by Neelly, his manservant and one of Neelly's servants, set out for Nashville on horseback, with two pack horses that were loaded with Lewis' papers and journals. One account indicates that a group of Chickasaw chiefs also left with the group, presumably for protection while crossing Indian lands.

Wearing his dress uniform, with two pistols stuck into his belt, Lewis got off to a shaky start, but his health improved with each passing day. That's not surprising, considering that the crudely built fort was small and accommodations were cramped, contributing to sanitation problems. On the trail, Lewis enjoyed a fresher food supply, and there were fewer sources of infection. Besides, the journey to Nashville put Lewis back where he was the most comfortable, under open skies.

In September, West Tennessee is usually hot and humid, with the temperature sometimes lingering in the mid-to-high eighties. The skies were clear when they left the fort, but twelve days into the journey the travelers encountered a storm. Thunderstorms in that area can be extremely violent, with black clouds commonly rumbling across the landscape at treetop level, generating a primeval fury of thunder boomers and electrical displays unknown to other parts of the country. Before the storm hit, the travelers made camp north of the Tennessee River.

When they awoke the next morning, they discovered that two of their horses had bolted and disappeared into the forest. Neelly offered to stay behind with the Indians to search for the horses. He insisted that Lewis proceed northward on the Natchez Trace and wait for him at the first house he found. Lewis set out on horseback, with his manservant following on foot, leading the packhorse at a slower pace.

At that time, the Natchez Trace was a haven for bandits. It penetrated dense forests that often gave the trail a dark and shadowy appearance. Treetops often intertwined, blocking out the sunlight, providing bandits with cover from which to launch surprise attacks against travelers. As governor of the territory, Lewis must have been aware of how dangerous the Trace was for solitary travelers, yet he did not hesitate to set out without Neelly. As he had proved on many occasions, he was a man of unimpeachable courage.

At sunset, on October 10, Lewis rode up to a roadside inn named Grinder's Stand. In the clearing were two crude log cabins and a livestock shed. Lewis asked for lodging for the night and said that his servants would arrive shortly. Mrs. Grinder, a wilderness-hardened woman in her mid-thirties, told Lewis that she was reluctant to allow him to stay since her husband was not at home. Lewis dismounted and, keeping a respectful distance, sat down to chat with the woman. Lewis was not accustomed to being told "No." Tall and slender, he had a masculine nose and a delicate, almost feminine mouth that would have been hard pressed to reflect malice. An early sketch of Lewis wearing an Indian ceremonial dress gives him a somewhat foppish appearance. Convinced of his sincerity, Mrs. Grinder allowed him to stay the night.

After dinner, Mrs. Grinder watched in discomfort as Lewis paced back and forth across the floor of the cabin, talking aloud to no one in particular. When she retired for the night, she locked her door. There was no sign of Neelly or the manservant yet, nor had Mr. Grinder returned to the cabin. Mrs. Grinder was unable to sleep. Late into the night she heard Lewis in the other cabin, sounding, she later reported, like a "lawyer." His behavior led her to believe that he was "deranged."

Sometime after midnight, Mrs. Grinder heard a gunshot. Moments later, she heard a second gunshot. The night dragged on as she lay wide awake in the dark. A few hours before dawn, there came a knock at her door. Lewis asked for water, saying that he was hurt and needed help. Despite the desperation in his voice, Mrs. Grinder refused to open her door. Finally, Lewis stumbled back into the night.

The next morning, Mrs. Grinder summoned the courage to enter the other cabin. With her was the manservant, who had arrived shortly before dawn. She found Lewis lying on the bed, still alive. He showed her a wound on his head and a second wound in his side. "I am no coward," he said. "But I am so strong, so hard to die."

Lewis died just as the sun came over the treetops. When Neelly arrived later that day, he had Lewis buried near the cabin. Lewis was wearing shabby, tattered clothing, not the dress uniform he had worn when he arrived at the inn. Neelly wrote a letter to Thomas Jefferson, informing him of Lewis' death: "It is with extreme pain I have to inform you of the death of His Excellency Meriwether Lewis...by suicide." Neelly shipped Lewis' trunk containing his journals to Washington. Missing from the trunk were Lewis' pistols and the one hundred dollars in cash he was carrying.

America was horrified to learn of the explorer's death, no one more so than the residents of the Mojo Triangle, who felt enormous collective guilt and anguish over his death. It was a major trauma for that time, similar to the 1963 assassination of President John F. Kennedy in Dallas, or the 2001 terrorist attack at the World Trade Center in New York. Meriwether Lewis, America's hero, had died on *their* watch—and in *their* backyard! Complicating the situation was the belief that Lewis had been murdered, either by bandits or by government agents who didn't want him to reach Washington.

Eventually, a monument was erected at his gravesite, a broken shaft, a symbol of a life cut short by violence. Almost from the moment of his death, scholars have debated whether Lewis committed suicide or was murdered. In 1993, James Starrs, a forensic scientist and law professor at George Washington University in Washington D.C., traveled to the gravesite in the hopes of solving that mystery. He was given permission to run ground-penetrating radar over the gravesite, but not to exhume the body.

"I look at Meriwether Lewis as an oddity in the scientific world because of the nature of the occurrence and the general claim that it was a suicide," said Starrs, who previously had helped solve the celebrated "Colorado Cannibal" mystery of 1874, involving an mountain guide convicted of killing and then eating his victims. "My immediate reaction was to smile a bit and shake my head, because from what I know about firearms, suicides in today's world, it would be a most unique suicide and extraordinary suicide. People who have written about it as suicide have looked at behavioral patterns.

I am only interested in the scientific, the hard science. My working hypothesis is that it was not suicide. The scientific evidence is entirely deficient that he committed suicide."

With a snow-white beard that makes him resemble a Civil War general more than a scientist—and an authoritative, military-like bearing that reinforces that distinction—Starrs arrived at the gravesite in 1993 with a team of forensic scientists and camped out, wilderness style, not far from Mrs. Grinder's cabin. That night, amid the campfires, Starrs paced and looked up at the stars, pondering his mission. "I think we can prove a case one way or the other, even without the remains, if we can find the projectile that was shot into him," he said. "If he had a chance to speak, what would he say? The only way he can speak is through his bones."

The next morning, the results of Starrs' ground-penetrating radar probe were inconclusive: The gravesite was an abstract picture of wavy lines, with no conclusive definition that would be helpful to a scientist—and no lead balls or potential projectiles were found in or around the grave, though that did not mean that none were there. Starrs pleaded with government authorities for permission to dig up the grave, to sift his fingers through the ancient soil that protected the secret, but the answer was no, based on an obscure federal law prohibiting the disturbance of burial sites. He returned to his Washington home, convinced that he could have solved the mystery.

The effect of Meriwether Lewis' death on succeeding generations in the Mojo Triangle cannot be overstated, for it established a legacy of defeat and dishonor, self-doubt and self-loathing, not to mention guilt and longing for history to be rewritten—not just because of the rumors of homosexuality, but because of what later was viewed as the abandonment of a great man in a time of need. And this was all long before the Civil War made such feelings understandable to the outside world. For the next two hundred years, the mythic memory of the event would stoke, albeit unknowingly, a fire in the belly of those who transformed their dreams and nightmares into the art of music and the written word.

◆ ▲ ◆ ▲ ◆

The Indians always knew. That might have been because, according to their legend, their people had come from the ground, deep beneath the surface, where rivers of molten earth flowed. They understood that what they saw on the surface was only part of the story, that for every river, every storm, every frightening atmospheric disturbance that thundered across the surface of the earth, there were corresponding frightening powers that moved with the same, if not greater, power beneath the surface.

Implanted in the genetic codes of the Choctaw and the Chickasaw were memories of great earthquakes that occurred five hundred, one thousand, ten thousand years before the arrival of the white man into the Mojo Triangle. In their eyes the whites were spiritually unsophisticated people who tended to view the natural world with a "what you see is what you get" mentality. The Choctaw and the Chickasaw knew that was not true, and they spoke to the white man of the great, always lurking, fearsome power of the earth, but the white man only laughed at them and their superstitions, telling them with great solemnity of the power of God Almighty in Heaven and of the power of Free Will.

Not until 1811 did the Indians and the white settlers come to a mutual understanding about the power of the earth. It began on Monday, December 16, at about two o'clock in the morning. John Bradbury, a Scottish scientist who had traveled to America to gather specimens of North American plant life, was asleep on a riverboat one hundred miles downstream from New Madrid, a small settlement south of where the Ohio River emptied into the Mississippi River.

Bradbury was awakened from a sound sleep by what he later described as a "tremendous noise." Before he could entirely rouse himself, he felt the boat lift into the air and then abruptly fall back to the water. He ran out on the deck and discovered that "all nature seemed running into chaos." The night was filled with horrific sounds—the screech of water fowl, the thundering sound of falling timber, the howl of a sudden wind, the roar of earthen banks collapsing into the river, the apocalyptic gurgle of the river changing course and flowing backward—but there was one sound that was more frightening than all the others combined, and that was the sound of the earthquake itself, an experience that Bradbury described as "equal to the loudest thunder, but more hollow and vibrating."

By first light, Bradbury had counted twenty-seven shocks. He and his crew were greeted by a raging river covered with foam, an obstacle course of entire trees carried by the currents—and ghost ships that passed, floating downriver, without crews and passengers. Bradbury's crew attempted to abandon their moored ship, but just as they made an effort to do so, a gigantic tree fell across their path, sending them scurrying back to the safety of the boat. Bradbury ordered the lines cut, and the boat ventured out into the channel, dodging the debris and the whirlpools, until, finally, he spotted a sloping piece of land that invited them to pull in to safety. They moored the boat and cooked breakfast before heading out again into the channel. Bradbury wrote, "Immediately after we had cleared all danger, the men dropped their oars, crossed themselves, then gave a shout, which was followed by mutual congratulations on their safety."

The earthquake that Bradbury and his men survived was the greatest in American history. Estimated to have been an eight on the Richter scale, it was centered at New Madrid, Missouri, where it leveled that small town and sent aftershocks that rumbled south to New Orleans and north to Detroit, and east to New England and the Canadian province of Quebec. Clocks stopped, and furniture moved about homes, as if being shoved by ghosts. Pavement was cracked as far away as Richmond and Washington.

The earthquake was not a one-time event. Jared Brooks, a Louisville surveyor, counted 1,874 shocks between December 16 and March 15, eight of which he classified as violent. Eliza Bryan, a New Madrid resident who survived the quake, described the event in a letter she wrote to a friend. "Beginning December 16, 1811, there were violent earthquakes in the area throughout the winter months. On some days, the atmosphere was so completely saturated with sulfurous vapors as to cause total darkness. Trees cracked and fell into the roaring Mississippi....The waters of the river gathered up like a mountain, fifteen to twenty feet perpendicularly, then receding within its banks with such violence that it took whole groves of cottonwoods which edged its borders. Fissures in the earth vomited forth sand and water, some closing again immediately."

Across the river, in northwestern Tennessee, the upheaval was so cata-strophic that the river changed course and created a thirteen thousand–acre lake that is today called Reelfoot Lake. Everyone dealt with the earthquake in different ways. The Chickasaw Indians, who lived on the land that was transformed into a lake, developed a legend to explain the event. According to the legend, the Chickasaw chief at that time was named Kalopin, which translated to Reelfoot, meaning he who walks with a rolling motion. One day, he was visiting his Choctaw neighbors to the south when he came across the woman of his dreams: Laughing Eyes, the daughter of the Choctaw chief.

When Kalopin asked for the woman's hand in marriage, the Choctaw chief was outraged. He did not want his daughter to marry a man with a physical deformity, so he told Kalopin that his daughter could only marry a man of Choctaw descent. If she were to do otherwise, he explained, the earth would tremble and the village would be swallowed up by a great wall of water.

Kalopin returned to his people, but he could not get the princess out of his mind. After many sleepless nights, he returned to Choctaw territory and rode into the village in the dead of night to steal away the princess so that she could become his wife. Once he returned to Tennessee, the tribe was so happy that he had found someone to love that they held a massive wedding party, during which the earth trembled and shook. To everyone's horror, the tremors were followed by a great wall of water that destroyed the village and killed everyone in it, including Kalopin and Laughing Eyes. The water that was left behind formed what is now called Reelfoot Lake.

A letter published first in the *Lexington Reporter,* and then reprinted in the *Pennsylvania Gazette,* described the terror of living through the earthquake:

> About two o'clock this morning we were awakened by a most tremendous noise, while the house danced about and seemed as if it would fall on our heads. I soon conjectured the cause of our troubles and cried out it was an earthquake, and for the family to leave the house, which we found very difficult to do, owing to its rolling and jostling about. The shock was soon over, and no injury was sustained, except the loss of the chimney, and the exposure of my family to the cold of the night. At the time of this shock, the heavens were very clear and serene, not a breath of air stirring; but in five minutes it became very dark, and a vapour which seemed to impregnate the atmosphere had a disagreeable smell, and produced a difficulty of respiration...The darkness continued till daybreak; during this time we had eight more shocks, none of them so violent as the first.

Once families escaped their homes, they gathered together their horses and wagons and fled to the countryside, where they felt they would be safe. That didn't make much sense, unless they lived in a city where buildings were tumbling to the ground, but their inbred response was simply to flee the scene of the destruction. One man later told of coming across a seventeen-year-old girl who had been left behind by her parents because her leg had been broken below the knee by a falling beam in the house. They left her on her bed, with supplies of water and cornbread, to fend for herself. The man who found her, took time to cook the girl a meal, but then he, too, left to find a safe place. Family loyalty and human kindness were no match for the blind fear engendered by the earthquake. Those who could run, ran; those who could not, perished.

Downriver settlements fared better than upriver settlements, though no one seems to understand why exactly. In the days following the earthquake, the *New York Evening Post* published a story that claimed, mistakenly as it turned out, that Natchez had sunk into the river, along with more than four thousand persons. The city suffered some structural damage, but the high bluffs protected it from a direct assault by the rampaging river, so there were remarkably few human casualties.

It took many years for scientists to understand what happened and why. Unknown to the residents who lived in the Mojo Triangle in 1811, New Madrid sat atop a fault that cuts through five states along the Mississippi River. At some places, the fault lies below more than three thousand feet of sediment, a ticking time bomb that the Indians understood for centuries, but were unable to communicate to their white neighbors. The psychological impact of that knowledge exacted a price in the years after the 1811 earthquake, for it was burned into the consciousness of every resident that death was only a tremor away. On any given night, another tremor could come, followed by the earth opening up to claim the lives of every living creature, human, and animal.

Modern science does not offer much comfort. Geologist Arch Johnston, who heads the earthquake center at the University of Memphis, has predicted that a magnitude eight earthquake could occur in the New Madrid zone every 550 to 1,000 years. Such a quake could cause tens of billions of dollars in damage from Mississippi to Michigan, leveling Memphis and seriously damaging St. Louis, he told the *Los Angeles Times:* "We have been accused of being alarmist, Chicken Little, the sky is falling, but we don't want to minimize what we see as a legitimate long-term hazard."

Scientists say that a level-seven earthquake is likely to occur within fifty to one hundred years, with a level six earthquake likely to occur at any time. "For the first time we can see how fast the earthquake engine is running and how long it takes to build up energy for a quake," geologist Karl Mueller told the *Los Angeles Times* in a 1999 interview. "New Madrid is the world's most spectacular example of liquefaction. When you take a fine-grained, saturated sediment like mud or silt and you shake it during an earthquake, it turns to the consistency of Jello. If you have a building that is sitting on top of Jello, the building falls down. The scary part about New Madrid is that...we see liquefaction all over the place there."

Scientists now know that the biggest threat for a catastrophic earthquake today is the New Madrid fault, not the San Andreas fault in California. When another level-eight earthquake comes—and it is not a matter of *if,* but rather when, for its arrival has been preordained—it will have the potential, according to the experts, to destroy Memphis, New Orleans, Natchez, Vicksburg, and perhaps even Nashville, returning America's premier music cities to the swampy, prehistoric mush from which they originally evolved...*and it burns, burn, burns, the ring of fire.*

◆ ▲ ◆ ▲ ◆

The plague began in New Orleans and worked its way up river, expanding throughout the Mojo Triangle, spreading the most agonizing death imaginable. In mild cases, the symptoms were similar to the flu, but in serious cases, known as the toxic phase, the patient developed a high temperature and then encountered a series of life-threatening conditions such as internal bleeding, kidney failure, hepatitis, and meningitis. The mortality rate for patients in the toxic phase was around fifty percent, with patients developing a yellow color and vomiting up large quantities of so-called "black" blood.

At first they thought it was malaria, typhoid, hepatitis, or poisoning of various kinds, but then, as the deaths mounted, people realized they were dealing with something new. Physicians gave it the name "yellow fever," because it left its victims badly jaundiced, but they were baffled by its causes; it took many years for them to discover that it is an infectious viral disease, with no known cure, that aggressively attacks the human liver and digestive tract. There had been signs of the disease early in the 1700s, but the outbreaks had never reached epidemic proportions, and the thinking then was that it was similar to a cold, an inconvenience but not a death sentence.

All that changed in the summer of 1796, when the disease blossomed into a deadly epidemic. Yellow fever is spread by mosquitoes, initially, but then can be transmitted by close contact with infected persons. Physicians did not know that at the time, and they looked to the environment for clues. In a report to the city council, the attorney general blamed "the stagnant waters that remain in the gutters of the streets, and the little cleanliness and care given to them, the dead animals abandoned on them, and on the margin of the river." The latter is a reference to flooding that left pools of water all about the city. Ironically, in his ignorance, the attorney general hit upon the real source of the problem: Stagnant water that allowed mosquitoes to thrive.

By winter, when the disease disappeared, more than two hundred of the city's six thousand residents had died. Other epidemics occurred in rapid succession. Between 1817 and 1905, more than forty-one thousand people died from yellow fever in New Orleans. As the disease made its way into the Mojo Triangle, it created conflicts as armed sentries took action to prevent travelers from New Orleans from entering their communities. Those who refused to turn back were shot dead on the spot.

In the spring of 1877, city officials were optimistic that the city would be spared a summer epidemic, because the previous year there had been no sign of the disease and all the "experts" had declared that the generous use of carbolic acid by public health officials had put an end to the city's suffering. By mid-July, they knew the horrible truth: Yellow fever had returned with a vengeance, giving the city its third-worst epidemic in history. Wrote one observer, "How it originated is a matter of dispute. Some maintain it was indigenous; others say it was imported here towards the end of May from the West Indies by the Steamer Emile B. Sonder and the germs remained latent until circumstances favored its development. Just a few days previously, our papers and people had been congratulating themselves on their being exempted from the intolerant heat which prostrated and killed hundreds of people in St. Louis and other western and northern cities. But scarcely did it become known that yellow fever had certainly made its appearance in our city than people began to leave it in the greatest fright and terror, so that the trains and boats could scarcely take away all who wanted to leave."

Within a matter of days, New Orleans was quarantined by the State of Texas and by individual cities such as Mobile, in an effort to keep the disease from spreading. "In some places, they drove out our refugees, refused them all shelter, kept them away with shotguns, refused all mails from this place," wrote one outraged citizen. "To the general rule, Louisville, Kentucky, was a most noble exception: She opened her doors to all our refugees, her hospitals to the sick, and her purse to the needy."

A person only had to walk through the streets of New Orleans during an epidemic to understand the terror that accompanied the disease. During the epidemic of 1853, one resident wrote: "As we passed the cemeteries, we saw coffins piled up beside the gate and in the walks, and the laborers at work, digging trenches in preparation for the morrow's dead. A fog, which hung over the moss-enveloped oaks, prevented the egress of the dense and putrid exhalations. The atmosphere was nauseating to a degree that I have never noticed in a sick room."

To "cleanse" the atmosphere, city officials ordered four hundred, six-pound discharges fired from the city's cannons. Barrels were filled with tar all over the city and then set afire in the belief that the thick, black smoke would drive away the illness. One diarist wrote: "When [the cannons] were simultaneously fired, a pandemonium glare lighted up our city. Not a breath of air disturbed the dense smoke, which slowly ascended in curling columns until it reached the height of about five hundred feet. Here it seemed equipoised, festooning over our doomed city like a funeral pall, and there remaining until the shades of night disputed with it the reign of darkness."

New Orleans doctors performed with courage and compassion during the epidemics, but that was not always the case with hospital workers. One elderly male nurse struck a writer as somewhat unusual:

The sick who were past recovery had for him a serpent-like fascination: when there was agony in the face or when the body writhed in contortions, he would chuckle. When the fatal symptom of the black vomit manifested itself, he grinned with a strange light—and the death-rattle was music to his ear. It turned out that the man had suffered from misfortune, deceit and ingratitude, and had become a hater of his kind, to whom remained no joy but that of seeing his fellowman in trouble and in pain.

As the epidemic made its way north, the Mojo Triangle became a string of outposts, as towns along the river, such as Natchez and Vicksburg, did the only thing they knew to do: Set up quarantines, so that no one could enter or leave the towns. One Natchez newspaper editor described his town as "closed up like an oyster." The most common emotion was panic, not unlike the fear associated with the earthquakes that occurred during this same period. The disease spread with the same unrelenting progress as creeping floodwaters, with towns all across Mississippi soon coming under its curse.

Memphis experienced major yellow fever epidemics in 1855 and 1867, which killed hundreds of luckless people, but those tragedies did nothing to prepare residents for what confronted them in the 1870s. In the spring and summer of 1873, after a long and unusually bitter winter, the city was hit by epidemics of yellow fever, cholera, and smallpox. The highest death toll resulted from fellow fever, which killed more than two thousand people. At that time, no one knew what caused yellow fever, but since there was considerable filth and standing water in the city, elected officials determined that the disease was the result of noxious gases that rose from the filth. To combat the gases, they fired cannons to dispel the deadly gases they imagined were hovering over the city.

As bad as that year was, it was nothing compared to what awaited the city in 1878. Within four days of the announcement of the first yellow fever death on August 13, more than half the city's forty thousand residents had fled to the countryside, where for a two-hundred-mile radius they were greeted by gun-toting vigilantes determined to prevent them from entering their communities.

Of the nearly twenty thousand residents who remained in Memphis, seventeen thousand contracted the disease. In a display of unprecedented heroism, most of the city's African-American residents, almost all of them former slaves, stayed in the city during the epidemic, supplying the majority of the three thousand nurses who cared for the sick and dying. They distributed the supplies that poured in from all over the country, and they collected and buried thousands of corpses. When the white police force fled the city in fear, African-Americans formed two militia companies that patrolled the streets to keep the peace and to prevent looting.

Of the six thousand whites who remained, virtually all were stricken by the fever, resulting in the deaths of about two-thirds of them. Incredibly, less than one thousand blacks died of the disease. Of the 111 physicians in the city when the epidemic began, 54 came down with the disease and 33 died.

A letter written in the 1800s by a Memphis man to a relative describes, in stark detail, the progression of the disease in a little girl that he cared for until her death:

> "Lucille died at 10 o'clock Tuesday night, after such suffering as I hope never again to witness. Once or twice my nerve almost failed me, but I managed to stay. The poor girl's screams might be heard for half a square, and at times I had to exert my utmost strength to hold her in bed. Jaundice was marked, the skin being a bright yellow hue: Tongue and lips dark, cracked, and blood oozing from the mouth and nose...To me the most terrible and terrifying feature was the 'black vomit,' which I never before witnessed. By Tuesday it was black as ink and would be ejected with terrific force. I had my face and hands spattered but had to stand by and hold her. Well, it is too terrible to write any more about it."

The Memphis experience with the disease, so far as African Americans were concerned, was indicative of the statistics throughout the region. For some reason, blacks possessed a high degree of immunity to yellow fever, presumably the result of a disease-resistant gene pool imported from Africa.

Yellow fever did not cease to be a major threat in the Mojo Triangle until 1905, when New Orleans suffered its last recorded epidemic. Some of the credit for the disease's disappearance must go to an army doctor named William Gorgas, who was sent to Panama to devise methods to protect canal workers from yellow fever. He implemented a program to destroy mosquito populations and to equip buildings with screen doors and windows. He also had buildings regularly fumigated, and he covered standing water with layers of oil. Within a year, Gorgas' common-sense approach to the problem brought the threat to a manageable level. Those techniques were brought back to the States, where they were put to widespread use in cities across the nation.

With efficient mosquito control techniques, improved treatment, and better sanitation, yellow fever was literally beaten back to Central and South America. However, there remains a mystery surrounding its precipitous demise. Screen doors and mosquito control, as important as they are, cannot explain why the disease disappeared. It may be that it entered a dormancy cycle, or it may be that the widespread use of vaccine in the 1950s, 1960s, and 1970s held the disease in check for the remainder of the century.

Today, the disease hovers in South America and Africa, infecting about two hundred thousand individuals each year and generating about thirty thousand deaths. If it again targets the Mojo Triangle, like a hurricane making a beeline to the swamp, its residents will be powerless to stop it: There is no known cure for the disease, and America's once impressive stock of vaccine has been depleted to the point of impotence.

For residents of the Mojo Triangle, yellow fever is a metaphor for the sins of the past, especially as they relate to slavery and the eradication of the Choctaw and the Chickasaw from their ancient lands, for deep in their hearts they don't believe in good and evil so much as they believe in an unfriendly world in which no bad deed ever goes unpunished. It is that belief that contributes to the burden that feeds their creativity.

Novelist William Faulkner had something similar in mind when he told an interviewer: "What time a man can devote to morality, he must take by force from the motion of which he is a part. He is compelled to make choices between good and evil sooner or later, because moral conscience demands that from him in order that he can live with himself tomorrow. His moral conscience is the curse he had to accept from the gods in order to gain from them the right to dream."

◆　▲　◆　▲　◆

At the outbreak of the Civil War, more than 92% of the country's manufacturing output was in the North. The South accounted for only 3% of the manufacture of boots and shoes, and its production of woolen and cotton cloth was less than one-tenth of that of New England alone. The South had one-fifth of the country's iron foundries, but most of them were located in Virginia, Tennessee, and Louisiana, and they quickly fell into enemy hands. The total white population of the eleven states in the Confederacy was 5.4 million, while the white population of the states in the North was 21 million. That translated to eight hundred thousand men between the ages of eighteen and thirty-five in the South, and 3.2 million men between the ages of eighteen and thirty-five in the North. The only area where the South had an advantage was in the production of corn and pork.

Was it possible to win a war with corn and pork alone? No rational person would think so, but after the attack of Fort Sumter by the Confederates in 1861, reason was the first casualty. Three months later, with an impressive Confederate victory at Manassas, the South was convinced that the war was winnable, especially with Mississippian Jefferson Davis as the Confederacy's first president—and the North realized that the war was theirs to lose. Nowhere in the South was the optimism more vibrant than in the Mojo Triangle, where the battle cry had less to do with slavery (in Mississippi, very few whites owned slaves—out of a white population of three hundred fifty-three thousand, only thirty-one thousand whites owned slaves, with only eighteen thousand slaveholders owning more than five slaves) than it did the nearly two-hundred-year old friction over individual rights. Almost all of the wealthy immigrants to the area were royalists who never agreed with the break from Great Britain. They never believed in the concept of the "United States," and with the beginning of the Civil War, they saw an opportunity to create a new nation that could align with Great Britain and adapt the same restrictions on individual rights—that is, that some people, by virtue of their breeding and success in life, were entitled to more rights than others. Today, the ideological descendents of those people are flag-waving members of the Republican Party, but in the 1860s they were the self-righteous minority, enemies of the Revolution that had elevated Thomas Jefferson and George Washington to hero status.

The main targets of Union forces in the Mojo Triangle were New Orleans, Memphis, Nashville, and Vicksburg, cities they wasted no time in conquering. Natchez was also invaded, but because it was considered of little strategic importance to the Union, no major battles took place there. That is not to say that residents did not undergo moments of terror. One day, the Essex, a gunboat manned by Union troops, anchored just off shore and sent a small boat filled with marines to the shore to collect ice for their ill and wounded. Spotting them from the bluff was a local resident who quickly mobilized a group of armed citizens and starting firing at the Yankees.

Annie Harper, a member of the plantation gentry, later wrote about the incident in a book published for her descendents. "The immediate response to this unwarranted piece of folly was a shell from the gun boat," she wrote.

"From two o'clock until six the bombardment was incessant. The roads leading from the town were filled with a stampeding throng...One circumstance alone prevented the destruction of life and property from being immense—very few of the shells exploded, a few went crashing though buildings full of people, where the carnage would have been very great had they exploded. One little girl running up the hill leading from the landing was killed by a piece of shell."

Up river, at Vicksburg, a major battle took place over a port that the Union army considered the most important on the Mississippi River. After forty-seven days of fierce fighting, nearly thirty thousand Confederate soldiers surrendered to General Ulysses S. Grant, who raised the Stars and Stripes over the county courthouse, thus sealing the fate of the South. Still, they fought—all up and down the Mojo Triangle.

In Oxford, Grant captured the Lafayette County courthouse, surrounding it with the tents of an Illinois regiment. Later, federal troops set fire to the courthouse and several Oxford residences, burning them to the ground. Wrote one Illinois correspondent: "Where once stood a handsome little country town, now only remain the blackened skeletons of houses, and smoldering ruins."

The Civil War was not an abstraction to the residents of the Mojo Triangle: It was a reality of everyday life, a life-altering descent into a hell that left deep wounds and fissures, scars—both physical and emotional—that are visible to this day. Most Americans were untouched by the violence of the war, but that wasn't the case for the men and women who witnessed the carnage firsthand and saw loved ones, property, and dreams for a better life turned to rubble by an invading war machine. The final months of the war were a nightmare for southern civilians, white and black. Federal troops burned, looted, and sometimes killed at random, showing little compassion to the slaves. Wrote a correspondent for the *New York Evening Post*: "Many, very many of the soldiers and not a few of the officers have habitually treated the negroes [sic] with the coarsest and most brutal insolence and inhumanity, never speaking to them but to curse and revile them."

By the end of the war, the Mojo Triangle was in a shambles. Federal victories at Nashville, Memphis, Vicksburg, and New Orleans had destroyed all symbols of stability, replacing them with a new military order. County and city governments were replaced by military districts that governed as harshly as an occupying foreign power. Of the seventy-eight thousand Mississippians who went off to war, more than fifty-nine thousand were killed or wounded. Mississippi allocated one-fifth of its total revenues during the first year of peace to purchase artificial arms and legs for returning soldiers.

During Reconstruction, federal troops prevented Confederate veterans from voting or running for elective office. Women were still half a century away from achieving voting rights, so that meant that the voting pool was made up of white males who never served in the Confederacy, black males who went from slavery to the voting booth, and the so-called carpetbaggers from the North who went South to make fortunes.

Ninety-three years after the cessation of hostilities, Oxford resident William Faulkner told an interviewer that passions ran high for many years after the war. "I can remember the old men, and they would get out the old shabby grey uniforms and get out the old battle flag on Memorial Day. Yes, I remember any number of them. But it was the aunts—the women—that had never given up. My aunt, she liked to go to picture shows, they had *Gone With the Wind* in the theatre at home and she went to see it, and as soon as Sherman came on the screen she got up and left. She had paid good money to go there, but she wasn't going to sit and look at Sherman."

The war was so traumatic that even today you can find individuals who can tell you the names of their kinfolk who died defending Atlanta, Vicksburg, Nashville, New Orleans, Memphis, Oxford, and a hundred other places, along with the dates of their deaths and the home addresses of their likely killers. In 2004, this author overheard an elderly white woman comment on the American invasion of Iraq: "They're doing the same thing to those Iraqis that they did to us, aren't they?"

Hard feelings die slowly in the Mojo Triangle. The South is the only part of America that has ever known defeat. That sense of loss is especially strong in the Mojo Triangle, where the betrayal that is felt, even today, among whites and blacks is not just the result of abuse that their ancestors suffered at the hands of federal troops, but because of the destruction of their ancestors' world view. For the majority of white southerners to believe that the plantation owners were better than they, they had to believe that they, in turn, were better than the blacks. The war destroyed that illusion, not just for the whites but for the blacks that had invested in the system in their own way, only to discover that freedom was just another word for nothing else to lose.

Throughout all the travail, the people took comfort in one of their most valuable resources: Their music. Musical instruments were played at all public events, during military ceremonies, and at gatherings called for the purpose of raising spirits. One song, a sad ballad called "Lorena," was a favorite of audiences across the South. Another favorite was "Battle of Manassas," a song composed by a Georgia slave named Blind Tom, who dazzled audiences with his virtuoso piano performances. It was said at the time that Blind Tom had perfect pitch and could play any song after hearing it once.

If there was a silver lining, it was that the cessation of the war meant that thousands of musical instruments used by the troops were sold as war surplus at cut-rate prices. Former slaves discovered that they could purchase trumpets, drums, fiddles, and flutes for pennies and then form bands and play for money, especially in New Orleans. Music had played an important role during the war, whether it was to inspire Confederate troops with "Dixie" or to inspire federal troops with "When Johnny Comes Marching Home Again." Actually, northerners wrote both songs and during the first years of the war, "Dixie" was just as popular in the North as it was in the South.

Indeed, when General Robert E. Lee surrendered at Appomattox, President Abraham Lincoln requested that the band play "Dixie," which he said was one of the best tunes ever written. Lincoln said, "I had heard that our adversaries over the way had attempted to appropriate it. I insisted yesterday that we had fairly captured it...I presented the question to the Attorney-General, and he gave his opinion that it is our lawful prize...I ask the band to give us a good turn upon it."

◆　▲　◆　▲　◆

And the flood was forty days upon the earth;
And the waters increased, and bare up the ark, and
It was lifted up above the earth.
And the waters prevailed, and were increased greatly upon the earth;
And the ark went upon the face of the waters.
And the waters prevailed exceedingly upon the earth;
All the high hills, that were under the whole heaven, were covered.
— Genesis

In 1927, before the Great Depression had sucked the last remnants of hope from those struggling to make a living in the Mojo Triangle, there was an event of biblical proportions in the Mississippi Delta, a turning of the wheel that had disastrous results. It began in March 1927, with the falling of a single raindrop, which is not an unusual occurrence in the Delta, where rain competes with sunshine for dominance on a daily basis. Only in this instance, the raindrop expanded to a downpour and then into torrential rains, accompanied by waves of horrific tornados, that continued day after day, week after week, until the forty-day, forty-night marker was met. The creeks and small rivers along the Mississippi River arm of the Mojo Triangle swelled, pouring water into the Mississippi River at such a furious rate that by April 20, the water level crept up the levees at Greenville, well past the danger point, sending residents into a panic as they envisioned the worst.

Then, it happened: On April 21, at 7:30 in the morning, there was a break eighteen miles north of Greenville at Mounds Landing. At the time the levee broke, black workers were straddling the earthen wall, feverishly tossing sandbags to the very end. They were swept to their deaths by a fourteen-foot wall of water as it rushed toward the cotton fields, crushing everything in its path. An engineer later calculated that the amount of water pouring

Supplies unloaded at Greenville during the Mississippi River floods of 1927. (Audie Turner)

through the levee equaled the amount of water passing over Niagara Falls.

When Greenville residents heard about the break, they panicked. It was too late to flee in cars, since the water would certainly overtake them, so the only avenues of escape were the trains that had come to the city in anticipation of an evacuation. The trains packed everyone into the railcars that they could, then fled from the city, their whistles screaming like a great beast in the throes of death. One train, the last to leave, was washed off the tracks just outside the city, the rails turned up on their side like a fence.

Those who remained were greeted by a wall of water with five-foot breakers. Families leaped onto kitchen tables to keep their feet dry, watching the water fill the inside of their homes, rising, rising, rising, until soon the tables were no longer adequate and they fled to the second floor or the attic—eventually using axes to cut their way onto the roof, where they remained, sometimes for days, until they could be rescued.

"Water was just rolling in, like you see the waves down in Gulfport," Jesse Pollard told author John M. Barry. "They were high—you saw horses and cows floating. If you were standing on the levee, you could see people floating who had drowned. It was a sight you never forget."

The water rushed well past Greenville, spreading out across the Delta with apocalyptic determination. At Metcalfe, four miles from Greenville, Fred Chaney ran for a boxcar, fearing the worst. Because the railroad tracks were elevated—and the boxcar was elevated a couple of feet beyond the tracks—he figured it would be as safe a place as any he could find. "At nine o'clock we could hear the rustle of waters in the woods a mile north of our boxcar haven," he later wrote in his reminiscences of the flood. "It sounded not unlike the rising rush of the first gust of wind before an oncoming storm, and a shiver shot up and down my spine as the rustling noise grew louder and its true significance plumbed the depths of my mind. Before I reached the railroad track, the water was swirling around my feet! From somewhere out of the night rose the piercing wail of a Negro woman's hysterical scream."

Amid the chaos, Alexander William Percy, Greenville's leading citizen and chairman of the Flood Relief Committee, took charge and ordered everyone to evacuate the city in boats that already were on their way. It was a controversial decision, because he meant to evacuate both whites and blacks, but he encountered opposition from planters who feared if their workers got on board the boats they would never return, and opposition from a significant number of blacks who refused to leave their homes, for fear that whites would seize their possessions in their absence.

"What should we do with the Negroes: Evacuate them in the same manner or feed them from centralized kitchens as the Belgians had been fed?" Percy later wrote in his memoirs. "There were seventy-five hundred of them. It was raining and unseasonably cold. They were clammy and hungry, finding shelter anywhere, sleeping on any floor, piled pell-mell in oil mills or squatting miserably

Greenville residents receive vaccinations during the Mississippi River flood of 1927. (Audie Turner)

on the windy levee. The levee itself was the only dry spot where they could be assembled or where tents by way of shelter could be set up for them. In spite of our repeated and frantic efforts we had been unable to procure a single tent."

Percy decided that evacuation was the only solution, but when he suggested that they get on the boats, they refused. The whites did not have to be persuaded; the first steamer out of Greenville, *The Control*, left with five hundred white women and children. Others soon followed. Once the boats were filled with white residents, Percy sent the remaining boats away still empty. One of the boats played "Bye Bye Blackbird" on its calliope, a slap in the face to the blacks who refused to budge from the levee. The following day, the sun came out and tents arrived from Vicksburg, enough to house the blacks in camps atop those portions of the levee that had not been breeched.

Once the hysteria of the moment passed, everyone did their best to keep warm and dry—and then they waited for the water to recede. It took a good four months for the nightmare to end. More than two million acres were flooded, affecting nearly two hundred thousand people. The water went down slowly, first soaking into the land, then evaporating in the hot sun, and finally making its way into the very tributaries that originally caused the problem. Left behind were thousand upon thousands of poisonous snakes, most of which were quite irritable over their changing fortunes.

"For months we Delta people have been suffering together, black and white alike," wrote Percy. "God did not distinguish between us. He struck us all to our knees. He spared no one. He sent His terrible waters over us and He found no one of us worthy to be helped by Him, so we had to help ourselves."

When everyone returned to their homes, they often found that their homes had simply disappeared, leaving cook stoves, anvils, and heavy tools and utensils that were rusted and mired in the mud, mocking them with reminders of better days. Federal statistics report that 162,017 homes were flooded in a seven-state area, though mostly in the Mississippi Delta and southern Louisiana, resulting in the destruction of 41,487 buildings and the deaths of approximately five hundred people. By the time Delta residents repaired and rebuilt their homes, about two years for most people, they were hit hard by the Great Depression.

◆　▲　◆　▲　◆

Night terror means one thing to those with chronic sleep disorders, but to those with roots in the Mojo Triangle, it has another, even more ominous, meaning: It is what many people felt from 1865 to the mid-1970s when the sun went down each evening, especially in the wild and untamed Delta, in the scrub pine forests around Tupelo, Jackson, Natchez, and Philadelphia, or in the urban jungles of Memphis, New Orleans, and Nashville. It was a frightening time that engendered nightmares among both whites and blacks.

Post-Civil War Reconstruction was chaotic for almost everyone in the Mojo Triangle. Southerners were the only Americans, other than indigenous Native Americans, ever to live as a defeated nation under military rule. Frustrated over losing their voting rights, not to mention their farms and businesses and any hope of gainful employment, former officers of the Confederate army organized into a secret society called the Ku Klux Klan, for the purpose of burning, looting, and killing families of newly freed slaves. They rode at night, hooded men on fast horses who felt that, by inflicting a wave of terror against freed slaves, they were somehow compensating for the terror that had been inflicted on them by federal troops.

As a military strategy, it didn't make much sense. The former slaves had taken nothing from them, other than their own freedom. Indeed, they had hoisted, without compensation or even the hope of compensation, the challenges of the wilderness on their backs to build a prosperous society for the very white men who now terrorized them. Logically, their anger should have been directed against the federal troops who abused and humiliated them at every opportunity, but they took the coward's way and turned on their own people (even if they did have different coloring on their skin— reminiscent of acts against the Chickasaw and Choctaw before them). It was a sacrilege against not only God, but the land itself, and, as is so often the case, it was not undertaken without a steep price.

One of the founding members of the Ku Klux Klan was General Nathan Bedford Forrest, who had grown up poor in Bedford County, Tennessee, where he received little education, but apparently enough to become wealthy by dealing in land and slaves. At the start of the war, he equipped a mounted battalion at his own expense and quickly rose to the rank of lieutenant general by leading some of the most daring cavalry raids of the war. He envisioned the Klan as an elite organization, whose purpose was to restore the South to some semblance of its previous glory; but the reality of the organization was that it was composed of uneducated men whose only mark of distinction had been the military ranks they had achieved during the war. When the war ended, they found themselves at the lowest rung of the social ladder, unable to compete for work against non-veterans or obtain loans for businesses; brash enough to be night riders that terrorized black men, women, and children, but not courageous enough to take on the United States army in broad daylight.

Looking back, one gets the impression that everyone involved was delusional, but the source of many of the problems of that era had more to do with a lack of accurate information than it did with mental illness. Whites felt threatened by the large numbers of African Americans assuming political office, and when they were told that the Klan was there to protect them from abuse at the hands of blacks, they believed it because there was no single source of unbiased news.

R. H. Henry, editor of the *Newton Ledger*, was like most white southerners: He didn't approve of the Klan's tactics, but the alternative—unfettered black power—worried him enough to allow him to look the other way. "The negroes [sic] and their carpet-bag friends were mortally afraid of the Ku Klux Klan, which has been organized to bring peace and order out of chaos in the South, and to make negroes and their associates behave themselves," he wrote in his memoirs. He described a situation in which white "renegades," one of whom had married a black woman, had "trumped up" charges that several leading citizens were members of the Klan, resulting in their being taken into custody by United States marshals. Prominent among the arrested men, wrote Henry, was the "well-known citizen T. M. Scanlan, sterling old Confederate soldier. He was carried before the federal court and, when asked certain questions about the order, refused to answer them. He was interrogated time after time, and told he would be committed to jail if he did not answer. He stood firm, refusing to give the court the names of the members of the Klan or divulge any of its secret work. He was ordered to jail, where he remained three months, when he was released by order of the court, but never gave away any of the secrets of the Klan." White Mississippians were so outraged by Scanlan's treatment that they encouraged Henry to relocate in Jackson and merge his newspaper with the *Clarion* in order to produce a newspaper with statewide clout that could better look after the interests of white citizens. Henry took their advice and established the *Clarion-Ledger*, a newspaper dedicated to the "establishment of an outspoken, white-line Democratic" viewpoint.

Violence was common in the years following the Civil War. In Memphis, there was a race riot in 1868 that left forty-six blacks and two whites dead. The riot began when a black man in a cart collided with a white man in a wagon. The collision seems like meager fodder for a race riot, but the collision was symbolic of a larger societal issue. Symbolically, the "right-of-way" issue extended to every level of society. Who has the right of way in a democratic society? In those days, it was a question over which normally reasonable men fought to the death.

Even amid the chaos, there were those in the Mojo Triangle that tried to come to terms with the past, even as they faltered in the present. Natchez diarist Annie Harper was brave enough to ask herself the tough questions. "Was there no dark side to the old plantation life?" she wrote. "Was nothing true of all we have heard of the horrors of slavery? Undoubtedly there was. Whenever unlimited power is given to one race over another, these evils will be found; and there were cruel, bad masters and mistresses in the South, but these were far in the minority. I can only say that, among the cultured and educated classes, it was considered a disgrace to be an unkind master.... In looking backward, I again record my thankfulness that African slavery is gone forever, with so many of the baleful things of the past. I thank God for so much of the purification of the earth—and pray that we may be led into the 'freedom of the truth.'"

The Klan was disbanded in 1869, by order of Grand Wizard Forrest, but it never went very far away, staying just close enough to re-emerge when needed— one generation, two generations, three generations down the road. The Klan returned in the 1920s with a nationwide membership, but the objects of hate were not blacks so much as they were Catholics and Jews. In fairness, it must be said that most of the racial violence that happened after the turn of the century had little or nothing to do with the Klan. It was mostly a string of unrelated occurrences, typically involving alleged theft or sexual advances by black men toward white women. In those instances, the terrorists typically were the victims of the theft, or the belligerent husbands or boyfriends of the women involved. Hangings took place on a regular basis throughout the Mojo Triangle.

It was not until the emergence of the civil rights movement in the late 1950s and early 1960s that the Klan returned in a big way to the Mojo Triangle, but it was not the old, aristocratic Klan envisioned by Forrest; it was more of a refuge for lower-class whites—down-on-their-luck truck drivers and gas station attendants eager to prove their superiority to higher-class, educated blacks. They were assisted in their efforts by super-secret state spy agencies called sovereignty commissions, the worst being located in Mississippi and Louisiana, where government links to the Klan were commonplace.

Perhaps the most famous non-Klan-related killings in Mississippi were the Medgar Evers and Emmett Till murders, two separate racial crimes that horrified the nation. The Till murder took place just outside Greenwood in the summer of 1955, when a fourteen-year-old black youth, who had traveled from Chicago to visit relatives, was dragged from his uncle's cabin, severely beaten, and shot in the head for allegedly whistling at a pretty white woman. His killers tied a seventy-pound cotton-gin fan around his neck with barbed wire and tossed his body into the Tallahatchie River. Roy Bryant, the woman's husband, and a second man, J. W. Milam, were charged with the murder. After a four-day trial, the two men were acquitted by an all-male, all-white jury. The following year, Milam admitted in a *Look* magazine article that he and Bryant did the killing: "'Chicago boy,' I said. 'I'm tired of them sending your kind down here to stir up trouble. I'm going to make an example of you, just so everybody can know how me and my folks stand.'" They couldn't be prosecuted again because of double jeopardy.

The Evers murder took place in Jackson, when the civil rights activist was shot in the back with a .30-06 deer rifle when he returned home from work. The bullet penetrated his right shoulder blade, ripped through his body, and then crashed into a window of the house, finally landing with a thud on the kitchen counter. Arrested for the murder was Byron De La Beckwith, an ex-Marine from Greenwood. Beckwith proclaimed his innocence at the 1964 trial, and the all-male, all-white jury was unable to reach a verdict. Prior to the trial, the Mississippi Sovereignty Commission screened the jury pool for the defense, providing Beckwith's lawyers with comments beside each name such as "fair and impartial" and "believed to be Jewish." One of the jurors belonged to the right-wing Citizens' Council, and another was a cousin of the Commission investigator. The second trial ended in a hung jury. Beckwith was released from jail, and he was not tried again until 1993. When the verdict was announced in 1994, people were stunned—not so much because he was found guilty, because everyone knew all along that he was guilty, but because justice would finally be administered after thirty years. Later, Rob Reiner made the story into a movie based on Maryanne Vollers' book, *Ghosts of Mississippi*.

The most famous Klan-related crime of the 1960s was the one associated with the murder of civil rights workers Michael Schwerner, Andrew Goodman, and James Chaney, who disappeared outside Philadelphia, Mississippi, not far from the Choctaw reservation. The Sovereignty Commission had had them under surveillance for months, but when they disappeared, the commission members pretended to be as shocked as everyone else was.

Nearly two months later, FBI agents, under the leadership of Joe Sullivan, found the bodies of the civil rights workers in an earthen dam near Philadelphia. Ballistic experts determined that Schwerner had been shot once in the chest, as had Goodman, but that Chaney, the African American, had been shot three times—all with a .38 caliber weapon. The weapon was never found, but the FBI compiled enough evidence to arrest twenty-one people, including the county sheriff, Lawrence Rainey, and his chief deputy, Cecil Price. To the FBI's dismay, federal judges dismissed charges against all the defendants, except Rainey and Price; prosecutors then took the case to a Jackson grand jury, where they were successful in obtaining indictments for eighteen of the twenty-one men originally charged. Later, the FBI identified the sheriff and two of his deputies as members of the Ku Klux Klan. Ultimately, seven defendants were convicted of civil rights violations—no one was ever prosecuted for the murder—but Sheriff Rainey and seven defendants were acquitted, with three defendants going free because the jury could not reach a verdict. The men received sentences varying between three and ten years. The judge defended his staggered sentences by saying: "They killed one nigger, one Jew and a white man. I gave them all what I thought they deserved."

The civil rights cases mentioned here, along with many others too numerous to name, had a profound effect on whites and blacks coming of age in the Mojo Triangle. Parents worried that their children would leave home in the morning and never return.

For the whites, the parental warning was: "Come home before dark, so the niggers don't get you." For the blacks, the parental warning was: "Watch

Ku Klux Klan rally near Tupelo, Mississippi, 1978. (Steve Gardner)

what you say, and don't look at white folks, even if they are looking at you, because you don't ever know what they're gonna do when the sun goes down."

Night terrors were a fact of life. During the daylight hours, if you had occasion to meet a man, you never knew, really, who he was or what he was capable of doing to you, whether he was crazy stupid or crazy smart, so you were careful what you said, where you went, and what you did when you got there. (It is one of the reasons that Southerners are so interested in knowing a stranger's family ties, for they are gene-obsessed: well aware that unstable behavior is often passed from generation to generation.) No matter how smart or beautiful or wealthy or talented you were, at the end of the day you still had to face the same darkness that greeted everyone else, and you knew that if you were to be held accountable for your actions, real or imagined, it would most likely occur on a moonless night, when you would be most vulnerable to the reckless will of others.

3 THE NATCHEZ TRACE
▼ Spiritual Aorta of the American Experience

The Natchez Trace is a two-thousand-year-old wilderness trail that snakes northeast from Natchez, across the heart of the Mojo Triangle, up through northern Mississippi and western Alabama, to its northern termination point in Nashville, Tennessee, a distance of about five hundred miles. The French first mapped the trail in 1733, but the actual path was created by Native Americans long before the voyage of Christopher Columbus. Ancient burial mounds along the trail have been dated to 100 B.C.

By 1810, the Trace was the most heavily traveled wilderness trail in the Old Southwest. By 1820, there were more than twenty inns along its route, many of which offered musical entertainment to weary travelers. With increased commerce came increased crime, and for years the Trace was traveled by roving bands of outlaws who hid within the trail's lush, green foliage to ambush unsuspecting travelers. It was for that reason that most travelers often went in groups of fifteen to twenty, walking single-file, with weapons at the ready.

In time, the Trace became the most notorious outlaw trail east of the Mississippi River. Because the trail was located on the southwestern edge of American "civilization," it was considered to be immune to traditional law enforcement restrictions. It was from this free, wide-open atmosphere of commerce and lawlessness that Southern music developed and spread throughout the region, enduring nightmarish floods, earthquakes, plagues, and man's inhumanity to man to express in art what history books could not capture.

For hundreds of years, first with Native Americans and then later with white settlers and explorers, the Trace has served as a magnet for the accumulation of hopes and dreams on a grand scale. As a result, it was on the Trace that many of the greatest passions and tragedies of American life occurred. Even today, travelers can feel the raw spiritual power of the Trace. (The author's advice to anyone suffering from a damaged spirit, or broken heart, is to spend a couple of nights alone on the Trace to tap into its ancient power.) The Trace is more than just another roadway: It is the spiritual aorta of the American experience.

Despite its outlaw past, the Natchez Trace is today a national park and falls under the jurisdiction of federal park rangers. That means that law-breakers, even those caught speeding, are prosecuted in federal court, which is an excellent deterrent to crime. Not only is the Trace one of the most interesting and scenic roadways in the South, today it is one of the safest.

♦　▲　♦　▲　♦

The Civil War had only been over for thirty-two years, when Jimmie Rodgers was born on September 8, 1897, in Last Gap, Mississippi, a small community near the city of Meridian. The state was still in turmoil over the lingering effects of Reconstruction. For example, in the 1870s, Mississippi had a black lieutenant governor, six consecutive black secretaries of state, a black state librarian, two black speakers of the House of Representatives, and a black superintendent of education, but a convention was held in 1890 to write a new state constitution (the one now in use), the main purpose of which was to restrict the rights and social development of Mississippi's African-American population.

Jimmie Rodgers grew up in and around Meridian, which General Sherman had terrorized and burned to the ground during the Civil War. Rebuilt from the ground up, it became an important railroad city that, despite its logistical importance to the railroad, was essentially in the middle of nowhere, even by Mississippi standards. Near the Alabama state line and about one hundred-fifty miles from the Mississippi River, Meridian was ninety miles from the Natchez Trace and less than fifty miles from the Choctaw Reservation. If a man didn't own a farm, or work on one, or have a good job with the railroad, he was pretty much out of luck in Meridian, because otherwise there were few economic opportunities.

When Rodgers was born, his father, Aaron, had a job with the Gulf, Mobile, and Ohio Railroad as an extra-gang foreman, which meant that he traveled a lot with his men to repair severed and faulty line sections. Not wishing to leave his wife alone with the baby, he left his railroad job to try his hand at farming. That came to an end shortly after Rodgers' mother died of tuberculosis when he was four. Aaron sent Jimmie to Alabama to live with relatives for a short while, and then he married a woman with a four-year-old son, Jake. To support his family, he returned to railroad work, this time taking a job with the New Orleans and North Eastern Line.

In 1906, Aaron and his wife, Ida, had a daughter they named Lottie Mae, and for a time it seemed that Jimmie would have a normal upbringing—at least normal by local standards—but by the time he was fourteen, he was again a motherless child, after the sudden death of his stepmother. After Ida's death, Lottie and Jake were sent to live with her relatives, and Jimmie stuck with his father, which meant that he spent a great deal of time hanging out with railroad workers, white and black.

Jimmie's interest in music began at an early age. He used bed sheets to construct a tent in which he performed for friends and relatives, obviously re-creating the mood of the blackface minstrel shows that passed through from time to time. By the age of twelve, according to authors Mike Paris and Chris Comber, he won a talent competition in Meridian with his rendition of "Steamboat Bill" and "Bill Bailey," also known as "Won't You Come Home Bill Bailey." Jimmie was enamored by the banjo music that was a staple in the minstrel shows, but the only people he knew who could play the banjo were black railroad workers. It is not surprising that black railroad workers would know how to play the banjo, considering that it is the only authentic African-American instrument to survive slavery.

Jimmie associated freely with blacks in his youth, but that was not unusual at that time. White women associated with black women, and white men associated with black men (and occasionally black women), with the only taboo being associations between white women and black men. Blacks and whites attended many of the same entertainment functions, although blacks were asked to sit in the balcony or in the back rows. Blacks enjoyed the minstrel shows as much as the whites, and when they played music, it was more likely than not to be the songs they heard at the minstrel shows. There was no black music, per se, only popular music that both races wanted to learn.

Jimmie also learned to play guitar while hanging out at the railroad yards. It is not known who taught him, but that expertise also probably came from the black workers. When the Spanish, and then the Scots, brought the guitar to the Mojo Triangle, African Americans didn't pick it up right away; for a long time, the guitar was considered more of a white man's instrument, more complicated than the banjo and less adaptive than the banjo to the up-tempo tunes that then were in vogue.

Jimmie Rodgers carried water for the railroad workers, and then was hired as his father's assistant. Finally, in 1913, at the age of sixteen, he was hired as a brakeman on the line's freight trains. He loved the work, for the most part, but one of his chores was to manhandle the hoboes that hitched rides on the freight cars, and he couldn't bring himself to kick them off the train. Typically, he bribed them into leaving by offering them fifty cents for lunch, an offer that was just too good for any of them to turn down.

It was around this time that Jimmie developed a distinctive yodel that he later named the "blue yodel." It is a style of singing that involves changing a normal singing tone to a falsetto and then back again in rapid succession. The yodel is most often associated with the Alpine mountaineers of Switzerland, but it existed long before that among Native Americans, who went in and out of falsettos while singing their sacred music. African Americans developed a yodeling style while attempting to imitate the Choctaw and Natchez Indians who greeted them upon their arrival in North America, and adapted it to popular white songs they heard at the plantations. Jimmie may have learned his yodeling style from black railroad workers, but it is more likely that he learned it from the Choctaws that he came into contact with as a railroad worker, or from the Indians who came into Philadelphia or Meridian to perform in traditional dress, a common occurrence on courthouse lawns in some parts of the state.

While still in his teens, Jimmie met and married a Meridian girl, but the marriage, which produced a daughter, lasted less than two years and ended in divorce. The following year, he met a thirteen-year-old schoolgirl named Carrie Williamson; they dated for about a year, then married in 1920, against her parents' wishes, when she was fourteen and he was twenty-three. Carrie later explained her attraction to Jimmie by saying, "I'd decided that having Jimmie was better than school."

They had a daughter they named Anita the following year, and Jimmie quit his job with the railroad so that he could find work closer to home. He tried farming and drove a truck for a while, at a dollar a day, but he had a difficult time supporting his family. When they had another daughter, Jimmie went out on the road to find work. During one of his absences, their second daughter died; they were too poor to pay for her funeral and had to rely on the kindness of their relatives to give her a proper burial. It was around this time that Jimmie started coughing up blood and realized that he, like his mother, had tuberculosis. He spent three months in a sanatorium.

Throughout all his family hardships, Jimmie never lost interest in music. He continued to play his guitar and banjo, and often woke Carrie in the middle of the night to tell her that he had written a new song. Unable to perform strenuous work, he began to view music as a way to support his family. His first job as a musician was with a traveling medicine show, for which he applied blackface and mimicked the speech and mannerisms of blacks. Not long after that, he put together his first band: A three-piece group he named the Jimmie Rodgers Entertainers.

In July 1927, Jimmie took his band to Asheville, North Carolina, where radio station WWNC broadcast a music show sponsored by the local Chamber of Commerce. Their performance didn't attract much favorable attention— Carrie later wrote that when a noted music journalist phoned the station to inquire about Jimmie, he was told, "He isn't anybody—just a bum"—but the following month, they were asked to record for Victor Records, which had been promoting so-called "hillbilly" records for several years. The session lasted almost two-and-a-half hours,

Jimmie Rodgers in a publicity photo made during his brief recording career. (Photofest)

and produced two songs: "The Soldier's Sweetheart" and "Sleep, Baby, Sleep." Jimmie received one hundred dollars for the session—pretty good pay for those days.

Encouraged by the modest success of the records, Jimmie went to New York in November 1927 to meet with record executives in the hopes of arranging another recording session. Carrie teased him that he should change his name to Jimmie Starr. Victor was agreeable to doing another session and arranged for him to do four new recordings at their New Jersey studio: "Away out of the Mountain," "Ben Dewberry's Final Run," "Mother Was a Lady," and "T for Texas," which was released as "Blue Yodel." The last song was an enormous success, selling more than five hundred thousand copies, and within months Jimmie Rodgers, or the "Singing Brakeman," as the newspapers called him, was a major star.

All of a sudden, Jimmie went from being an obscure "hillbilly" performer to becoming Victor's best-selling artist. Because of the success of "Blue Yodel," he went on to record twelve additional "Blue Yodel" tunes, giving each song a number. "Blue Yodel #9" was unique in that it featured two fellow Mojo Triangle musicians, Louis Armstrong on cornet and Lil Hardin Armstrong on piano. In addition to the "Blue Yodel" songs, he recorded more than two-dozen similar songs, all with a blues foundation, with some recordings featuring a clarinet, a tuba, a cornet, or a piano.

Jimmie's fame spread so quickly that he was asked to tour with humorist Will Rogers, easily one of the most popular Americans of the 1930s. He also was asked to make a fifteen-minute film, "The Singing Brakeman." Soon he was billed as the "Father of Country Music," a title that was richly deserved. He became America's first country music star simply by doing what came naturally, and by drawing on the simmering power of the still-evolving musical tradition of the Mojo Triangle.

In May 1933, Jimmie traveled to New York to attend what was to be his final recording session. He had scaled back on his touring, due to his failing health. Tuberculosis had killed his mother, and now it was slowly squeezing the air from his lungs. He started the session strong, completing four songs on the first take, but when he returned to the studio the following day, he was so tired that he had to record while sitting down. Afterward, he returned to his hotel and rested several days before going back to the studio. On May 24, 1933, with his health failing rapidly, he went to the studio and recorded four songs, including "Mississippi Delta Blues," a tune that referred to his inability to shake the "muddy water" from his shoes.

The following day, he rested all day in his hotel room, feeling strong enough the next day to go on a sightseeing tour of Coney Island with his nurse. While on the island, he suffered a spasm attack and was rushed to the hospital. Jimmie Rodgers died in the early morning hours of May 26. His recording career had lasted only five years, but his impact on American music was immeasurable.

Jimmie made the long ride home in the baggage car of a train and was buried next to his daughter. Nearly twenty years after Jimmie's death, country singer Hank Snow was instrumental in helping to erect a memorial statue of the Singing Brakeman in Meridian. The inscription reads, in part: "His is the music of America. He sang the songs of the people he loved, of a young nation growing strong. His was an America of glistening rails, thundering boxcars, and rain-swept night, of lonesome prairies, great mountains, and a high blue sky."

◆　▲　◆　▲　◆

When Jimmie Rodgers was five years of age, another musical Jimmie came into the world in Fulton, about a dozen miles off the Natchez Trace, near Tupelo, Mississippi. Born on June 6, 1902, Jimmie Lunceford was the grandson of slaves brought to Mississippi from North Carolina in the late 1850s. After emancipation, they worked as farm laborers about five miles northeast of Fulton, saving their money until they were able to purchase 320 acres of former Chickasaw farmland. In time, they deeded about 15% of their land to one of their sons, James Riley, who married a woman named Idella Shumpert in 1900. Two years later, James and Idella had Jimmie.

Jimmie's musical talents became obvious at a young age, which was why his parents—his father was a choirmaster—sent him to Fisk University in Nashville, a black school founded in 1865 by the American Missionary Association of New York City and the Western Freedman's Aid Commission of Cincinnati for the purpose of providing the sons and daughters of former slaves with a Christian education that was strong both spiritually and academically. By the time Jimmie enrolled in the school, music education had become a major focus of the institution, primarily because of the world-famous Jubilee Singers, a student singing group that was the school's most important fund-raising tool.

After graduating with a bachelor of music degree, Jimmie moved to Memphis in 1926, where he got a job as a music teacher at Manassas High School. Because he had a passion for music, apart from teaching, he organized a select group of students into an orchestra named the Chickasaw Syncopators. It was an interesting choice of names, not just because of Jimmie's ancestral land in Chickasaw territory, but because syncopation is a characteristic of Native American music. Was Jimmie thinking in terms of Native American contributions to music, or did he simply like the sound of the name? The latter seems unlikely because neither word was commonly used in Memphis in the 1920s; the Chickasaws had left many years before.

Jimmie's student dance band played in and around Memphis for several summers, attracting so much attention that he imported three professional musicians from Fisk to add to the band's commercial appeal. They recorded a couple of records that went over quite well locally, and by 1930, the Chickasaw Syncopators was one of the hottest dance bands in the region, booked mainly by white social organizations. In addition to his talents as a bandleader, Jimmie was a master showman, who dressed elegantly and used a long white baton with great flare.

Surprisingly, Jimmie wouldn't let the band perform anywhere near Beale Street. He felt that the rough-and-tumble atmosphere of the blues district was not up to the high standards he set for his students. He did not drink or use drugs, and he constantly preached to his students about responsibility. If they didn't respect themselves, he told them, then society would have no respect for their music.

Soon Jimmie received offers for the band to tour the northeast. After one such tour, the famed Cotton Club offered them a booking. That was simply too good to turn down, so Jimmie resigned from his teaching job—and his students presumably dropped out of school—so that the band could compete with the big-name orchestras of that time. The band was renamed the Jimmie Lunceford Orchestra.

Jimmie went on to have a significant influence on the development of swing. He did not have a gift for composition, but he had a genius for arrangement. By the 1940s, Glenn Miller and Benny Goodman were building on his precise, melodic arrangements to take swing to a new level. "The music of Lunceford's mid-thirties glory years was, for a moment in time, the very best that jazz had to offer," observed music historian Gunther Schuller. "The Lunceford band, second only to Ellington and, for a few brief years, even more consistent than his, reigned supreme for a while."

Lunceford's popularity was such that he was asked to appear in several movies, *Blues in the Night* being perhaps the best known. The band's highest level of success occurred in 1934, when it recorded a series of hit records for Decca, including "Organ Grinder's Swing," "Margie," "Cheatin' On Me," "My Blue Heaven," and "For Dancers Only." Jazz critic George Simon later wrote: "For those of us lucky enough to have caught the band in person it has left memories of some of the most exciting nights we ever spent listening to any of the big bands."

In the summer of 1947, Jimmie was signing autographs at a music store in Seaside, Oregon, when he collapsed and was taken to the hospital. He died on July 12, with the cause of death listed as food poisoning. Rumors circulated that he was murdered, but foul play was never proved. Ed Wilcox, Jimmie's pianist, and saxophonist Joe Thomas tried to keep the band going, but without the elegant sizzle offered by the dapper bandleader, the orchestra lost momentum and finally broke up in 1949.

◆　▲　◆　▲　◆

About twenty-five miles from the Trace—and about fifty miles from Jimmie Lunceford's birthplace—is the small town of West Point, Mississippi, located in Oktibbeha County; Oktibbeha is a Choctaw word that means "icy water." The name probably came from the creek north of West Point that served as a boundary between the Choctaw and Chickasaw tribes.

During the Civil War, Oktibbeha County was devastated by federal troops, as raiders passed through on their way south, burning and looting as they went. General Nathan Bedford Forrest was successful in turning back one raid just south of West Point. After the war, residents went through some hard times, but by the turn of the century, they rebounded, enough at least to allow the United States Army to build an airfield in West Point so that army pilots could be trained for overseas service.

Chester Arthur Burnett, later known as Howlin' Wolf, was seven years of age when the airfield was built in 1917. Yankees were no longer hated quite so much, at least not to their faces, and blacks were segregated from both the Yankee soldiers and whites native to the city. The political successes blacks enjoyed during Reconstruction had died down by the start of World War I, and most lived quiet lives, their main pleasure being the traveling minstrel shows where they were allowed to sit in the back of the tent and enjoy the latest music of the day.

At the age of thirteen, Chester moved with his family to the Mississippi Delta, to the Young and Mara Plantation near Ruleville. Because he was a difficult child—not to mention menacingly large, topping off as an adult at six-foot-three and three hundred pounds—his parents nicknamed him Howlin' Wolf. He lived a pretty standard life for the times, working from sunup to sundown for meager wages, and giving his pay to his parents as part of their "furnish" for working the land. He may have felt like complaining, but he never did, because he knew that was the way the system worked.

Howlin' Wolf. (Photofest)

For his eighteenth birthday, the Wolf's father bought him a guitar. He learned to play well enough to make pocket change while performing on street corners, but not to the point where he could call himself a professional musician. He kept his day job picking cotton, hanging out in juke joints where he could pick up pointers on his guitar. Eventually, he moved to Arkansas, where he felt economic opportunities were more varied. It was during those footloose years that he met Charlie Patton, one of the first Mississippi bluesmen to get a record deal. However, to call Patton a bluesman is to limit his abilities, because he performed various styles of music: Ragtime, folk, and the type of "country" music that Jimmie Rodgers made popular. In those days, African Americans didn't call themselves "bluesmen," because the blues didn't yet exist; whites adopted the term bluesman as shorthand for identifying a performer as black.

Patton was a quarrelsome, violent man, who was deficient in social skills. What he had that endeared him to other blacks was a reputation for making money by playing his guitar, no small distinction in the Delta, where poverty was the norm. The Wolf once said about Patton, "It was he who started me off to playing. He took a liking to me, and I asked him would he learn me, and at night, after I'd get off work, I'd go and hang around."

Despite some first-rate tutoring, the Wolf couldn't sell himself as a performer. Part of it may have to do with his intimidating size, since in a smoke filled juke joint—most of which weren't much larger than a normal sized living room—he seemed to suck the air out of the room, looming against the wall like a King Kong creature in bondage. It also could have had something to do with his style of playing: Raw, powerful, simmering with the violence of passions that could frighten people who didn't know him.

One quality that all successful black entertainers had in common at that time was affability—the ability to make people laugh and smile, while presenting nothing in the way of an impending threat—and that quality was popular with both black and white audiences. Music was God's gift for the good times, and the last thing that black or white audiences wanted was trouble while they were escaping the unpleasantness of their daily lives. However, the Wolf did not exude affability. Even when he was happy and laughing, there was always something about the look of him that made people suspect that his mood could take a bad turn on a moment's notice.

Perhaps for that reason, the Wolf had little success selling himself as a musician while in his twenties and thirties. He spent his daylight hours working on farms in various parts of Arkansas, and he spent his nights pursuing live music wherever he could find it. All that was cut short in the early 1940s, when he was drafted into the United States Army, where he served in a racially segregated unit that was given few responsibilities in the war effort. Everyone figured that the war would extinguish the Wolf's musical flame once and for all; few men had returned with the same passions they had when they left.

◆　▲　◆　▲　◆

It can be argued that the Mojo Triangle provided America with its greatest novelist (William Faulkner), its greatest short story-writer (Eudora Welty), and its greatest playwright (Tennessee Williams)—and it would be difficult to quibble with that assessment, for although writers from other regions may approach their genius, none have yet been able to surpass it. That is because the same ancient land, the same myths, the same apocalyptic battles over good and evil that have shaped America's original music have also shaped its most powerful literature. The creative force, whether it is directed words or music, rises from the same wellspring.

If Faulkner had not become a writer, it is easy to imagine how he might have become an innovative jazz pianist, or how Welty might have composed cut-to-the-chase folk songs with lyrics to die for, or how Williams could have channeled his brooding energies into heavy-metal rock 'n' roll. In fact, music often interested Faulkner, especially where his writing career was concerned. "I would say that music is the easiest means in which to express [creativity], since it came first in man's experience and history," he told interviewer Jean Stein. "But since words are my talent, I must try to express clumsily in words what the pure music would have done better. That is, music would express better and simpler, but I prefer to use words, as I prefer to read rather than listen. I prefer silence to sound, and the image produced by words occurs in silence. That is, the thunder and the music of the prose take place in silence."

What all three of the above-mentioned writers have in common—besides depicting man's inhumanity to man, and complicated emotions in their work—is that they were born on or near the Natchez Trace. Welty took her first breath on April 13, 1909, in Jackson, Mississippi—about as close to the Trace as one can get—where her father worked for an insurance company and her mother doted over their three children.

William Faulkner, circa 1962. (Ralph Thompson for Random House)

Eudora was the eldest, and her earliest memory was of her mother singing "Wee Willie Winkie's," and her parents whistling back and forth to each other from different parts of the house.

There was a Victrola in the dining room that Eudora was encouraged to operate at a young age, and songs like "Kiss Me Again," "Overture to Daughter of the Regiment," and "When the Midnight Choo-Choo Leaves for Alabam" set her tiny feet to dancing. Actually, music was everywhere in Jackson at that time: On the street corners, in the juke joints on the outskirts of town, on the main streets where school bands proudly marched, and in every home that managed to rise above the poverty level. By the time Eudora was nine, her mother had saved enough from her housekeeping money to buy her an upright Steinway piano, so that her daughter would be able to play the music that she heard on the Victrola.

In later years, Welty came to understand the relationship between music and writing, and the inner voice that gave rhythm to her words: "Ever since I was first read to, then started reading to myself, there has never been a line read that I didn't *hear,*" she wrote in her memoir, *One Writer's Beginnings.* "As my eyes followed the sentence, a voice was saying it silently to me...It is to me the voice of the story or the poem itself. The cadence, whatever it is that asks you to believe, the feeling that resides in the printed word, reaches me through the reader-voice."

Eudora heard that music, or voice, at an early age. It told her to get up and move, to explore her surroundings. She went off to college at sixteen, attending first Mississippi State College for Women, and then the University of Wisconsin in Madison, where she graduated at the age of twenty. She moved on to attend the Columbia School of Business in New York, to study advertising, but her father's sudden death in 1931 brought her back to Mississippi, where she worked first for a radio station and then as a society correspondent for the Mid-South's largest newspaper, the *Memphis Commercial Appeal*. That led to work with Franklin Roosevelt's Works Progress Administration (W.P.A.), which enabled her to travel the back roads of Mississippi, photographing and writing about the people that she encountered.

By then, she knew that writing would be her life's work. She published her first short story in 1936, brought out her first short story collection, *A Curtain of Green,* in 1941, and she was quickly signed up as a staff member of *The New York Times Book Review*, where she reviewed World War II battlefield reports from North Africa, Europe, and the South Pacific. When an editor in another department complained about a lady from the "Deep South" being *The Times'* primary war critic, she adopted the pseudonym Michael Ravenna and provided the newspaper with reviews that were featured prominently in publishers' ads.

As a Mojo Triangle writer, she drew heavily on the same material that influenced musicians of her time, as can been seen in the subject matter of novels such as *The Robber Bridegroom,* which took place on the Natchez Trace, and titles of stories such as "Keela the Outcast Indian Maiden." She was so moved by the murder of Medgar Evers that she wrote a story based on the event titled "Where Is the Voice Coming From?" After it was published in *The New Yorker,* she received a telephone call from a newspaper reporter who wanted to know if she had suffered any repercussions. "Had anyone burned a cross on my lawn, he wanted to know," she told Walter Clemons of *The Times.* "I told him, 'No, of course not,' and he wanted to know if he could call back in a few days, 'in case anything develops.' I told him I couldn't see any sense in his running up his phone bill. The people who burn crosses on lawns don't read me in *The New Yorker.* Really, don't people know the first thing about the South?"

Although she was best known for her short stories, it was her short novel, *The Optimist's Daughter,* that won her a Pulitzer Prize in 1973. The award placed her in the same class as Faulkner (who, in addition to winning the Nobel Prize for Literature, also won Pulitzer Prizes for *A Fable* and *The Reivers),* and with Tennessee Williams, who was awarded Pulitzers for *A Streetcar Named Desire* and *Cat on a Hot Tin Roof.*

Eudora Welty at her home in Jackson, Mississippi. (Photofest)

Tennessee Williams and Eudora Welty had still more in common. They both lived their entire lives without intimate contact with the opposite sex; Williams was homosexual, and Welty simply preferred the company of her family and female friends. And both were attracted to the "music" of Southern speech, which is to say the underlying innuendo and the dark imagery that is characteristic of the Mojo Triangle.

Thomas Lanier Williams was born on March 26, 1911, in Columbus, Mississippi, where Welty, who was two years his senior, attended college as a teen. Williams' family lived there for five years, then moved to Canton, just outside Jackson, for a short time, and then on to the Mississippi Delta, where he lived with his mother and her parents in Clarksdale until he was eight. At that time, they moved to St. Louis. Williams was essentially raised without his father in the home, because his father worked as a shoe salesman and was constantly on the road. He later described his Mississippi upbringing as "the most joyously innocent of my life."

At age eighteen, Williams enrolled at the University of Missouri to study journalism, but he dropped out of school after his father interfered with his romance with his childhood sweetheart, Hazel Kramer. He had a nervous breakdown as a result, and he was sent to Memphis to recuperate. While there, he joined a local theater group and realized that he had a flair for dramatic writing. Once he recovered from his breakdown, he enrolled at the University of Iowa, where the plays he wrote were performed on campus. After graduation, he moved to New Orleans and changed his name to Tennessee Williams, a childhood nickname that came about because his father was from Tennessee.

Williams' first play, *The Glass Menagerie,* opened on Broadway in 1945. With its focus on the psychology of dysfunctional family relationships, it revolutionized American theater. His second play, *A Streetcar Named Desire,* was an enormous success and earned him not only a Pulitzer Prize, but a Drama Critics' Award. No playwright in American history had ever depicted human relationships in such stark terms. It was as if he had distilled all of the generations of human travail and geographic disaster of the Mojo Triangle into words, so that even when his characters seemed to be carrying on an innocuous conversation, they were actually navigating the most menacing terrain of the human condition.

Northern people have an image of the South as some sort of hillbilly enclave for incomplete thoughts. In reality, Southern writers and musicians have always had a genius for the exploration of complex emotions, such as pride, honor, love, hate, and obsession, and a genius for peering into the void of time and historically lost space. "[There's] the mystical belief that there is no such thing as was," William Faulkner once explained to an interviewer. "That time *is,* and if there's no such thing as was, then there is no such thing as *will be.* That time is not a fixed

Tennessee Williams at work. (Photofest)

condition, time is in a way the sum of the combined intelligences of all men who breathe at that moment."

Faulkner could seem obsessed with time—time passing, time standing still, time lost to the future or the past. Perhaps more than any other writer or musician produced by the Mojo Triangle, Faulkner understood, and more importantly *felt*, the power of the land and its people. Born on September 25, 1897, in New Albany, Mississippi, not far from Oxford—on land that had been taken from the Chickasaw and then later fought over during the Civil War—William Cuthbert Faulkner came into the world knowing that his existence was predetermined by the past.

Named after his great-grandfather, William Clark Faulkner, he had a great deal to live up to at birth, because W.C. Faulkner, or Colonel Faulkner as he was called, had enjoyed an illustrious career in the Civil War. He raised a volunteer regiment, the Second Mississippi Cavalry, which he took to the first Battle of Manassas. Later, with the rank of colonel, he served under General Nathan Bedford Forrest. After the war, he co-founded a railroad line and wrote a novel, *The White Rose of Memphis*, which was a bestseller in its day, with one hundred sixty thousand copies sold.

Perhaps because of his great-grandfather, when William Faulkner came of age, he was eager to serve in World War I. He went to Canada and joined the Royal Air Force, and trained as a pilot. The war ended before he could complete his pilot's training, but not before he had occasion to crash his plane, upside down, into the hanger. Back in Mississippi, he took a job for a short while in the post office at the University of Mississippi, then headed south to New Orleans to begin his writing career.

After a couple of false starts that included a book of poetry, Faulkner started writing about what he knew best—a history of the Mojo Triangle that reflected the struggles, victories, and burdens of the inhabitants, including the Chickasaw and the Choctaw. Most of his stories took place in a fictional county that was remarkable for its resemblance to Oxford's Lafayette County, but he named it Yoknapatawpha County in honor of the Chickasaw that had lived on the land for thousands of years before the arrival of the white man.

Faulkner viewed the dispossession of the Indians in the Mojo Triangle as something of a curse, a ghost of that "ravishment" that lingered long after the act was done. "They were paid for it [the land], but they were compelled to leave it, either to leave—to follow a chimera in the West or to stay there in a condition even worse than the Negro slave, in isolation," he said in 1957 at a class conference at the University of Virginia. "There are a few of them still in Mississippi, but they are a good deal like animals in a zoo: They have no place in the culture, in the economy, unless they become white men, and they have in some cases mixed with white people and their own conditions have vanished, or they have mixed with Negroes and they have descended into the Negroes' condition of semi-peonage."

Beginning with his first Yoknapatawpha County novel, *Sartoris*, Faulkner wrote a series of books that were dazzling, not just in their vision, but in their language, establishing him as America's most accomplished novelist. In *The Sound and the Fury*, he used inner monologue and the distortion of time to tell the story of a once-proud Southern family, and in *Light in August, Absalom, Absalom!* and *Intruder in the Dust,* he dealt with racial prejudice and a wide range of problems that existed between blacks and whites. Actually, his books cover the early history of the Mojo Triangle, drawing upon early events such as the Civil War and the mistreatment of the Chickasaw, to weave a rich fictional tapestry.

As for the source of his extraordinary talent, Faulkner was himself often baffled. "I realize for the first time what an amazing gift I had: Uneducated in every formal sense, without even very literate, let alone literary, companions, yet to have made the things I made," he once said in a letter. "I don't know where it came from. I don't know why God or gods or whoever it was, selected me to be the vessel. Believe me, this is not humility, false modesty: It is simply amazement."

◆ ▲ ◆ ▲ ◆

Times were already bad in Tupelo, Mississippi, on January 8, 1935, when Elvis Aron Presley was born on former Chickasaw land near the Natchez Trace. The Great Depression was in full gear, and events went from bad to worse on that day for the Presley family with the stillbirth of Elvis' twin brother, who was to have been named Jesse Garon.

Elvis' parents, Vernon and Gladys Presley, pretty much lived day to day. Vernon was a laborer and accepted any type of work he could find. (He even worked for a while at this author's family's feed store.) Gladys worked at a garment factory. With a son to feed, they felt the hard economic times even more acutely over the next two years, which may be the reason that Vernon took a chance on altering a check made out to him in payment for a hog. He was sentenced to three years at the state penitentiary, Parchman Farm (where this author's grandfather was a warden), but he was released after only eight months, largely due to a petition that was submitted by his friends and neighbors. Unfortunately, he didn't get out early enough to help Gladys keep from losing their home.

Unable to find work, Vernon moved his family to the Gulf Coast, near Pascagoula, to work on a W.P.A. project for eight months; then it was back to Tupelo to get Elvis situated to start school. During the World War II years, Vernon took a job in Memphis at a munitions plant and commuted to Tupelo on weekends to be with his family. By the time the war ended, Vernon had saved enough—two hundred dollars—to make a down payment on a house for his family.

Elvis started singing with his mother and father in the Assembly of God choir during this time, and when he was ten, he shocked his mother by taking the stage to sing Red Foley's "Old Shep" at the Mississippi-Alabama Fair and

Dairy Show. Not long after that, Elvis got his first guitar and discovered that he had a passion for music. Whether it was a substitute for his lost brother, or simply a substitute for material wealth, is of little consequence; what was important was that, even as a young child, he felt the power of music.

By the time Elvis started the seventh grade, Vernon and Gladys had lost their home and moved to a rented house in a predominately black neighborhood, where Elvis came into contact with students from the black school. A classmate told Elaine Dundy, author of *Elvis and Gladys*, that Elvis was a loner, and a second classmate described him as a "sad, shy, not especially attractive boy" who was made fun of by the other students for playing hillbilly songs on his guitar.

In November 1948, feeling that he would never be able to better himself in Tupelo, Vernon loaded his family and all their possessions into a road-weary Plymouth and struck out for Memphis, a drive of little more than one hundred miles on Highway 78. He had done well in Memphis during the war; perhaps he would be able to make a good living there again. Before they arrived, Vernon had a father-son talk with Elvis, a conversation he later related to *TV Radio Mirror:* "I told Elvis that I'd work for him and buy him everything I could afford...I also said, 'But son, if you see anything going on, promise me you'll have no part of it. Just don't let anything happen so that I'd have to talk to you between bars. That's the only thing that would break my heart.'"

The Presleys found it difficult to live on Vernon's 85-cents-an-hour wage as a loader at a paint company, and they moved from rooming house to rooming house several times that first year in Memphis. Finally, they applied to the Memphis Housing Authority for admission to a subsidized housing development called Lauderdale Courts. That same year, Elvis started his freshman year at Humes High, walking the ten blocks each day to school with a sense of wonderment. And why not? He had moved from a small town to a big city, and he was attending a school that was large enough to afford him a certain amount of anonymity as he struggled with his music.

In the eighth grade, insulted by his music teacher's observation that he couldn't sing, he took his guitar to school and sang "Keep Them Cold Icy Fingers off of Me," a song that he was convinced would win her over to this way of thinking. Elvis told his teacher that she just didn't appreciate his style of singing. He played and sang, the teacher listened, along with the entire class, but when it was over, she told Elvis that he was right after all: She didn't appreciate his style of singing.

Undeterred, Elvis kept playing and singing at every opportunity. That no one took him seriously didn't seem to bother him; he listened to the inner voice that told him that he had no choice but to continue on the road that he had chosen. What choice did he have, really? He had seen life through his father's eyes, and he didn't like what he saw. His mother was different. She felt that her only surviving child was special, that he had been anointed with greatness. Whenever Elvis looked at life through her eyes, he was encouraged by the hope and self-confidence that she instilled in him. A young man can take a lot of abuse from his peers if he feels that his mother is on his side; her vision became his guiding light.

◆　▲　◆　▲　◆

Back home in Mississippi, a young girl by the name of Virginia Wynette Pugh—she later changed her name to Tammy Wynette—tapped into the same grand vision. Perhaps only in the Mojo Triangle could a child dream of becoming a music star and not be considered a candidate for confinement in a mental hospital. Truthfully, her odds of becoming a star were every bit as good as, if not better than, they were of becoming a doctor, or a lawyer, or president of the United States.

Seven years Elvis' junior, Tammy was born in a tar-paper shack in Itawamba County just east of Tupelo. She was only eight months old when her father, guitarist William Hollis Pugh, died, a tragedy that sent her mother to Alabama to find work, which meant that Tammy had to be placed in the care of her grandparents. As a child, Tammy worked on her grandparents' farm, chopping weeds and picking cotton along with the hired workers—and for the same wages, a consideration that boosted her self-esteem considerably. Her mother returned in 1945, after her job in Alabama played out, and they continued to live with Tammy's grandparents.

Tammy started singing in her church, and she liked it so much that she joined a second church so that she could sing twice as often. The first country song she ever learned was "Sally Let Your Hands Hang Down," a tune that delighted her grandfather. Then she learned a Kitty Wells song titled "How Far Is Heaven."

As she grew older, Tammy became more interested in the musical instruments that had belonged to her father. There was a guitar, an accordion, a mandolin, bass fiddle, and a piano. Her mother agreed to allow her to take music lessons, but only on the condition that she never consider music as anything other than a hobby. As the wife of a musician, she well knew the heartbreak and rejection that accompanied a career in music, and she didn't want that life for her daughter.

Tammy and Elvis lived in the same general vicinity for six years, but there is no record that they ever met in Tupelo (though it seems likely that they would have attended the same fairs and carnivals that took place each year). As it turned out, Tammy followed in Elvis' footsteps at the age of ten, when she and her mother, who had remarried, moved to Memphis so that her stepfather could find a better job. Tammy's mother took a job in the office at the University Park Cleaners, which was owned by a man named Carney Moore.

There, as fate would have it, Tammy came face to face with Elvis Presley, for the first and only time.

◆　▲　◆　▲　◆

The first music that Marty Stuart ever heard growing up on Route 6 in Philadelphia, Mississippi, came from church bells that he heard while being held in his mother's loving arms. The bells were rung to announce Sunday services, or to celebrate special holidays, or to warn of impending disasters such as floods, tornados, or raging fires. Always, the sound of the bells merited full and immediate attention.

Later, when he was of school age, it was the music of the school bands that were forever marching up and down the streets to announce an important football game, or to celebrate Christmas or the Fourth of July, that stirred him. Born on September 30, 1958, Marty's childhood development occurred during one of the most turbulent eras since the Civil War—the Sixties. He was five years old when Medgar Evers was gunned down in Jackson, and he was six when civil rights workers Schwerner, Goodman, and Chaney were murdered just outside of Philadelphia, sending dozens of FBI agents into the community and putting the city on the front pages of newspapers across the country.

"I had a very happy childhood, then all of a sudden the race thing occurred," Marty later recalled. "And Jimmie, the black lady that I loved, she couldn't come to my house and I couldn't understand it....My mother came home from the bank and talked about how the FBI was there all day questioning people. I remember one Sunday we went to church, and most of the men there had guns and baseball bats in the trunks of their cars because of a church bombing. It really confused my mind. The only time I felt relief was on a Saturday afternoon, when Flatt and Scruggs came into our living room on TV. When they were on TV the air was different. It was like it used to be before all the darkness came in, and it was wonderful. When their show went off the air, I missed them and it left a big hole in the air, and things went back to being heavy. Flatt and Scruggs was the first time I realized how powerful music could be as a healer and a soother."

After kindergarten, before the arrival of the "dark days," Marty sometimes stopped by the Busy Bee Café, a cheeseburger stand/shoeshine parlor/weekend dive with a red-hot jukebox. With its pungent smells, Christmas tree-like lighting, and rich array of town characters, the café pushed buttons inside Marty that he didn't even know existed. The first live music Marty ever saw was a black youth playing a guitar on Church Street in front of the café. Once the racial troubles began, he was forbidden to enter its doors—at least, until things got back to normal.

For a time, Marty had to look elsewhere for musical inspiration. One of the places he found it was with the Choctaw at the Neshoba County Fair. "I remember the dances they used to do—and the chants," he said. "Even as a young kid, I remember them doing chants around the drummer. I recognized the black blues moan that I heard on church music. I felt like it was the same kind of struggle trying to come out. Oddly enough, I later heard the same strand in the Otis Redding songs, 'Try a Little Tenderness,' and those songs—and I head the same things come out of George Jones in Nashville. It was that common blues strand of struggle."

Marty was so fond of the Choctaw that his parents once dressed him up like an Indian and took his picture. "At that time, the Choctaw used to walk to town and they still dressed in traditional dress. On Saturday afternoons, you could see lots of Choctaw sitting around the lawn of the courthouse in their traditional dress. I had my picture made with lots of them. I knew they were special. They were a beautiful people. Their costumes were beautiful. Their hair was beautiful. And the Choctaws were in a world unto themselves. Like most Native Americans, they seemed to know a whole lot more about ourselves then we knew about them. And a lot of them liked Borden's buttermilk. I remember that."

Another place Marty found music was in the church. "We were Southern Baptists. Right down the street from our house was a Pentecostal church, and some of the touring acts like the Dixie Echoes came down, and that's where people shouted to the music and stomped their feet and clapped, which we didn't do in our church."

Marty was surrounded by music. Philadelphia radio station WHOC, 1490 on the dial, was owned by a man named Howard Cole. Looking back, Marty considers him a "pioneer and a visionary in a quiet sort of way." WHOC signed on with country music, featuring a disk jockey named Rex Smith, who kept Philadelphia in a country mode up until noon, when the station offered the news and then switched to gospel during the lunch hour. At one o'clock, the play list was changed to rock 'n' roll. That continued until late afternoon, when rhythm & blues music was put in the spotlight. They closed out the day with easy listening music, thus providing their listeners, during the course of the day, with a full range of music, most of it indigenous to the Mojo Triangle.

The most impressive event in Marty's childhood was always the county fair, which offered the largest musical and political gatherings in the state. Politicians such as Governor Ross Barnett, who caused a riot at the University of Mississippi when he said the federal government would have to shoot its way into the state to enroll a black student at the university, was a frequent speaker at the fair, as was country singer Jimmy Swan, who once claimed to have shined Jimmie Rodgers' shoes. Swan was a speaker in 1966 when he ran for governor as a segregationist. Politicians such as Barnett Swan, Paul Johnson, and myriad others had honed public speaking into an art, especially concerning segregation: They could tell spellbinding stories, jab their fingers into God's heaven, and lift the crowd to its feet, generating a thunderous rhythm of human passions that were as complicated and lyrical as an Italian opera.

Somewhere between the race-baiting speeches and the promises of a brand-new tomorrow when whites, blacks, and Indians could live in separate-but-equal perfect worlds approved by God Almighty, were the entertainers. In the 1960s, the fair was a major stop on the fall touring circuit, which meant that all the big-name country artists made appearances there at one time or another.

In 1970, when Marty was twelve, country music star Connie Smith was booked at the fair. At that time, she was the toast of Nashville, where she recorded a string of hits, including "Once a Day," "Nobody But a Fool (Would Love You)," and "Cry, Cry, Cry." In addition to being the "Sweetheart of the Grand Ole Opry," as Roy Acuff dubbed her, she was Marty's mother's favorite singer. "It was a big event in our house that Miss Connie Smith was coming to town," Marty recalled. "I wanted to impress her, and so mama took me to the store to get me a yellow shirt so that Connie would notice me. That night, at the concert, she didn't notice me, so I went and got her autograph—and, still, she didn't say anything. That was when I went and borrowed mama's camera and stuck it right in Connie's face and took her picture. On the way home, I said, 'Mama, I'm going to marry her!'" And, of course, many years later, he did marry her.

The first two records that Marty owned were *The Fabulous Johnny Cash* and *Flatt and Scruggs Greatest Hits,* which is ironic since as those two bands were the only real jobs he ever had in his life. "My whole life revolved about music," said Marty. "The earliest pictures of me, as a baby in the crib, I had a Mickey Mouse windup guitar. I had my first cardboard guitar when I was five or six. The first band when I was nine—and I was gone when I was thirteen."

The way that happened—the leaving part—was that his father took him to a bluegrass festival in Indiana, where Marty, then eleven, made friends with the mandolin player in the Lester Flatt and Earl Scruggs band. The following year, when Flatt and Scruggs traveled to Philadelphia for the fair, Marty's mother invited the mandolin player to their house for dinner. It became clear to the mandolin player during dinner that Marty had a future as a musician, so he invited him to Nashville for the weekend so that he could show him around. "I rode the bus to Nashville, and I was so excited that I stood up all the way," said Marty. "Finally, I sat down and went to sleep about halfway between Jackson [Tennessee] and Nashville."

That weekend visit was expanded to a week, and then, in Marty's words, to "an eternity," when his parents gave permission for him to join Flatt's band as a picker. "Lester and me hit it off just like that. I knew his songs, and it kind of dazzled him that a thirteen-year-old had that much knowledge of his music. If it had been Led Zeppelin or Steppenwolf, my parents never would have allowed me to stay, but Lester assured them it wasn't a rowdy band and told them I would be well looked after."

Marty traveled with Flatt's band, playing about two hundred dates a year, until Flatt's death in 1978. Marty was only twenty years old then, but he felt like he already had lived a full life. Once the whirlwind stopped, it took him a couple of years to get his bearings again. The next step in his career occurred when he decided to produce a memorial album to honor Flatt. He was in a producer's office to discuss the album with him, when he spotted an address book opened to a page with Johnny Cash's telephone number in full view.

"I thought, 'Naw, I can't do that.' Then I thought, 'Yes, I can.' So I called Cash up point blank and introduced myself and asked him to be on the album." Cash didn't hesitate; he agreed to play on the session. When he showed up at the studio and heard Marty play, he offered him a job in his band. Marty knew then that he wouldn't be going back home again, maybe ever. Even so, the images of all that he had loved back home in Mississippi haunted him: "...just the simple mysteries of life that came to me in the summers. The smell of the dirt, the smell of rain on top of the tomatoes. In the fall, the shotguns would come out and we would go out and hunt....There was a dipper on the back porch and a water bucket....The trains, the stars, the moon—they all still do their job. It is the same moon that shined on Muddy Waters and the Choctaws. There is a magic about the place."

Marty Stuart taking a spin around Nashville in his Jeep. (James L. Dickerson)

◆　▲　◆　▲　◆

In May 1975, when Faith Perry was seven years of age, she learned that Elvis Presley was coming to Jackson, her hometown, for a concert at the Mississippi Coliseum. She was beside herself. Elvis was her very favorite entertainer in the whole world. His songs were the first that she had learned, skipping from room to room, her hairbrush for a microphone, singing, "Don't be cruel to a heart that's true..."

But when she said that she wanted to go to the concert, her adoptive mother's response was, "No way."

Faith was devastated. "Why?" she asked.

Her mother explained that she didn't want her daughter exposed to the evils of rock 'n' roll, especially in a coliseum with several thousand half-drunk rednecks doing Lord knows what in between songs. Faith reminded her that she had thought it was cute when she imitated Elvis with her hairbrush.

"No way," repeated the mother.

Faith wasn't grown-up yet, but she was as stubborn and persistent as she needed to be—in later years when she became pop superstar Faith Hill, those traits would work to her advantage—so she went next door and pleaded with a neighbor woman to help her dreams come true. Faith was so innocent looking then, so appealing in her wide-eyed naiveté, that the neighbor didn't have the heart to say no. Taking up Faith's cause, she marched next door and pleaded her case, making slow progress at first, but then winning the day when she volunteered to take Faith herself and sit beside her to protect her against whatever vileness that rock 'n' roll tossed their way.

Faith was blown away by the energy of it all, the pageantry of Elvis at his Las Vegas-style best: Strutting about the stage, confident, taking away everyone's breath with little more than a glance. She knew then that when she grew up, she wanted to be a star, just like Elvis.

Not long after that, Faith's family moved twenty miles south of Jackson, to Star, Mississippi (population five hundred), where the Perrys thought they would escape the violence and temptations of city life and raise their children to be hard working, God-fearing Christian Americans. Faith worked hard—at becoming a singer—but the God-fearing part sometimes took a backseat to the demons that occasionally danced about inside her head. One time, she grabbed a couple of rolls of toilet paper from her bathroom and rolled the lawn of the music director of the Star Baptist Church; another time she stole a candy bar from a local store; and there were the many times when she walked the railroad tracks, playing chicken with the fast freight trains that sped through Star three times a day. The part of church that she embraced without question was the choir, for that was where she could rise above the rest and soar to places that others could only dream about.

Faith's first taste of stardom came at the Bienville National Forest near Raleigh, Mississippi, where the United States government sponsored the national Tobacco Spitting contest on the porch of a two-story log cabin at Billy John Crumpton's farm. At sixteen years of age, Faith was one of the featured performers; for an aspiring singer in Mississippi, it was the equivalent of singing the National Anthem at the Super Bowl.

The daylong festival was broken up into a series of events, including canoe rides on a nearby lake, and watermelon-eating, weightlifting, and face-painting contests. Faith reveled in the party atmosphere, but she was careful not to sample the barbecue or corn dogs before she took the stage for fear of weakening her voice. Finally, at the end of the final qualifying spit—the world record had been set by Jeff Barber in 1979 with a juicy wad that was propelled thirty-one feet, nine-and-a-half inches—Faith was told that it was her turn to shine. She stood on the side of the porch, waiting patiently for someone to run out on the stage and wipe away the spit, then she took a deep breath and strode out onto the stage and began in a cotton-soft voice what she knew to be Elvis Presley's favorite hymn: "Amazing grace, how sweet the sound that saved a wretch like me..."

When Faith returned to Star that day, she just knew, deep in her wildly beating heart, that she was destined for better things. And why not? Tammy Wynette, another one of her heroes, was a Trace girl who had made it as a recording artist. If Tammy and Elvis could do it, why couldn't she? Everyone she knew asked Faith, "Honey, don't you know that's crazy?" But she just couldn't put those thoughts away.

By the time Faith was graduated from high school in 1986, the Natchez Trace had produced an incredible array of stars, in addition to Elvis and Tammy. Country singer Mickey Gilley was born in Natchez, though his family later moved to Ferriday, Louisiana, to be near his cousins, Jerry Lee Lewis and evangelist Jimmy Swaggart. (Gilley recorded seventeen Number One records, but he is probably best known for his Texas nightclub, Gilley's). Bluesman Willie Dixon, born in 1915 just north of the Trace at Vicksburg, was a prolific songwriter whose songs—"The Red Rooster," "The Seventh Son," "Wang Dang Doodle," "I Just Want to Make Love to You," and others— helped define the blues as an art form. Grammy-winning jazz vocalist Cassandra Wilson was born in 1955 in Jackson to a school teacher and a father who was a bass guitarist; her album *Blue Light Til' Dawn* earned her *Downbeat* magazine's 1994 "Singer of the Year," and two years later *Time* magazine proclaimed her America's "most important and daring jazz vocalist." Songwriter/producer Glen Ballard, another Grammy-winner, was born in Natchez in 1955. He moved to Los Angeles, after graduating from the University of Mississippi, to work first for Elton John and then to become Quincy Jones' protégé, writing hit songs for Kiki Dee, James Ingram, Patti

Austin, George Strait, and Michael Jackson. However, it was Ballard's 1996 collaboration with Alanis Morissette on her *Jagged Little Pill* album that brought him his greatest fame (so much fame that a Mississippi legislator introduced a bill praising him for his accomplishments, only to have the resolution killed when the sexually explicit lyrics to Morissette's song were made available to the lawmakers).

Further south, the Mojo Triangle's no–man's–land that stretches from Jackson to the Gulf Coast gave birth to an array of recording artists, including: Jimmy Buffett, who was born in 1946 at Pascagoula, Mississippi, then later educated in Hattiesburg at the University of Southern Mississippi. He scored in the 1970s with a series of hits such as "Come Monday," "Margaritaville," and "Cheeseburger in Paradise." (Buffett started his career as a writer for *Billboard* magazine in Nashville, but then switched to music and recorded several Platinum albums, including *Changes in Latitudes, Changes in Attitudes*.) Brandy Norwood, born in 1979 in McComb, Mississippi, signed with Atlantic Records when she was fourteen, and when her first self-titled album was released in 1994, it was certified Gold in two months and went on to triple-Platinum status. (Soon after, she became an actress, appearing in several motion pictures, including *Demolition Man* and *I Still Know What You Did Last Summer* and in the television sitcom "Moesha"). And Lance Bass, who was born in Laurel, Mississippi, in 1979, and later moved to the Trace town of Clinton, where he went to high school before joining the popular group N'Sync (which also included Mojo Triangle alumnus Justin Timberlake, who was born in Memphis in 1981).

◆ ▲ ◆ ▲ ◆

Perhaps one of the most quintessential products of the Mojo Triangle was rhythm & blues guitarist/singer Bo Diddley, who was born in 1928 in McComb, Mississippi, located about twenty miles from the Louisiana state line. His real name was Ellas Bates, and he was born to a sixteen–year–old girl who had neither the means nor the knowledge to raise him, and so turned him over to the cousin who had raised her, Gussie McDaniel.

"I'm classed as a negro, but I'm not," Bo Diddley once said. "I'm what you call a black Frenchman, a Creole. Just like Fats Domino: French, African, Indian, all mixed up. My great-grandmother was actually supposed to have been a Blackfoot Indian, an' I got some people in my family that look like they're white."

When Gussie McDaniel's husband died in 1935, she gathered up her family and moved north to Chicago, where she made certain that Bo Diddley attended the Ebenezer Missionary Church on a regular basis. It was through church that he was introduced to music, first the violin—after the congregation took up a collection to purchase him one—and then later the guitar his sister gave him for Christmas when he was twelve years old.

Bo Diddley didn't have a guitar teacher, so he made it up as he went along, adapting the same rapid wrist movements that he used on the violin to form a very distinctive style of guitar playing. He never learned to move his fingers with great speed or precision, which is why he never became a great lead guitarist, but that hardly mattered, because he could use his wrist motion to create the exotic rhythms that later became his signature sound.

The distinctive Bo Diddley rhythm, which he used to great effect on "Hey! Bo Diddley," "Bo Diddley," and "Pretty Thing," to name a few, was little more than a tom-tom sound derived from his Native American ancestry. It is one of the best examples of how the music of the Natchez and the Choctaw influenced African-American musical development. Whether he had memories of Indian music growing up in Mississippi, or simply laid down a rhythm that he felt from deep within, hardly matters: The Bo Diddley sound was unmistakably born of two cultures.

Bo Diddley was never a huge success with black audiences, but he influenced other black recording artists, such as Muddy Waters, who used his popular "I'm a Man" in his own repertoire. And, during the sixties, he influenced British groups such as the Rolling Stones, the Animals, and the Beatles, who used his music to expand the rhythmic perimeters of rock 'n' roll.

Early in Bo Diddley's career, music critics often described his music as "Chicago style" blues. It is debatable whether Chicago ever produced any original music, since every style identified as Chicago blues or jazz, was imported, in one form or another, from the Mojo Triangle. Rather, that music results from an undisguised merger of the fiddle (brought by the Scottish and the Irish), the tom-tom rhythm developed by the Native Americans, and the vocal chants brought by African slaves.

Once, when asked by author George R. White, if his music had come from Africa, Bo Diddley replied, "I ain't never been to Africa. Truthfully, I don't know where it came from exactly. I just started playin' it one day."

◆　▲　◆　▲　◆

Throughout the music explosion that took place on the Trace in the later half of the twentieth century, a literary renaissance tapped into the same power source to produce a number of new writers. These included Ellen Douglas, who was born Josephine Haxton in 1921 at Natchez. Her novel *A Family's Affair* was awarded the Houghton Mifflin fellowship in 1961 and was hailed as one of the five best novels of the year by *The New York Times*. Barry Hannah, who was born in Clinton in 1942, won the William Faulkner Prize for his first novel, *Geronimo Rex*, and his other novels, such as *Ray* and *High Lonesome* were also praised. The late Larry Brown, a native of Oxford, was born in 1951 to a sharecropper and worked as a firefighter for the Oxford Fire Department before trying his hand at writing; his novels *Joe*, *Fay*, and *Billy Ray's Farm* all received extravagant reviews. Lewis Nordan, born in 1939 in Forest, Mississippi, but raised in the Delta, has written more than half a dozen books, including *Wolf Whistle*, *The Sharpshooter Blues*, and *Lightning Song*. *The Philadelphia Inquirer* said he is "...among the best American writers in any genre and form." John Grisham was born in Arkansas but had the good sense at a young age to move to Mississippi, where he served in the Mississippi legislature and built a home in Oxford. His best-selling thrillers, such as *The Firm* and *The Testament* have made him one of the wealthiest novelists in the world. (In its review of *The Rainmaker*, *Time* magazine wrote, "As he reels off another No. 1 best seller, the lawyer turned supernovelist can seemingly do no wrong. Deal with it."). And Beth Henley, who was born in Jackson in 1952, is a screenwriter and playwright whose three-act play *Crimes of the Heart* was the first drama to win the Pulitzer Prize before going on Broadway.

Fitting into this music and literature wellspring along the Trace are two media stars who have had a major impact on the way music and literature are perceived by the public. Jackson-born Bob Pittman co-founded MTV in 1981 and revolutionized the way music is presented to the public (he later went on to become a major player in America Online). Oprah Winfrey, was born on the Trace in Kosciusko, Mississippi, and later moved to Nashville, where she began her broadcasting career at WVOL radio. Her award-winning daytime talk show first aired in 1986, and within two years she was able to purchase the show, making her the first woman in history to own and produce her own talk show. By 2003, *Forbes* magazine was able to announce that Oprah had become the first African-American billionaire.

◆　▲　◆　▲　◆

Of course, none of that was going through Faith Hill's head as she plotted and schemed a way to escape Jackson for the bright lights of Nashville. By 1986, she had enrolled in Hinds Community College in Jackson, where she landed a position on the school's recruiting team. (Her boss, Jackie Granberry, said that the main thing she remembered about Faith was that she was always singing and humming, always "peppy.") Nor was it on the mind of a much younger Jackson girl by the name of LeAnn Rimes. She was just four when Faith started college, but was already entering talent competitions, convinced that she had what it took to become a star.

LeAnn, who started singing at age two, was so impressive by age five that her dance teacher asked her to work up a song-and-dance routine to "Getting to Know You" for a local contest. "She won, and from that moment, she was hooked," said her mother, Belinda Rimes. "She told me, 'I'm going to be a singer, and I want to be bigger than Barbra Streisand!'"

The following year, when LeAnn was six, the Rimes family moved to Texas, where she began her career as a singer. By age eight, she was a champion on television's "Star Search," where she sang "Don't Worry About Me," and by age eleven, she had recorded an album for an independent label. The execs at Curb Records of Nashville were so impressed by the album that they picked it up for national distribution, elevating the single, "Blue," into the Top 10 on the country charts. "Blue" had been written by radio DJ Bill Mack for Patsy Cline, but she died before she could record it, and he had held onto it for more than forty years, hoping that someone would come along that could do it justice. With her crystal-clear voice and precise phrasing, LeAnn seemed much older, which made her success seem even more amazing. At age fourteen, she had record sales of more than twelve million copies—a feat she topped off by becoming the first country singer to win a Grammy in the Best New Artist category.

LeAnn's lightning-quick rise to stardom with "Blue" was amazing, but what was most meaningful about the song was Rimes' singing style. She used a Jimmie Rodgers yodel that was so pure, so infused with his genius, that it sent shivers up the arms of those who understood its significance.

4 MISSISSIPPI DELTA
▼ Highway 61 Revisited

Twelve thousand years before the arrival of the white man and his black slaves, Indians farmed the fertile land that is now called the Mississippi Delta. Their culture has largely disappeared, but their spirit remains in the land that the Mississippi River first offered as a sun-bronzed gift of life, and then periodically reclaimed with deadly floodwaters.

More recently, approximately fourteen hundred years ago, a tribe of Indians, similar in custom to the Natchez, thrived in an area just north of Greenville, Mississippi, where they built burial mounds now called the Winterville Mounds. The cluster of mounds—there were at one time more than two dozen, but highway construction and modern farming long ago obliterated all but a dozen—indicate a sophisticated culture that farmed the land and valued faith in spiritual matters.

The largest of the existing mounds is called the Temple Mound, because there is evidence that the fifty-five-foot-high earthen structure contained a building of religious significance and was, perhaps, the home of the tribal chief. Archaeologists' findings indicate that the building, constructed of wooden posts and covered with mud plaster, was destroyed by a great fire that took place in the 1300s. The cause of the fire is still a mystery, but the site was used until 1450, when it was abandoned. It is not known if the tribe was wiped out by disease or flood, or simply left the Delta for higher ground. Whatever their reason for leaving, they left behind the building blocks for a cultural landscape that is shrouded in mystery and spiritual ambiguity.

Since prehistoric times, the Mississippi Delta has stretched from just below what is now Memphis, southward 220 miles to Vicksburg, arching toward the Mississippi hill country. Fifty to seventy miles in width, the delta offers some of the darkest, richest farmland on earth. Until the 1830s and 1840s, when white settlers started establishing plantations along the river, it was a jungle filled with bears, panthers, rattlesnakes, poisonous water moccasins, and bobcats. The vegetation was as lush and dense as any jungle growth in Africa. It was a dark and dangerous place, a wild and untamed hatchery for evil.

One of the first settlers in the Delta was Charles Percy, a twenty-year-old Alabama plantation owner who abandoned everything he owned to travel to what is now Greenville, Mississippi, to start a new life. With him, he took boatloads of furniture, farm equipment, white overseers, and African slaves, who cleared a fifteen-mile path from the river to Deer Creek, near what is now Leland. He quickly learned that farming in the Delta was a roll of the dice, depending entirely on whether the Mississippi River chose to overflow its banks during that fragile time between planting and harvesting. He never lived to see levees built along the river, but his descendents did. By 1858, a rather stable network of levees was built that protected the farmland from flooding, thus opening up the entire Delta to adventuresome planters. After the Civil War, blacks poured into the Delta to work the farmland for wages or as sharecroppers, but there was not enough manpower to do everything that needed done, so Chinese and Italian workers were imported, creating one of the most racially diverse populations in the Mojo Triangle.

Perhaps because of that diversity, which soon included Jews, Syrians, and Lebanese, the Delta gained a reputation as one of the most hospitable locations in the South for African Americans. Free black families moved to the Delta from all over the country, lured by sharecropper land and the prospect of economic independence. Greenville became an oasis of liberalism, where lynching was frowned upon. But there were exceptions. In the late 1800s, a white man was lynched by whites in Greenville after he boasted of having killed a black man. Despite moments of liberal enlightenment, the Delta was a frequent target of nightriders from all over the state, creating a climate of terror that continues to this day.

Mississippi native son Willie Morris, the editor of *Harper's* magazine in the 1960s and an accomplished author for the remainder of the century, once gave a description of the Delta that merits repeating. While driving from his hometown of Yazoo City, to Greenville, he came to terms, finally, with the mysterious power of the landscape near a small Delta town named Onward. With a sense of wonderment, he wrote:

> **This, I knew from my boyhood, was one of the most desolate and treacherous drives in the whole state. My gasoline gauge pointed to empty, and I beseeched the Lord that I would not be stranded here in a storm, with**

not even a road shoulder to drive the car to, much less a Seven-Eleven or a Bun 'N Burger. I drove for miles in a mindless fright until, praise eternally be His name, there was the town of Onward, Mississippi, with a general store plastered with patent-medicine posters and a gas pump sitting precariously on the edge of the swamp. Back in the car again, stopping every so often to read in the eerie glow of the headlights the historical markers about the early Indians, the Spanish explorers, or the French settlers, I felt for the hundredth time the pull of that powerful and unremitting delta land, its abiding mysteries and strengths—retrieved from the ocean and later the interminable swamp—and the men of all colors and gradations known to the species who had fought it into its reluctant and tentative submission. No wonder there is no other state remotely like this one, I thought, no other so eternally wild, so savagely unpredictable, so fraught with contradictory deceits and nobilities; societies are shaped by the land from which they emerge, and on this night in a dark and relentless November storm, the land from which I and my blood-kin had emerged was scaring the unholy hell out of me.

The author of this book made that same drive in 2003—with much the same visceral reaction—though going much deeper into the Delta on U.S. Highway 61 to Clarksdale, to meet with Hollywood actor Morgan Freeman, who had been born in Memphis, but raised in the Delta near Greenwood. Over dinner conversation at his restaurant, an upscale establishment named Madidi, the actor talked about growing up during the same era in Greenwood. The previous week, Freeman had been in Memphis to promote a new film, *Levity*, co-starring Billy Bob Thornton, Holly Hunter, and Kirsten Dunst. On that night, when the bright lights of publicity were upon him, he had been dressed in a black suit, with a blue shirt and a white collar, but on this night, accompanied by his lovely wife, Myrna, and his assistant, Samantha, he drove in from his Delta home, wearing blues jeans and a baseball cap, the modern-day uniform of Southern leisure.

Freeman recalled Greenwood in the 1950s, when it was a town filled with contradictions. Segregation was the law. Blacks and whites attended the same movies in the Paramount movie theater (mostly westerns starring Roy Rogers and Gary Cooper, and World War II films starring John Wayne and James Stewart), but custom dictated that the whites sit in the seats on the floor, and the blacks sit in the balcony. Blacks and whites marched in the same parades, but their school bands were separated by enough mechanized floats to mark a clear boundary between the white bands and the black bands. And they walked the same streets, seeing the same sights and hearing the same political posturing about the civil rights movement.

What he remembered most about growing up in the Delta town, he said, was not racial discord. (Greenwood was where the killer of civil rights leader Medgar Evers called home), but rather the fact that a doctor once diagnosed him as suffering from malnutrition. "I didn't know I wasn't getting the right food," he said. "There seemed to be enough food on the table for everyone to eat."

The question this author most wanted to ask Freeman was how he had grown up in such an unfriendly environment, but had then moved on to become a movie star of liberal sensitivities—someone who could live anywhere in the world he chose, but wanted to live in the Mississippi Delta. The question hung there for a moment: "How did you go though everything that everyone else went through, but turn out so different?" And the answer came in the form of a question: "How did *you* do that and turn out the way you did?" It is a good question, for it goes to the heart of the Delta experience. It is a place where passions run deep, and the power of the land dictates roads taken and roads not taken, and where the myth of time and place stir the creative juices, sometimes to the boiling point and other times to that point where everything in the past is frozen fast, just the way it was. And, of course, it is a place where great art grows in the soil alongside the tomatoes, snap beans, and sweet corn. Where every man, woman, and child is born with an innate ability to play the guitar or piano, or write a clever verse.

Toward the end of the conversation, the restaurant filled with an interracial group of high school students from Freeman's hometown. Whites and blacks sitting at the same table—black boys, white girls. Weren't people once lynched for doing much less? The teacher spoke to Freeman, and he graciously acknowledged the students. "Isn't that something?" he asked, lowering his voice so that they would not hear him. "They've come to my restaurant to learn the proper etiquette for eating in a restaurant. Things have really changed since I grew up."

◆   ▲   ◆   ▲   ◆

Just as the people crept into the Delta like meandering flood waters, so did the music, first from Natchez, where the Scottish and the Irish planted the seeds of a folk tradition, and the Indians contributed harmony and exotic rhythms, and the African-American slaves, after experiencing both the white and the Indian worlds, embraced the Christian hymns that gave them hope—and then south from Memphis, where the slave trade brought new arrivals from Africa and a type of folk music that was expressed in chants or hollers, seamless streams of dialogue that had neither form nor direction.

When African Americans played musical instruments, whether it was their native banjo, the white man's guitar, or the Indian's drum, it was almost always done for the benefit of whites or Indians, who invariably rewarded them for their efforts. When they performed for other blacks, the music was carried by the rhythms of their vocals, whether it was expressed as spirituals or chants and hollers. Blues, as we know it today, did not make the journey from Africa with the slaves; rather, it was constructed in America in much the same way that a quilt is made, by adding bits and pieces of musical fabric into a coherent design that could stand alone.

Early on, the word "blues" was used by whites to describe any type of music played by blacks, who were routinely referred to in a derogatory way as "blues boys," but as time went by, blues came to mean a type of "relationship" music whose lyrics expressed a longing for a better time or place, whether in the past or the future. The word "blues" did not come into widespread use until 1912, when W.C. Handy published "The Memphis Blues." Before that, black music was simply called black music.

The most important thing that black musicians took with them to the Delta was the understanding that there was money in music, as evidenced by the Indian musicians who serenaded wealthy white settlers in exchange for coins, or staple goods, or whiskey. African Americans emulated that behavior and quickly learned, after the demise of slavery, that they could earn more playing music than they could working in the fields. For decades, the only music that blacks played for money was the music that whites wanted to hear—European style music that had a lively beat (for dancing) or a slow tempo (for drinking or reminiscing). They played the popular hits of the day—ragtime, show tunes, minstrel music, waltzes, and polkas. They didn't choose songs that appealed specifically to blacks, because blacks had no money with which to pay them.

At the turn of the century, one of the most popular string bands in Mississippi was fronted by Ezell Chatmon, who worked out of Jackson. For a while, he was accompanied by his nephew, Charley Patton, but for the most part, he called on his sons to staff his band. By the late 1920s, three of Ezell's natural sons (Lonnie, Bo, and Sam) and one adopted son (Walter Vincson), formed a separate band they named the Mississippi Sheiks. The Chatmons were exceptional musicians and consummate showmen. They sometimes switched instruments in the middle of a song—with the fiddle going to the guitarist and the guitar going to the fiddle player—and their play list included ragtime, popular songs of the day, and the music of Jimmie Rodgers.

In 1930, a white record store owner in Jackson, H. C. Speir, took the Mississippi Sheiks into a recording studio. Speir was not a music expert, just a businessman who wanted product for his record store, but he had a fine ear for music. One of the records that emerged from that session was "Sitting on Top of the World," a song that became a national hit and ended up selling millions of copies, its success no doubt influenced by the hard times associated with the Great Depression. Later, the song would be recorded by Frank Sinatra, Howlin' Wolf, Bob Wills, and the Grateful Dead, to name a few. The Mississippi Sheiks followed up that success with "Stop and Listen," making them one of the most famous African-American bands.

By 1935, however, interest in them had waned to the point where they stopped recording and went their separate ways. Bo Chatmon, who sometimes used the stage name Bo Carter, launched a solo career that produced more than one hundred songs, making him the single most popular black entertainer in Mississippi. Walter Vincson moved to Chicago, where he also found success as a recording artist. Sam Chatmon pursued his solo career on the West Coast, then in Memphis, before moving to the Delta town of Hollandale, Mississippi, to live out the remainder of his life.

In Hollandale, Sam became a fixture on the street corner outside Booth's Drug Store. When he wasn't touring around the country, or making trips overseas, he made himself at home on that corner and played for passersby.

Most Hollandale residents, the white ones anyway, thought that he was a bum asking for a handout, and that was because no one had any idea that he was revered in Paris and London, and most other places outside Mississippi. Nor did they know that he was receiving royalty checks for "Sitting on Top of the World" and other records made with his brothers.

Supposed grave site of Robert Johnson. (Steve Gardner)

Sam didn't say much, preferring to let his guitar do his talking for him, but when he looked at you, he looked right through you, his icy blue eyes letting you know whether he was glad to see you or not. Sometimes, Sam disappeared from the street corner for weeks at a time. Everyone figured he was home sick or something. It never occurred to anyone that he might be on a bus to an exotic location.

Sam didn't like to fly, and that sometimes caused him to turn down bookings. He once rejected a booking in Europe because he thought the eight-hundred-dollar paycheck was too small, and he wasn't interested in flying across the ocean. "My boy told me once, 'Oh, Dad, go ahead over there with Memphis Slim. Boy, eight hundred dollars would be good for a week. You ain't going to die till your time come,'" Sam told Margaret McKee and Fred Chisenhall. "I told him, 'Yeah, but I'd look like a fool. I'd be way up over all that water, and somebody else's time come, and I had to follow him down for him to die. I'd look like a fool following him down to die.'"

At the time that the Mississippi Sheiks were attracting national attention with their music, a guitar player from Hazelhurst, Mississippi, named Robert Johnson, set his sights on the same type of fame and fortune. For most blacks of that era, music was one of the few options available to them to escape the drudgery of plantation life. That was not lost on Johnson, who learned to play first harmonica, then guitar, when he was a young boy. He grew up listening to Delta musicians such as Son House and Charley Patton, both of whom incorporated chants and hollers into a more structured form that came to be known as folk blues, so that when the time came to develop his own style, Johnson looked more to Patton and House than to the popular music of the day. He wanted to be a success, but he wanted to do it on his own terms.

When white Mississippians show an interest in improving the lives of blacks, their efforts do not stay a secret. Their names are spread by word of mouth, from one end of the state to the other. Johnson did not have to read about the success that H. C. Speir was having with his recording acts; he heard it on the street, which was why he strolled into Speir's store in 1936 and introduced himself. After an audition, Speir referred him to Ernie Oertle, a talent scout for ARC records. Oertle liked what he heard and offered to take Johnson to San Antonio later that year to record a number of sides.

During a three-day session, Johnson recorded sixteen songs, including "Kind Hearted Woman," "I Believe I'll Dust My Broom," and "Sweet Home Chicago." Then, he returned to Mississippi to await the release of the records. When his copies arrived by mail, he went door to door to give them to his friends and relatives. In June 1937, he was called back to Texas to make more recordings.

This time, when he returned to Mississippi, he traveled throughout the Delta, then into Memphis, and over into Arkansas, performing at every venue he could find, finally winding up in Greenwood by late summer 1938. There he died. Some say he was poisoned or stabbed by a jealous husband, without ever knowing that the recordings he made would be recognized as legitimate music. As the years went by, more and more people discovered his legacy. Soon he became an icon, revered because the boogie-woogie bass line incorporated into his recordings was so unique, and because his lyrics were full of poetry.

Johnson's music is also important because of obvious Choctaw influences. Both use $^6/_4$, $^5/_4$, and $^4/_4$ time signatures, and both use short $^6/_4$ introductions that quickly change to $^5/_4$ or $^4/_4$ after one or two bars. For example, Johnson's "Little Queen of Spades" has a one bar introduction in $^6/_4$ that changes to $^4/_4$, an identical time signature to the Choctaw's "Wedding Dance," which also goes $^6/_4$ to $^4/_4$. Johnson did not hear time changes like that in the field hollers and chants that he listened to in the Delta, because that music was totally unstructured in its stream-of-consciousness flow, but he would have heard those unique changes in the music performed by the Choctaw on courthouse lawns in the counties surrounding Jackson.

So little is known about Johnson's life and the origins of his art, that rumors about his past range from unsubstantiated to mystical. Some say he made a pact with the Devil at a Delta crossroads, where he traded his soul for musical immortality. Certainly, strange things have happened in the Mojo Triangle. Some point out that Johnson's life paralleled Jesus' in the sense that he didn't discover his purpose until late in life, suffered for his beliefs, and had only two years to bring his mission into fruition. Unlike Jesus, however, he led a scoundrel's life—and then he was gone, leaving behind a mystery that seems to grow with time.

In August 2001, a headstone was erected at the Little Zion Missionary Baptist Church cemetery in Greenwood. No one is certain the bluesman is actually buried there, but it seems to be the most likely location for his grave. However, the black community did not welcome this well meaning gesture. In June 2004, a Little Zion deacon protested the publicity that the grave was attracting from tour groups. She asked that the church be removed from the tour, saying, "The blues and the church are separate, and they should not be mixed." What went unsaid, perhaps, is that, if Johnson did make a pact with the Devil, his music should not be associated with the church.

Today, Johnson's legacy and mystery continue to inspire blues musicians. Eric Clapton released an album in 2004 titled *Me and Mr. Johnson*, which featured fourteen Johnson covers. Clapton had discovered Johnson's *King of the Delta Blues Singers* at the age of fifteen, and when the time came for him to make his first recording, it was a cover of Johnson's "Ramblin' on My Mind." *Me and Mr. Johnson* serves as a tribute to Clapton's musical roots.

◆ ▲ ◆ ▲ ◆

Rice Miller, who later adapted the stage name Sonny Boy Williamson, was born around 1910 on a plantation in Glendora, Mississippi, about thirty miles northwest of Greenwood. By the time he became a young adult, in the early 1930s, black musicians were a common sight throughout the Delta: On street corners, in black juke joints on Saturday nights, and at barbecues held by white plantation owners. Using fiddles, banjos, and guitars, they played the popular tunes of the day, bits and pieces of Jimmie Rodgers' new country music, and original folk progressions that were increasingly being identified as the blues.

Sonny Boy learned the harmonica and the guitar, but he was unable to distinguish himself from other black performers in the Delta, most of whom had strong followings. It eventually occurred to him that if he was going to be successful, he would have to out-think his competition, not out-play them.

On occasion, Sonny Boy traveled to Clarksdale so that he could cross the Mississippi River on Mr. Jenkins' ferry into Arkansas. (Jenkins was the father of future country music star Conway Twitty). He was a fresh face at the juke joints in and around Helena, a small town about sixty miles south of Memphis. On one such trip in 1941, he learned that the town had a radio station. Fearless, he approached the white owner of KFFA and asked him if he would air a blues show. The owner, who could see the economic potential of a show that appealed to black shoppers, explained the realities of radio to Sonny Boy: If he wanted a blues show, he would have to find a sponsor to pay for the air time.

Sonny Boy didn't know a soul in Helena who was capable of paying for a radio show, but the station owner sent him to talk to Max Moore, the white owner of the Interstate Grocery. Once Sonny Boy explained his idea to Moore, the businessman understood that sponsoring a radio show could be a good way to market his own brand of flour and corn meal to the black community. He agreed to sponsor the show, but only if Sonny Boy would allow him to use his image and name on his corn meal. Soon the grocery's shelves were stocked with row after row of Sonny Boy Corn Meal, with Sonny Boy's smiling face on the side of the bag, right beside the bags that already bore the name King Biscuit Flour.

Moore wanted to call the radio show "King Biscuit Time," and that was fine with Sonny Boy, who liked the way it sounded. The show's format was simple. Each day at noon, Sonny Boy and whatever band he could put together played live music that was interspersed with commercials for Sonny Boy Corn Meal and King Biscuit Flour. It was an immediate success, not just in Helena, but all across the Mississippi Delta, where it could be heard as far south as Indianola and Greenwood.

"Sunshine" Sonny Payne, one of two white announcers on the show, later recalled that Sonny Boy showed up on the first day wearing a derby hat, a style that Payne had never before seen. "I don't mean to be insulting," Payne recalled, "but he had a nose just like a buzzard's beak. A lot of the blues performers called him the Buzzard Beak."

Payne was impressed with Sonny Boy's professionalism. "When he came in, he always had a big smile on his face," Payne recalled. "He would greet all the musicians, and naturally the guy who would be hosting the show, in most cases myself. After that, everything was strictly business. He got serious. He didn't want anybody to foul up. He wanted you right then and there on the spot to do your thing and do it right....He got real serious about his music."

From 1941 to 1981, "King Biscuit Time" did for the blues what the Grand Ole Opry had done for country music; it made the blues accessible to a mass audience. At that time, there were no black radio stations in the area, and few white-owned stations showed any interest in airing black music, much less an entire show devoted to the blues.

So, that was how Sonny Boy outsmarted his competitors. Soon, he was the most famous blues musician in the Delta, able to attract other name musicians to his show, people like Robert Junior Lockwood, Elmore James, Houston Stackhouse, and boogie-woogie pianist Pinetop Perkins, who was born in Belzoni, Mississippi, a town known as the catfish capital of the world. Asked in 1989 about working with Sonny Boy, Perkins said, "Me and him could get along all right. He was kinda' crabby, but he never did bother me too much." Then, as if to further explain their relationship, he added, "My first wife was his first cousin."

"King Biscuit Time" made Sonny Boy famous, but it didn't make him rich. Throughout the 1940s, he tried to use his fame as leverage to get a recording contract, but with no success. It was not until 1951 that he was able to interest someone in recording his music. Ironically, the person who believed in him the most was not a Chicago record executive, or a Los Angeles or New York record label that specialized in recordings by African Americans, but rather a twenty-eight-year-old white furniture store owner, Lillian McMurry, who started up a record label after test-marketing rhythm & blues records in her store over a public address system. The more records she played, the more furniture she sold. She named the label Trumpet Records and set out to discover a wide array of talent, recording everyone right there in the store, using mattresses as baffles. Her roster was eclectic, to say the least, varying from white segregationist and gubernatorial candidate Jimmy Swan to Sonny Boy, discovered by Lillian in her second year of operation. In all, Sonny Boy recorded about twenty songs for Trumpet, including "Dust My Broom," which he performed with Elmore James.

Three years later, Sonny Boy signed with Chess Records in Chicago, turning out rhythm & blues hits such as "Bring It on Home" and "Don't Start Me Talking." He stopped performing on "King Biscuit Time" on a regular basis, but throughout the 1950s and early 1960s, he would stop by the station to do another show whenever he was anywhere near Helena. In 1964, he returned to Helena, thinking he might stay a while—or at least long enough to justify renting a room upstairs over the Dreamland Café. When Payne ran into him, Sonny Boy said he had come home to die:

"No one ever knows when they are going to die," answered Payne. "That's God's thing."

"I know," Sonny Boy said, shaking his head.

Payne wrote his comments off as the product of a creative mind, but, sure enough, Payne was at the radio station when he got word that Sonny Boy had died in his sleep. "When I actually saw his body, I knew he was gone, and it hurt," said Payne. "I felt kind of dead myself—I cried."

By the time Sonny Boy died, the blues had gone off on an entirely new tangent, thanks, in large part, to McKinley Morganfield, who was born in 1913 on a plantation near Onward, Mississippi, in the majority black county of Issaquena. Like Sonny Boy, Morganfield—whose stage name was Muddy Waters—was a slow starter. He began making music during his childhood, but he spent most of his daylight hours driving a tractor. His big break came in the summer of 1941, when folk music researcher Alan Lomax went to Mississippi in search of Robert Johnson so that he could make some recordings for the Library of Congress. He didn't find Johnson, but he did run across Muddy Waters at Stovall Plantation.

Muddy was taken aback at first, thinking that perhaps Lomax was a government agent on a mission to bust Muddy's small bootlegging operation, but when he brought out a tape recorder, Muddy realized that Lomax was serious about capturing music. Even before he heard Muddy play, Lomax was impressed by his looks—with a round, somewhat flat face and high cheek bones and slanted eyes, he looked more like an Indian than an African American. He almost certainly had Choctaw or Chickasaw blood somewhere in his family tree.

Lomax was "bowled over" by Muddy's artistry: "He sang and played with such finesse, with such a mercurial and sensitive bond between voice and guitar, and he expressed so much tenderness in the way he handled his lyrics, that he went right beyond his predecessors...His own pieces were more than blues; they were love songs of the Deep South, gently erotic and sentimental."

Encouraged by his impromptu recording session with Lomax, Muddy spent more time on his music, performing wherever he could, whether it was at fish fries or on Saturday night at a local juke joint. When Lomax returned the following year to do more recordings, Muddy felt that, finally, his time had come. It was not long after that he started listening to "King Biscuit Time." "Every time there wasn't a radio around, I'd run to the next house where one was at, to hear 'em play—they was good," Muddy told *Living Blues* magazine. "They played ever little things, called theirself playing every little thing, but after I found out they wasn't playing no jazz—they'd get sweet sometime, but they wasn't jazz people, just like I wasn't, you know. But you know, you could jive the public that he was playing different stuff. They'd play a lot of good church songs on there sometimes."

One day, late in 1949, Muddy called the KFFA station manager and asked him if he would give him a show like Sonny Boy's. After being paired with a sponsor called Katz Clothing Store, Muddy and his band moved to Helena, where they got up early in the morning to perform live at five o'clock. It wasn't a good time slot for the blues, so the sponsorship lasted only six weeks. He later discovered that, although he was unpopular in Helena, he had been well received in Mississippi, well beyond traveling distance to Katz's Clothing Store. No hard feelings. Just thank you, but no thanks.

In 1943, convinced that he could do better, Muddy boarded a train in Clarksdale and traveled north to Chicago, where he landed a job in a paper mill making containers while he attempted to establish himself musically. By the end of the decade, he had signed with Chess Records and released a series of unforgettable sides, fueled by his high-voltage electric guitar. Songs like "Rolling Stone," "Honey Bee," and "Baby, Please Don't Go" made it clear that Muddy Waters was a major star.

By the early 1950s, Muddy was playing music that had moved far beyond the folk music he had listened to growing up in the Delta. He had a more sophisticated style of playing, combined with clever and, at times, poetical lyrics that mimicked the power of the jazz bands in previous decades and hinted at the beginnings of rock 'n' roll.

◆　▲　◆　▲　◆

Growing up in Indianola, Mississippi, located on Highway 82, about halfway between Greenville and Greenwood, Riley Ben King—who would later settle on the stage name B.B. King—was sixteen when "King Biscuit Time" went on the air

B.B. King with friends at his hometown of Indianola, 1991. (Steve Gardner)

in 1941. "It used to come on about twelve-fifteen weekdays, Mondays through Fridays, and we would be in the fields and we would go home for lunch," said King. "We always hurried to be there so that when twelve-fifteen came we could catch the program. I heard them so long, it seemed like I really knew them."

Indianola was a cotton town about fourteen miles from Leland, where U. S. Highway 82 crosses the famed U. S. Highway 61 that goes from Memphis all the way to New Orleans. (Highway 82 goes from Greenville to Columbus and beyond into Alabama.) Clarksdale, through an effective promotional campaign, dubbed itself the "blues crossroads" of America, because it is where Highway 61 meets with Highways 49 and 6, but it's not actually a crossroads, because Highways 49 and 6 don't cross Highway 61, they terminate there.

The *real* blues crossroads is located at Leland, for that is where Memphis is connected to New Orleans, joining Beale Street to the French Quarter, and Greenville is connected to Columbus, joining the Mississippi River with the Mississippi-Alabama state line. Greenville would qualify as a second "mini" crossroads, because it is where State Highway 1, which runs from across the river from Helena south to Rolling Fork, crosses with Highway 82. Clarksdale is a fine town, with a fabulous music history, but it is not located at the blues crossroads.

Riley Ben King wasn't worried about any of that growing up near Indianola; he was more concerned about helping his family earn a living in the cotton fields. He grew up during a time when rituals were important, when the spiritual world was not separate from the workaday world. It was through the rituals of daily living that music entered King's life at a very early age, long before "King Biscuit Time" stirred his imagination. "A lot of my people were very religious," King explained. "Going to church was one of the things we all cherished. We used to go house to house. Every Wednesday night they would meet at some family's home. Everyone would sing and have food. That's how I got into music."

Indianola was a county seat (Sunflower County), which gave it a cosmopolitan edge over the small communities that surrounded it. People were constantly streaming from other places into the town to conduct business in the stores, attend court, go to the doctor and the dentist—but King had the best of both worlds; he was able to go into the city when he wished, and able to avoid the city when he wished. "I guess I was just a normal Mississippi boy," he explained. "I was one of those guys who enjoyed all the fun guys usually did—hunting and fishing, those kinds of things. There was a lot of area for guys to romp around and have a good time."

King gravitated to the guitar for economic reasons. "That was all I could afford. It was rare to see a piano or an organ in someone's home. We had a guitar in our family. It is an instrument that most people can play. Very few people can't play any licks on a guitar—and they are within the reach of the average family, which is why I call the guitar the people's instrument."

King formed a quartet in his late teens, and began playing around Sunflower County at social functions. They got a reputation as hard working musicians, but they were a long way away from being able to compete with the blues professionals that roamed the Delta, going from juke joint to fish fry to plantation barbecue. Still, he worked at getting better, with the same work ethic that he displayed in the fields.

"King Biscuit Time" filled King's head with music—blues, spirituals, pop tunes—so that he was convinced that he could have a future in music if he worked hard at it. If Sonny Boy could do it, anyone could do it—or so his reasoning went. Of course, there was more going out over the airwaves than music. Black boys and girls all over the Delta also heard black men standing toe-to-toe with white men, bantering, laughing, communicating man to man, having a good time the way the Lord meant them to do, and it had a profound effect—instilling not just pride in their race, but hope that they, too, could find a way to discover the American Dream.

In 1925, not far from King's birthplace—about halfway between Indianola and Leland—on a plantation near Dunleith just off the indomitable Highway 82, yet another future African-American musician was born. Jimmy Reed did as much as B.B. King or Muddy Waters did to attract white audiences to electric blues.

Growing up, Reed spent much of his time in Leland, a sleepy town located on the banks of Deer Creek. Reed was only two years old when the Great Flood of 1927 sent several feet of muddy, snake-infested water through the town's streets and beyond, to towns such as Dunleith, where most share-croppers' shacks were destroyed. The flood had a great impact on Reed; it introduced him to an unfriendly world in which death and destruction were a real possibility that lingered menacingly in everyone's thoughts and dreams.

In those days, black children were not required to go to school during

Sharecropper shack in the Mississippi Delta, 1990. (Steve Gardner)

the chopping and picking seasons; they were expected to be in the cotton fields alongside their parents, grandparents, and aunts and uncles. It was hard work, and it often took place in temperatures that ranged from the mid-nineties to well over one hundred degrees. Typically, workers were given water breaks many times a day, but the only extended break occurred when they were allowed to go home to lunch.

Like B.B. King, Jimmy Reed rushed home at noon to listen to "King Biscuit Time." It was his first introduction to the blues. "Now that used to be my stone rundown, when I'd slip out of the fields and go up to the house to listen at them do that fifteen minutes he [Sonny Boy Williamson] had to do over the radio show," Reed told Jim O'Neal. "I listened to them play, and I said, 'Well, I'll keep on tryin' to play this thing, first and last. I might be able to do it too.' So, I just kept on it. It took me quite a few years, but I finally got around to it."

Reed lived on the Dunleith plantation until he was in his mid-teens, then moved on to other plantations in the area, never venturing too far beyond walking distance of Leland. Reed went to church and participated in church events, so he heard a lot of sacred music, but the secular music he heard in his youth came into his home on the radio. There was no one around that could teach him how to play the guitar, so he picked it up on his own, starting at age ten, by imitating the songs on the radio, learning the music note by note.

When Reed was eighteen—the year was 1943—he underwent a life-altering experience. He was working in the fields behind a brace of mules, steering them in a straight line so that they would plow a furrow for cottonseeds, when he took a water break. His boss man, not happy to see him stop working, started pushing him with his feet—not kicking him, just gently pushing him across a ditch, back to where the mules were waiting for him. Reed allowed himself to be pushed across the ditch, but then he just started walking away from the mules, away from the boss man, all the way into Leland, where he boarded a train to Chicago, where he moved in with relatives.

No sooner did he arrive in Chicago, than he was drafted and ordered to report to the naval boot camp in Brainbridge, Maryland. It probably was not a coincidence that he was drafted so soon after leaving the Mojo Triangle. In those days, and for many years afterward, draft boards in the Delta were controlled by plantation owners, and in some instances, Grand Dragons of the Ku Klux Klan. It is entirely within the realm of coincidence that Reed was drafted soon after turning eighteen, but more likely his walk away from the cotton field was reported to the draft board by Reed's boss man.

When he was discharged from the Navy after two years' service, Reed returned to Mississippi to live with his parents, who had relocated to Clarksdale. He hung around there for another year or two, then decided to return to Chicago. It was then that he honed his skills on guitar and learned how to play the harmonica. By 1953, he was good enough to be signed to a recording contract by Vee-Jay Records. His first record, "You Don't Have to Do," was written by his wife, Mama Reed.

Reed had a deceptively simple boogie-woogie style that he played over and over again in a moderate $4/4$ time. Fellow Mississippi refugee Eddie Taylor was recruited for his band, and together—with Mama Reed's considerable help—they recorded one hit after another, including "Big Boss Man," "Bright Lights, Big City," "Shame, Shame, Shame," and "Baby, What You Want Me to Do." He was especially popular with white audiences and musicians such as the Rolling Stones, the Animals, the Spencer Davis Group, and the Yardbirds, all of whom recorded his songs in the 1960s and early 1970s.

Reed never really considered his music as being blues. That was just a label that white people put on his music because he was black. "I never did name one of my records 'the blues,'" Reed told O'Neal. "Everybody else called my sounds what I made 'the blues,' but I always just felt good behind 'em. I didn't feel like I was playin' no blues. I felt like it sound just as good to the spiritual people as it would to somebody in a bar."

What Reed did like about the blues were isolated notes and phrases that touched his heart. He took those notes and phrases and worked his magic on them to shape a new kind of music that gave him a distinctive edge over his competitors. Reed's live music was different from his recorded music, in that it had an actual physical presence, a melancholy air that flowed in waves, his guitar marching onward with the symmetrical certainty of a railroad locomotive, and his harmonica rising above it all with a spiritual sweetness that stood in bold contrast to the darkness of the slurred lyrics that often spoke of failure and rejection.

Furry Lewis on the porch of his Memphis apartment. (Courtesy of the Mississippi Valley Collection, Univerissty of Memphis)

Reed played hard, and he lived hard. As a result, his final years were a nightmare for him, marked by the effects of alcoholism and epileptic seizures that kept him in and out of hospitals until his death in 1976. None of his music was played at his funeral in Chicago, which is the way he would have wanted it. In the funeral program, his son, Jimmy Reed Jr., wrote: "There can never be another Jimmy Reed, but his music will live forever in our hearts and lives, because in today's world, life is only more or less the blues anyway."

In addition to Jimmy Reed and B.B. King, the 61-82 Crossroads produced an impressive array of talent, including Furry Lewis, who was born in Greenwood. He ended up in Memphis, where he had two impressive careers, the first on Beale Street in the 1920s and 1930s, and the second in the 1970s during a blues revival that catapulted him from obscurity onto concert stages with major rock stars. There was also Mary Wilson, the Greenville-born member of Motown Record's top female act, the Supremes; Indianola's Albert King, whose real name was Albert Nelson. He scored a minor hit in 1961 with "Don't Throw Your Love on Me So Strong," but his career didn't take off until he moved to Memphis and signed with Stax Records. Leland's Boogaloo Ames was educated in music at Michigan State University and traveled with bands led by Louis Armstrong and Louis Jordan. James "Son" Thomas, also born in Leland, is a country blues performer whose best album is *Highway 61 Blues.*

Jacqueline Gooch, a white teenage guitar wizard and blues singer from Clarksdale attracted the attention of top producers in Los Angeles after Morgan Freeman praised her talents; and last but not least, there's Greenville's

Blues guitarist James "Son" Thomas, 1986. (Steve Gardner)

Little Milton, who moved at a young age to Memphis, where he learned to play blues from Sonny Boy Williamson during his visits to the city in the 1940s. Asked in the late 1980s if he thought growing up in Greenville helped or hurt his career, Little Milton answered: "I think it helped. I learned a lot about people. I learned how to respect myself. You have to know how to respect yourself before you can respect other people. I think if I had grown up in a major city or something I might have been a little too cocky."

◆　▲　◆　▲　◆

"I wanted to come home—it's no more complicated or simple than that," former *Harper's* magazine editor Willie Morris told William Thomas in 1980. "I'm at a kind of juncture in my life, and I felt it was time. Besides, my nerve ends come alive when I cross the Mississippi line. I'm not exaggerating. It's got to have something to do with that whole business of the burden of memory—the memory that serves one's imagination as a writer....I have no doubt but what this business of coming home is stronger for Southerners than it is for any others in the country. And, among Southerners, the feeling is strongest in Mississippi. Why? Because there's just something about Mississippi that's different...different than any other place...absolutely different. It is something profound in our emotions."

In 1980, Morris returned home to teach at the University of Mississippi, after spending most of his adult life outside Mississippi. That is rare for a Mojo Triangle writer, the returning part of it, because most writers born in the region—Tennessee Williams is another exception—remain there to be close to their material, as frightening as that prospect may be to them at times. The "memory" that haunted Morris is the same prehistoric recollection of time and place that has driven, inspired, and sometimes terrified creative minds in the region; whether through music or literature, it is another manifestation of the power of the Triangle.

Morris was born in Yazoo City, a geographical citadel that overlooks the Mississippi Delta from high above the bluffs. (Yazoo is an Indian word meaning, "river of the dead," a reference to the Yazoo River that runs near the city.) Morris is not a Delta writer, by a mere technicality of a few yards of rocky soil, but his literary sensibilities were certainly Delta-like in his understanding of the dark swampland, and his acceptance of the liberal tradition that has characterized the

Delta, almost from the day that white men and women first stepped foot there.

The Delta literary tradition essentially grew out of the Charles Percy family of Greenville, who, after proving that fortunes could be made in the cleared swampland in the 1800s, proceeded to mine that section of the Triangle for its literary riches. William Alexander Percy was an aristocratic planter, born in 1885 in Greenville, but educated at Sewanee and Harvard Law School, who believed that public service was an obligation mandated by his family's control of the Delta's economy. He served in Herbert Hoover's relief commission in Belgium, he fought in World War I—with enough enthusiasm to be awarded the French Croix de Guerre—and, upon his return to Mississippi, he and his father fought hard against the Ku Klux Klan.

In 1941, Percy published a memoir titled *Lanterns on the Levee.* It is a curious book that argues for the assimilation of blacks into white society, albeit at a snail's pace, while sounding an alarm against sexual experimentation. "In the South the one sacred taboo, assumed to be Southern, but actually and universally Anglo-Saxon, is the untouchability of white women by Negro men," he wrote. "It is academic to argue the wisdom or justice of this taboo. Wise or unwise, just or unjust, it is the cornerstone of friendly relations, of interracial peace. In the past, it has been not the eleventh but the first com-mandment. Even to question it means the shattering of race relations into hideous and bloody ruin. But I fear it is coming to be questioned."

Today, that reads like racism of the worst kind, but by the standards of that era, it qualified Percy as a liberal. There were two kinds of racial fears in those days—fear of black economic dominance, and fear of black sexual dominance. Percy's most telling flaw as a human being was his fear of black sexual dominance. Despite that fear, he was instrumental in establishing Greenville as a liberal oasis that opened its doors to Jewish, Syrian, Chinese, and Italian immigrants, who gave the city a character unlike any other in the Triangle. At a time when Jews were banned from country clubs all across America, the Greenville Country Club had a Jewish president. And so it went.

Percy's greatest fear came true, of course, beginning in the 1960s, but it had less to do with black sexual dominance than it did with the centuries-old subjugation of white women, who began to see the civil rights movement gaining rights for blacks that white women did not possess. These women rebelled by taking black men as lovers. Consider, for example, a socially prominent, married white woman in Greenville who, had sex with a black meter reader for reasons she could not really explain. "He came over to read the meter," she said, "and it just happened." When asked if he was her first black lover, she answered no, and then proceeded to explain that she had sexual relations with her boss at the bank. Her boss was an affable black man who was, no doubt, hired because he was affable, and therefore was assumed not to be a threat. However, when a supervisory job had opened up, all the white women, most of whom were married, slept with him in the hopes of getting a promotion.

That black bank manager, to a great degree, had Percy to thank for his good fortune—not just for the job, but for the side benefits—though Percy would surely have had a heart attack if he had lived to see it happen. Besides putting his reputation on the line for racial moderation, Percy recruited a newspaperman from Louisiana named Hodding Carter, who would have an even more profound impact on Delta race relations. With Percy's financial support—and the backing of other leading citizens—Carter and his wife, Betty, moved to Greenville in 1936 from Hammond, Louisiana, where they published the *Daily Courier*.

Carter named his new newspaper the *Delta Star*. It was tough going at first, because Greenville already had a newspaper, the *Democrat-Times*, but he assembled a strong staff—including a reporter and proofreader named Shelby Foote—and methodically went about the business of undercutting his competition.

No one quite knew what to make of Hodding. He seemed familiar and different at the same time. Toward the end of the newspaper's first year, Hodding wrote a page-one editorial that left no doubt about where he stood on the important issues of the day. Midway across the state, in Duck Hill, not far from where the Delta meets the hills, a black man was lynched after being charged with the murder of a white storekeeper. In his editorial, Hodding wrote: "In Washington, congress debates a federal anti-lynching bill extreme in its encroachment on state's rights. To the vindicators of that encroachment, Mississippi has now contributed a mighty bludgeon...Is there justice in Mississippi? Then, punish the Duck Hill mobsters."

Carter followed that by publishing a photograph of black athlete Jesse Owens, who had won four gold medals at the 1936 Summer Olympics. Owens had come to the all-black Delta town of Mound Bayou to celebrate its fiftieth anniversary, and Carter thought that was newsworthy. A firestorm of protest followed. Few newspapers in the nation published photographs of

African Americans, much less newspapers in the South. Carter reveled in the controversy. He responded by writing an editorial that defended his publication of the photograph: "Jesse Owens is a remarkable athlete. And so we printed his picture. We'll print it again when we feel like doing so."

As newspaper wars go, Carter's competition with the conservative *Democrat-Times* didn't last long. In 1938, with the help of his influential friends, Carter bought out his competitor and renamed his new newspaper the *Delta Democrat-Times*. William Alexander Percy kicked in twenty thousand dollars in United States Steel stock as collateral to secure the annual notes.

Although he was conservative in many areas—he shared Percy's apprehension about interracial sexual coupling—Carter went on to become a legendary liberal newspaperman, largely responsible for the speed with which racial equality was greeted in the Delta. It was tough to be an overt racist in Greenville simply because Carter, fire-breathing democrat that he was, was ever ready to name names in his newspaper—and publish photographs, if available.

Hodding Carter was awarded the 1946 Pulitzer Prize for editorial writing, but it wasn't necessarily for his editorials about race relations. There was a second issue dear to his heart during World War II: Right across the Mississippi River, in Arkansas, the federal government had established internment camps for Japanese Americans. Carter was indignant that the government would herd law-abiding American citizens of Asian ancestry into what amounted to prison camps, simply because of their skin color, and his editorials criticized the government for its actions. In the 1970s, long after Carter's death, his business partner John Gibson told this author that he had personally packaged the editorials that were sent to the Pulitzer committee, and he was certain that the editorials that were cited in the award were those written about the internment camps.

Besides leaving behind a glorious journalistic legacy, Hodding left behind two talented sons: Philip Carter, who worked at *Newsweek* for a time and then married a Virginia socialite and settled in New Orleans, where he started up a weekly newspaper; and Hodding Carter III, who took over leadership of the *Delta Democrat-Times* after his father's death and served as editor until he accepted a position with the State Department during Jimmy Carter's presidency. Hodding III, or "Little Hodding," as he's called by locals, went on to become an author and television news analyst.

After getting his start at the *Delta Star*, Shelby Foote went on to become an authority on the Civil War, probably best known for this three-volume history, *The Civil War: A Narrative*. He also published fiction, including the novels *Shiloh, Jordan Country,* and *September, September,* but his non-fiction made him a household name, at least among history enthusiasts.

As a young adult, Foote moved to Memphis, where he lives today, but he never stopped marveling at the influences the Percys and the Carters had on Greenville. "The Ku Klux Klan never made any headway, at a time when it was making headway almost everywhere else," he said. "In most places, nobody would stand up to the Klan in politics. It represented too many votes for you to stand up to. You might explain to your friends that you thought the people in the Klan were a bunch of rednecks and nuts, but you didn't tell them that. In Greenville, they did."

Another author who made Greenville home for a time was novelist Walker Percy, who moved there at a young age, following the death of both parents, to be raised by his father's cousin, William Alexander Percy. Walker didn't begin life thinking he wanted to be a writer; he was much more interested in science. He earned a degree in chemistry at the University of North Carolina, and received a medical degree from Columbia's College of Physicians and Surgeons. It was not until he contracted tuberculosis while working as a pathologist at Bellevue Hospital in New York that he began to see himself as a writer. He returned to the South and married a woman he had met in Greenville, and they settled down in Covington, Louisiana, where he tried his hand at writing novels. His first novel, *The Moviegoer,* was published in 1961 and was awarded the National Book Award. Other novels—*The Last Gentleman, Love in the Ruins: The Adventures of a Bad Catholic at a Time Near the End of the World,* and *Lancelot*—won him more accolades and established him as a major talent.

Any discussion of Greenville literary talent would have to include James Maury Henson, born in 1936 at King's Daughter's Hospital. The family actually lived in Leland, where Henson's father worked for the United States Department of Agriculture, but King's Daughter's was the closest hospital. Growing up, Henson walked the same streets as Jimmy Reed, B.B. King, Hodding Carter, the Percys, Little Milton, and others, but the inspiration he received from the Triangle led him neither to music nor to the type of writing that distinguished others mentioned in this section. Henson wrote, but he didn't write for humans, at least not directly—he wrote for puppets.

James Henson is, of course, the Jim Henson who invented the muppets—unforgettable characters such as Bert and Ernie, Oscar the Grouch, Big Bird, and Cookie Monster, all known to fans of television's "Sesame Street." Henson, who died in 1990, was an innovator who used advanced technology to transform the dark, mythical visions of the Mojo Triangle into bright, colorful images suitable for children. All of those wonderful creations that have influenced millions of kids around the world, began as dreams, then as ideas committed to paper that progressed to written dialog, creating the stuff of which legends are made. In that context, Henson, the writer, was a dramatist of Shakespearean caliber—even if it was all just for the kids.

◆　▲　◆　▲　◆

Born in 1944 in Chickasaw County, just south of Tupelo in the piney hill country, Roberta Lee Streeter, later known to the recording industry as Bobbie Gentry, moved to Greenwood at the age of six. She lived there until the age of thirteen, when she moved to Palm Springs, California, with her mother. After high school, she attended the University of California at Los Angeles, where she studied philosophy, and then enrolled in the Los Angeles Conservatory of Music, supporting herself by doing secretarial work.

In 1967, she took several songs that she had composed to a Los Angeles publisher in the hopes of getting representation. The publisher was impressed by the freshness of her music and played the tapes for Kelly Gordon, an executive at Capitol Records, who immediately signed her to a recording contract. The first side she did for Capitol was "Mississippi Delta," an up-tempo song inspired by her childhood in Greenwood. Because it was to be released as a single, and they needed another song for the flip side, they sent her home to compose another song with a Delta theme. It took her less than three hours to adapt one of her short stories into "Ode to Billie Joe," which she recorded while accompanying herself on acoustic guitar. A dense bed of strings was subsequently added to the track by the producer. "Ode to Billie Joe" was viewed by the record label as a throwaway song, something to take up space.

When "Mississippi Delta" was released in July 1967, radio programmers greeted it with a yawn; they felt it didn't fit any of their prefab format categories. It wasn't rock 'n' roll. It wasn't blues. It wasn't country. What they did like was the flip side, "Ode to Billie Joe." That song didn't fit any of their formats either, but it was so innovative, so charmingly irrepressible in its imagery, that they started airing it. The song left two questions on everyone's lips: What was thrown off the Tallahatchie River Bridge, and why did Billie Joe McAllister make a death leap from the bridge?

As "Ode to Billie Joe" shot up the charts in August 1967—by the end of the month, it was the Number One record in the country—Chickasaw County organized a home-coming celebration for Gentry in Houston and invited her back to Mississippi. This author was sent to cover the event for *Mississippi Magazine*, a student publication at the University of Mississippi. When he attempted to schedule an interview, producer Kelly Gordon's reply was, "Absolutely not. She's not going to do any interviews for you or anyone else."

Later, at a luncheon given in her honor, the author persuaded her to do the interview, much to Gordon's displeasure, because the record label wanted to maintain an air of mystery about the song, and the best way to do that was to keep her away from reporters. Strikingly beautiful—and more attractive in person than in her photos or on television—she quickly proved that she could handle herself in an interview situation. To the nervous producer's great relief the interview ended without Billie Joe's secret being divulged.

She did admit that her songs were drawn from her own life experiences. "I find writing easy, and I can do it almost anyplace," she said. "However, I prefer creating in solitude, probably because I have lived most of my life alone. I try to write wherever I am. My writing is large- *Bobbie Gentry recording in* ly autobiographical, so I find that keeping notes helps me *Muscle Shoals. (David Hood)* to remember."

In 1976, when "Ode to Billie Joe" was made into a film starring Robby Benson and Glynnis O'Connor, Gentry told a reporter for the *Delta Democrat-Times* that the movie company wanted to leave the Billy Joe issue unresolved. She opposed that approach and insisted that the film answer the questions about the song that she had steadfastly refused to answer for nearly a decade. "I don't think there was anything to do but give an answer," she explained. "The movie will put the song back into focus. The movie is about Billy Joe and why he jumped off the bridge."

So many people came to the Delta looking for the fictional bridge mentioned in "Ode to Billie Joe" that Lieutenant Governor Evelyn Gandy used the occasion of the making of the movie to declare "Bobby Gentry Day" and to rename the Roebuck Bridge, located near the village of Rising Sun, the Tallahatchie Bridge, thus converting fiction to fact—a transaction that occurs all too often in the State of Mississippi.

The movie's explanation for Billy Joe jumping off the bridge was that he was uncertain about his sexual preference. Was Bobbie Gentry writing about herself? Or was she writing about a friend? Because of the mystery associated with the song, the singer's sexual preference became the topic of tabloid gossip and rumor. Two years after her stunning debut on the national charts, she addressed that debate by marrying Bill Harrah, president of the Desert Inn Hotel in Las Vegas, and by retreating from public view. When that marriage didn't pan out, she married singer-songwriter Jim Stafford, a marriage that lasted less than three years.

Gentry's first album generated several hits, in addition to "Ode to Billie Joe," including "Mississippi Delta," "Chickasaw County Child," and "Papa, Won't You Take Me to Town With You." Her follow-up album, *The Delta Sweete*, which was released in 1968, did not sell as well as the first album, but it is of interest because it included songs by other Mojo Triangle artists, such as "Big Boss Man," a hit for Jimmy Reed, and "Parchman Farm," a hit for Mose Allison. In 1968, Gentry won three Grammys—and she spent the 1970s steadily booked as a nightclub entertainer.

During the 1980s and 1990s, Gentry shied away from making public appearances and adopted a reclusive lifestyle, although her name surfaced briefly in the early 1990s, when Reba McEntire had a Number One hit with Gentry's 1970 song "Fancy." By that time, Gentry was pigeonholed as a country artist, an ironic legacy for a pop artist who, in 1967, had a record that out-charted the Beatles, the Doors, the Monkees, and Aretha Franklin. That business of not fitting any existing mold is common for innovative recording artists from the Mojo Triangle. Early on, no one knew what to make of Elvis Presley or Louis Armstrong, or Jimmie Rodgers, either, and the list goes on and on.

Three artists from the Delta that encountered similar confusion were Conway Twitty, Charley Pride, and Mose Allison, all born near Clarksdale. When Conway Twitty, whose real name was Harold Jenkins, was ten he formed his first band, the Phillips Country Ramblers, a group that was good enough to have its own radio show at KFFA, across the river in Helena.

However, the older he got, the less interest he showed in country music. Instead, he put all his efforts into baseball; he was good enough to be considered a star on his high school team, and he was able to land a contract with the Philadelphia Phillies. Unfortunately, the draft board had other priorities and he was ordered into the army before he could report to the Phillies training camp.

When Jenkins was discharged from the army, he realized that the rock 'n' roll revolution, which had gone into full swing while he was out of the country, was where he belonged, not baseball, so he put together another band and chased after the hits being recorded by the likes of Elvis and Jerry Lee Lewis. It was at that point that he changed his name to Conway Twitty, at an agent's insistence, and signed a recording contract with Mercury Records. Twitty and his band released three singles, none of which hit. Then, one night while they were performing in Toronto, Twitty and band member Jack Nance wrote "It's Only Make Believe." The song went to the top of the charts in November 1958 and sold more than a million copies, establishing Twitty as a major new rock 'n' roll star. (He later became the model for Conrad Birdie in the Broadway musical *Bye Bye Birdie*.)

Twitty continued to release hit records for the remainder of the decade and into the early 1960s, his most important being "Lonely Blue Boy," which was certified Gold in 1960, but by mid decade he was eclipsed by the British rock "invasion," a career downer that sent him back to his first love, country music. After that, critics were at a loss as to how to classify him. Was he a rocker doing country on the side? Or was he a country artist who had once crossed over into rock? As rock 'n' roll became louder and more aggressive in the late 1960s and early 1970s, Twitty realized that it had passed him by, and he reconciled to living out his life as a country artist.

Charley Pride's career took a parallel path. Growing up in the Delta in the 1940s, he heard all sorts of music, but the sounds that touched him the most were the records made by Jimmie Rodgers and Hank Williams, the yodels and plaintive cries that accompanied fiddles and guitars strummed and picked to ancient folk rhythms. That was unusual because Pride was black, and the music he enjoyed was considered white music.

Pride bought his first guitar when he was fourteen, and he learned the top country songs of the day simply by listening to the radio and picking them up note by note. He was pretty good by his late teens, but he never considered music as a career. Instead, he focused on his athletic talents, becoming good enough at baseball to play in the all-black league with the Memphis Red Sox, a promising career that was interrupted by two years of military service. After his discharge, he landed a position with a minor-league team in Helena, Montana, where he surprised his teammates by singing between innings. Reaction was so encouraging that he decided to perform in a local club.

Word soon spread about the black man from the Delta who could sing like Hank Williams, and in 1964 he was invited to Nashville by RCA Records head Chet Atkins for an audition. Atkins was warned by industry insiders that it would be impossible to promote Pride as a country singer, simply because country was "white" music and fans would reject the suggestion that a black man could do the music justice. Atkins signed him anyway.

Pride released his first single in 1966, "Snakes Crawl at Night," and it made the charts and stayed there for several weeks. He followed that with another hit, "Just Between You and Me." When his album, *Country Charley Pride*, was released in 1967, it went to the top of the charts and earned Pride his first Gold record. Pride had proved that country audiences, despite their inability to classify him, cared more about his songs than his skin color. It was a proud moment in country music history.

Equally hard to classify, though for entirely different reasons, is Mose Allison, a jazz pianist who has been called the "William Faulkner of jazz." Allison grew up in the late 1920s and early 1930s in Tippo, a crossroads community that contained little more than a country store and a cotton gin in the way of urban development. He listened to the folk blues being developed by the black musicians who passed through Tippo on their way to the next plantation. Fascinated by the blues, he started piano lessons when he was five, but then dropped out when he realized that he could play what he wanted to play by ear. "My piano teacher is still living," Allison said in 1987. "She doesn't take any credit for what I do." He breaks out into laughter that sounds remarkably like a lead-in to a blues song. "She says, 'I never taught him any of that!'"

By the time Allison was a teen, he had found a way of expressing the blues through jazz, an innovative approach that had been used successfully by Louis Armstrong to create the first jazz recordings. With its reliance on musical integration—and simply feeling what the Delta land offered up to him—it was a technique that was in the best tradition of the Mojo Triangle.

Unfortunately, Allison didn't know what to do with that knowledge.

He didn't think he could make a living playing his kind of music, so he attended the University of Mississippi for a while, then enlisted in the Army for a two-year hitch. After his discharge, he enrolled at Louisiana State University, where he studied philosophy and literature. It wasn't until he left the university that he realized that his musical skills were more marketable than his degree. He moved to New York City and started working as a sideman to legendary figures such as Stan Getz and Zoot Sims.

Allison's debut album, released in 1956, was instrumental music, and that was the way he was promoted, until he started singing during his nightclub performances. When his record label, Prestige, heard his unique voice, executives insisted that he include vocals in future releases. Not until 1963 did his record label combine his vocals into an all-vocal album titled *Mose Allison Sings*. The result is an inspired collection that pays tribute to the fabulous music of the Triangle, featuring songs by Sonny Boy Williamson ("Eyesight to the Blind"), Willie Dixon ("The Seventh Son"), Jimmie Rodgers ("That's All Right), and several songs composed by Allison, including the one that made him famous, "Parchman Farm." It wasn't until that album was released that his unique style as a jazz pianist and blues singer blossomed. It was his best moment—and his worst moment—for it left critics confused over whether he was a jazz or a blues musician.

Aware of the confusion, Allison once explained it this way: "I'm a jazz play-er, a jazz pianist, and I sing a style that is mostly blues-oriented. Some people call me a blues singer, and some call me a jazz singer. As far as the singing goes, I think I'm more a blues singer than a jazz singer, but I'm not a blues singer in the traditional sense, and I don't sing blues all night...Well, it's hard to describe."

By 1987, when this author interviewed him, Allison had stopped doing "Parchman Farm" in his nightclub act, primarily because "cotton sack" songs had become politically incorrect. Besides, Allison explained, "You go to the Mississippi Delta, and there are no cotton sacks; it's all machines and chemicals." He wrote the song during what he calls his "local color" phase, a time when he was trying to depict the Delta through his music. "Growing up near Parchman Farm and hearing about it all my life, and hearing the blood-hounds coming through every once in a while looking for somebody, it was just on my mind," he explained. "After I had written the song and recorded it, this blues aficionado in New York came up with a record by Bukka White and he had done a tune called "Parchman Farm" in the 1930s or 1940s. He played it for me, and it wasn't exactly like mine, but it had some similarities. So I don't know whether I heard that as a child and forgot about it or what."

Allison has made a good living for the past nearly half-century, not from his early albums, which typically earned him $250 each, but because best-selling mainstream recording artists such as Bonnie Raitt, The Who, Eric Clapton, and Elvis Costello have recorded his songs. Even so, the super-star status that he deserves eludes him. Despite clear evidence that he is an innovator—and belongs in the same class with Elvis, Robert Johnson, Jimmie Rodgers and all the rest who drank from the pure wellspring—he has continually battled the misconception that his jazz renderings of the blues are somehow "stolen" music. "Every now and then I still get people saying, 'Oh, he's just trying to sound black,'" Allison told the *Tucson Weekly* in a 1997 interview. "And I say, really? Which black singer is it that I sound like? I got a review in London a couple of weeks ago where the guy said I was almost as good as the real thing. It's just something that never goes away."

◆　▲　◆　▲　◆

Founded in 1848, Clarksdale is about eighteen miles from the Mississippi River, as the crow flies, and about twenty-six miles from the river at the nearest crossing at Frairs Point-Helena. Perhaps because it is not a port city, it never became a melting pot for people and ideas, as did Greenville, its neighbor to the south. It thrived as a city because it was about halfway between Greenville and Memphis, and provided cotton planters with a base of operations from which to gin their cotton and then ship it, first by river, then by rail when the Illinois Central Railroad laid tracks through the city.

Clarksdale also thrived because it was the nearest large city to Mississippi State Penitentiary, also called Parchman Farm. Constructed in 1904, the penitentiary had a tremendous economic impact on the area because its rehabilitative program was based on putting inmates, white and black, to work on farms to grow the prison's food and to grow cotton that had to be ginned and processed through Clarksdale. Parchman was a feared place, not just because of the hard labor expected of inmates—at the turn of the century, prisons were considered places where prisoners literally "did" their time by seldom leaving their cells—but because of the prison's reputation for enforcing its work rule with beatings meant to break the prisoners' spirit. On

the positive side, the prison was one of the first in the nation to allow prisoners to have conjugal visits from spouses. This author had occasion to tour
the prison in 1960 and found it to be dreary and foreboding, especially the
execution chamber, which resembled an empty storage room with pale,
almost colorless, walls and a concrete floor that sweated in the summer
months. The executioner was an alcoholic from Clarksdale who was paid a
per diem rate for his services. The tour guide joked that he would be an alcoholic, too, if his only source of income was putting people to death: "Some
of those boys they put down are right nice fellahs"—the words still echoing,
the tone similar to what you would expect to hear at the local dog pound.
At that time, female prisoners were expected to work in the laundry and
kitchen, instead of the fields, and they bunked together in a large, wooden
building with no interior walls, and they all slept in the same room on soft
mattresses filled with chicken feathers plucked from the carcasses of long ago
dinners. Most wore cotton dresses, grey in color, and all had ashen faces that
looked ghost-like when they stared at visitors, especially those visitors
marching past single-file, munching on candy bars.

All of it—the nearby prison, the cotton fields, the ever-present poverty—
made Clarksdale a gathering place for African Americans who assuaged their
pain and suffering with copious amounts of alcohol and music in juke joints
that sprang up in black neighborhoods all over the city. For decades, Clarksdale
ignored its musical heritage, primarily because white society thought that the
blues was a black mark on a city that liked to think of itself as a cotton capital, but today music has come to the forefront, with a blues museum that
attracts visitors from all over the world, and nightclubs that recapture the
nightlife of previous generations of African Americans. The most significant of
these clubs is Morgan Freeman's nationally known club, Ground Zero.

From 1917 to 1931, Clarksdale produced a number of talented African-
American entertainers, including guitarist John Lee Hooker, who learned to
play guitar by strumming on strings made from strips of inner tube nailed to
a barn, and then went on to become an influential bluesman with hits such
as "Boom, Boom," "I'm in the Mood" (which sold a million copies), and
"Crawling Kingsnake Blues," to name a few. Sam Cooke, who moved to
Chicago when he was three years of age, became America's first superstar of
soul. Another of Clarksdale's well-known offspring was guitarist Ike Turner,
who was born in 1931—the same year as Sam Cooke—and a later teamed

with Tina Turner to form the Ike and Tina Turner Revue, one of the most successful rhythm & blues acts of all time.

Of course, long before Ike Turner ever met Tina, he entertained dreams of stardom, beginning at the age of eight when a Clarksdale deejay at radio station WROX taught him how to spin records. Ike got so good at it that the DJ would sometimes leave him alone in the control room and go across the street to get a cup of coffee. Not long after that, Ike was walking home from school when he passed a house that was rocking with the sounds of piano music. Curious, Ike went inside and met Pinetop Perkins, who was demonstrating piano skills for a friend. Soon after, Ike had his own piano—the result of a good report card at school—and Pinetop consented to give his young friend lessons. By the late 1940s, Ike had traded his piano for a guitar, and put together his own band. Despite still being in his teens, he gained a reputation around Clarksdale for being a showman destined for greatness, a reputation based as much on his energetic personality as on his musical skills.

◆　▲　◆　▲　◆

The influence of the Mississippi Delta on the Mojo Triangle is incalculable. Next to the Natchez Trace, it has had more impact on American music than any other geographical area: A place that exists in that razor-thin dividing line between shadow and hellfire, a place that percolates artistry from an ancient wellspring that is protective of its offspring—a place ever ready to express its passion in music or words.

"In August in Mississippi, there's a few days somewhere about the middle of the month when suddenly there's a foretaste of fall, it's cool, there's an ambience, a luminous quality to the light, as though it came not from just today but from back in the old classic times..." William Faulkner once told an interviewer. "It lasts only a day or two, then it's gone, but every year in August that occurs in my country...a luminosity older than our Christian civilization."

Faulkner was explaining the title of his book *Light in August*, but his comments go deeper than just an explanation of the weather, for they address the source of the creativity that has given the world so much great music and literature, a source that is identifiable as "luminosity older than our Christian civilization," which is another way of saying that it comes from the land itself. Nowhere is that luminosity greater than in the Mississippi Delta.

5 MEMPHIS
▼ Great Balls of Fire

Memphis sits on ancient Chickasaw land, precariously balanced on a precipice: At any moment, the New Madrid Fault can belch and level the city and topple its downtown district into the Mississippi River. The Chickasaw favored the location because of the high bluffs that made the land immune to flooding, but they were aware of the dangers associated with earthquakes, and each day they prayed to the Great Spirit to give them just one more day of peace—and the Great Spirit sometimes listened, for intervals that often stretched for a hundred years or more.

In the late 1700s, when Spanish explorers arrived, the Chickasaw traded them a small strip of land along the bluff in exchange for food, brandy, and weapons. They didn't think to warn the Spanish of the great beast that sometimes awakened and shook the sleep from its eyes, sending great shards of the bluff tumbling into the river, and the Spanish didn't think to ask. No sooner did the trade take place than the Spanish built a fort with an imposing stockade, along with an Indian trading post.

When Spain ceded the land to the United States in 1795, the fort was abandoned and the site was occupied by American troops that, for a few months, were under the command of Captain Meriwether Lewis. Not long after Lewis' departure, the fort was relocated several miles downriver and named Fort Pickering, after Secretary of State Timothy Pickering. One of the fort's commanders was a lieutenant named Zachary Taylor, who later became America's twelfth president.

With the site of the former fort abandoned, settlers poured in and built the city that is now Memphis. One of the surveyors who laid out the boundaries was Marcus B. Winchester, the son of James Winchester, who had been instrumental in obtaining more land from the Chickasaw (and an ancestor of singer/songwriter Jesse Winchester, who fled Memphis in the 1960s because of his opposition to the Vietnam War to go to Canada, where he became a popular recording artist and wrote songs later recorded by Wynonna, Emmylou Harris, and others). Because the Winchesters were instrumental in the founding of Memphis, a major east–west thoroughfare was named

Winchester Road. It is one of only two thoroughfares in the city that connect Highway 61, Elvis Presley Boulevard, and Highway 78, the road to Tupelo.

When the time came to name the new city, its three owners—Winchester, Judge John Overton, and future president Andrew Jackson—looked to the Middle East and borrowed the name of an Egyptian town located on the Nile River near the Abu Sir Pyramids. In later years, the pyramids became both the spiritual and the promotional symbol of the city, an ironic reflection of Memphis' apex position in the Mojo Triangle. In the 1980s, the importance of the pyramid was affirmed with a multi-million-dollar, downtown sports and concert arena constructed in the shape of a pyramid.

Because of its location, Memphis soon became a wide-open frontier outpost, resembling a shantytown more than it did an emerging city. The streets were muddy, and most of the buildings were constructed of logs instead of planking. As the years went by, the city's importance as a port increased, so that by 1852 it was the third most important port on the Mississippi, a distinction that allowed it to become, by the end of the decade, the fastest growing city in America. A great deal of that growth can be attributed to its development as a marketplace for the cotton that was brought up from the Mississippi Delta, and to its reputation as a major slave market, where African-American men, women, and children fetched prices that averaged a thousand dollars each. Prior to 1860, only 17 percent of the city's residents were black, but the whites were so fearful of a revolt that they instituted a 10 p.m. curfew and imposed a ten-dollar fine on violators, if they were free, and ten lashes across the back if the violators were slaves.

At the start of the Civil War, there was some doubt whether the city would go with the South or remain in the Union, where most of its business connections were located. In the 1860 presidential election, 90% of the city's voters sided with pro-Union candidates, but by the time of the firing on Fort Sumter, Memphians had had a change of heart and voted overwhelmingly in favor of secession. The war had a devastating effect on the city, throwing it into bankruptcy and racial turmoil, as blacks poured into the city by the tens of thousands. For fifty years after the war, Memphians were exposed to successive waves of yellow fever epidemics that accomplished even more destruction than the war.

By 1905, there were those who felt that the city had been damned by a curse: Not only did Memphis have a national reputation as the murder capital of the United States, it was in the throes of cocaine and morphine addiction that approached epidemic levels, and a booming sex industry that attracted young white girls by the thousands from Mississippi, Arkansas, and Louisiana. The city never came up with a plan to reduce the murder rate, but it did address addiction by sponsoring treatment centers, and it attempted to control prostitution by setting up the Women's Protection Bureau.

Beale Street became a marketplace for prostitution, gambling, drug use—stores sold dime boxes of cocaine and morphine, along with tonics and headache remedies—and entertainment, primarily because of its location; it began at the edge of the bluff and proceeded east for several blocks. Although almost all of the stores and nightclubs on the street were owned by Jews and Italians—and not far from the street was an upscale white neighborhood—most of the visitors to the street were black.

Beale Street offered a concentrated form of all the paradoxes that existed in isolated pockets throughout the Mojo Triangle. It was dark and dangerous, a place where a man could lose his life on the spot by looking at someone the wrong way, but it was also a place of hope, where a man or a woman of color could earn money in ways not associated with farming or housecleaning or cooking. It did not take long for Beale Street to become black America's Main Street, a status that was enhanced by the city's decision to make the street a safe haven for women: Female performers were treated as equals with male performers, giving the city a reputation as an entertainment center that was wide open for both men and women. Beale Street was a beacon that shone southward across the Delta, beckoning the most talented with unspoken promises of fame, fortune and, for the lucky few, a type of immortality that white money could not buy.

◆　▲　◆　▲　◆

In 1903, after several years on the road with traveling minstrel shows, W.C. Handy moved to Clarksdale, Mississippi, where he formed a band. He was thirty years old, an advanced age for a musician at that time, and his wife, Elizabeth, felt that it was time they put down roots. They had met in Henderson, Kentucky, after he performed at a society barbecue. At the barbecue was Carl Lindstrom, a cornet soloist in the Patrick Gilmore Band, which once counted John Philip Sousa among its members; he heard Handy play cornet and encouraged him to stick with a career in music. Handy stayed in Henderson for a while, and when he left, he took Elizabeth with him.

In Clarksdale, his nine-piece orchestra performed for the usual functions—fish fries, barbecues, political rallies, any type of event that attracted a crowd. Summer was always a profitable time, as was the fall, when white politicians took to the stump to work voters up to a fever pitch over the "nigger problem." Black musicians actually had no problem performing at such events, as long as they were adequately paid, because they had heard that type of talk all their lives from their employers, even from strangers on the street.

Handy was a classically trained cornet player who performed all the current music of the day: The German marches, the waltzes, the sentimental ballads from Ireland and Scotland, the same tunes that the white bands played. One day, he was performing at Cleveland, a farming town south of Clarksdale, when someone requested that he play "native music." Baffled, he played an old Southern melody that he thought would pass for "native music." It didn't. A second request followed: Would he mind if a local "colored" band took the stage to perform some of their original songs? Handy moved his band out of the way and allowed a three-piece band—guitar, mandolin, and bass—to take the stage. The "native" music that followed was the folk music that had migrated north from Natchez: A formless, free-flowing music, consisting more of chants and hollers than harmonics, that had neither beginning nor middle nor end. What Handy heard was the merger of African, Choctaw, and European music, if not in its earliest form, at least in an undeveloped form that contained elements of all three cultures.

Handy found the music unsophisticated but "haunting" in its emotional appeal to the audience. He had never heard anything like it growing up in Florence, Alabama. As he listened, he wondered if the music could be profitable. The answer came soon enough. "A rain of silver dollars began to fall around the outlandish, stomping feet," he wrote in his autobiography. "The dancers went wild. Dollars, quarters, halves—the shower grew heavier and continued so long, I strained my neck to get a better look. There before the boys lay more money than my nine musicians were being paid for the entire engagement. Then I saw the beauty of primitive music. They had the stuff the people wanted. It touched the spot. Their music wanted polishing, but it contained the essence. Folks would pay money for it."

Handy left the engagement that day baffled. The music that he had heard had potential, but without structure, it could not be adapted to orchestra music. As it existed, it was not the kind of music that any band could perform; in truth, it was not even music—it was as much a burst of energy as anything else, its charm derived from its rawness. Handy thought about the primitive music often, but he couldn't think of a way to incorporate it into his orchestra.

Two years later, Handy and his family moved to Memphis, where they were dazzled by the bright lights of Beale Street. He set up shop in Pee Wee's Saloon, owned by Vigello Maffei, an Italian immigrant who allowed black musicians to use his bar as an office; a friendly fellow, he even took telephone calls for them. Handy was fascinated by the constant flow of humanity that entered the bar's swinging doors. "They ranged from cooks and waiters to professional gamblers, jockeys, and racetrack men of the period," he later wrote. "Glittering young devils in silk toppers and Prince Alberts drifted in and out with insolent self-assurance. Chocolate dandies with red roses embroidered on cream waistcoats loitered at the bar. Now and then, a fancy gal with shadowed eyes and a wedding-ring waist glanced through the doorway or ventured inside to ask if anybody had set eyes on the sweet good man who had temporarily strayed away."

Like most of the other musicians in town, Handy made his living, primarily, by performing at white parties and political events. To solicit business, he marched his band up and down Beale Street, where they could be seen and heard by whites that stopped by the street to shop for a band. It was in that setting that Handy was approached by the political committee for a novice politician named E. H. Crump, a tall, awkward redheaded man from near Tupelo. Handy was asked if he would compose a special song for Crump's mayoral campaign, an assignment he took without hesitation. What was called for was a song that would appeal to black voters without alienating white voters.

Handy thought long and hard about his assignment, and the idea that kept popping into his head was a merger of the "primitive" music he had heard in Clarksdale with the classical familiarity of orchestra music. Sixteen bars was the standard measure for popular music of that era, so Handy played around with the primitive music until he had put together a twelve-bar, three-line structure. He added a bass line in tango rhythm and a three-chord harmonic structure and then he wrote parts for the individual instruments in his band. When he finished the song, titled "Mister Crump," he had a tune with Delta rhythms and European instrumentation—and lyrics that promised nothing but good times ahead if Crump was elected.

With Handy's help, Crump was elected mayor by a margin of seventy-nine votes and thus began a four-decade rein as Memphis' political boss. Later, Handy rewrote the lyrics and poked fun at Crump and his promises of reform. He renamed the song "The Memphis Blues," and submitted it to every publisher in New York, only to have it rejected on each occasion. Frustrated, he went to a local music store and asked for advice. The white store manager told him that if he would print copies of the song he would sell the sheet music in his store. Handy self-published the song, convinced that he would be able to place it in stores all over town. That wasn't the case, and he was left with only one sales outlet for the music. When sales in that one store trickled away, the manager offered to reimburse Handy his printing costs in exchange for the copyright to the song. Handy agreed, thinking that he had reached a dead end with the song.

Once he owned the rights to the song, the store manager placed it with a publisher that knew how to market it properly. Soon, "The Memphis Blues" was the talk of the nation, especially in New York where it was a major hit. Encouraged, Handy wrote additional songs— "The St. Louis Blues," "Joe Turner Blues," and "The Beale Street Blues," to name a few— and moved to Chicago, and then on to New York, where he established his own publishing house. He did not receive any royalties for "The Memphis Blues" until the copyright expired twenty-eight years later.

Because Handy was the first person to publish the blues, he was given credit for being the "Father of the Blues," a label that stuck for decades, until socially conscious critics decided that Handy had not so much invented the blues as stolen its thunder from the poor blacks in the Delta. Today, it is obvious that those who labeled him "Father of the Blues" were correct the first time around. The music that we call blues today did not exist when Handy wrote "The Memphis Blues."

At the time that Handy lived in Clarksdale, the word "blues" was applied to any type of music that black performers played that had a "woe is me" appeal, whether the music was country, popular, or of European origin. The unstructured music that Handy heard from the field hands who crashed his party was not the blues; it was a type of folk music that had evolved from field chants and hollers, and then merged with Choctaw and European

W.C. Handy (seated right) returns to Memphis to jam with friends. (James L. Dickerson)

influences. Handy borrowed the energy of the music he heard in Clarksdale, not the structure, for "The Memphis Blues."

Ironically, after the success of Handy's "blues" songs, the musicians in the Delta who had been playing folk music applied Handy's structure to the new songs that they wrote. In other words, Robert Johnson, Son House, Charlie Patton, and all the others, borrowed from Handy, and not the other way around. They did so for a very good reason: Because Handy's blues appealed to everyone, black and white, it was profitable to perform at social gatherings. Handy's contribution to music was the essence of the Mojo Triangle, and the father of everything that followed.

◆　▲　◆　▲　◆

Memphis has one of the most illustrious music histories of any city in America, yet almost all of the music created there was by individuals who migrated to the city from other locations. The only major recording artists that were born there were Justin Timberlake and Aretha Franklin, both of whom left at a very early age; Bobby "Blue" Bland; and Lil Hardin, who married Louis Armstrong after leaving the city while in her teens. Compounding the oddity of that statistic is the fact that Memphis, unlike the Delta, New Orleans, or the Natchez Trace—and a population that has always been more than twice that of the Delta—has never produced a major literary talent. Shelby Foote later made the city his home, but he could hardly be called a Memphis product.

Of all the people associated with Memphis music, it is Lil Hardin Armstrong who has put the most enduring shine on the city's music legacy. Born in 1898 into a household that included her grandmother, who was a former slave, in Mississippi, she grew up within earshot of Beale Street, where she could hear W.C. Handy's band marching through the neighborhood, drawing everyone out into the street to clap and dance.

Lil's mother, Dempsey, didn't much care for Handy's music. She wanted her daughter, an only child, to grow up to play organ in the church. Like many African-American women of that era, she equated the blues with prostitution and drug addiction, simply because that was the connection that she saw on Beale Street. To keep Lil's mind off the streets—and to prepare her for a career as a church organist—she enrolled her in piano lessons. When she was older, Lil was asked to be the organist for her Sunday school, an honor that made Dempsey proud until the day she learned that Lil had played a jazzy version of "Onward Christian Soldiers" in church, drawing a disappointing look from the pastor. Despite Dempsey's best efforts, Lil seemed hell-bent on gravitating to Beale Street. Desperate to make a lady out of her jazz-crazed daughter, Dempsey sent her to Fisk University in Nashville. Lil took all of the academic courses required of her, but she was mainly interested in her music classes. When she returned to Memphis at the end of the school year, she made the mistake of purchasing the sheet music for Handy's "St. Louis Blues." Outraged, Dempsey beat her with a broomstick and told her to pack her bags: They were going to move as far away from the evils of Beale Street as they could get and still live in America, all the way to Chicago.

That was in 1917, and Handy followed them to Chicago in 1918, leaving a void on Beale Street that was filled during the 1920s and 1930s by dozens of talented blues musicians, all either from the Delta or from the Memphis area, such as Lizzie Douglas, whose stage name was Memphis

Minnie; Sam Chatmon; Bukka White, whose real name was Booker T. Washington; Peter Chatman, who used the name Memphis Slim; Furry Lewis; Sleepy John Estes; and others.

Collectively, they engineered the second wave of blues artists. They took the structure given to them by Handy and reworked the folk blues of the Delta to make it more commercially acceptable. They did such a good job that people later thought that Handy had lifted the music from them. When opportunities on Beale Street dwindled, they took their music to Chicago, where they tinkered with it some more, allowing the Windy City to take credit for its own style of blues, a style that it nurtured but did not create. Sleepy John was among those who made that trip. When he arrived, he learned that Memphis had a bad reputation because of Beale Street. He didn't disagree with the reputation—he once called Memphis "the leader of dirty work in the world"—so he never argued about it, but he did learn to keep his Memphis connections to himself.

Of all the country blues performers that perfected their craft on Beale Street, Memphis Minnie probably had the greatest impact. Born in Walls, Mississippi, she learned to play the guitar at an early age, developing a passion for music that made her run away on several occasions to Memphis where she walked the streets, listening to the music, until a family member located her and dragged her back to the farm, with admonitions that the Devil was on her trail.

Memphis Minnie was not too worried about the Devil, but she knew that if she ran away to Memphis again, she would be hunted down by her family and punished. So, she did what many other restless youths of that age did—she joined the circus and toured the South. When she returned, she was old enough to do as she pleased. What pleased her most was working on Beale Street, a place more exciting than any of the small towns she visited while with the circus.

Throughout the 1920s, Memphis Minnie dominated the music scene on Beale Street. Petite and attractive, she used her sexuality to draw attention to her music, even to the point of using the dresses she wore during her performances to entice men into looking up her skirt. In her off hours, she sometimes worked as a prostitute, if accounts from her contemporaries can be believed. The first thing that newcomers to the city learned about Memphis Minnie was that they didn't want to cross her. When angered, she would reach for a knife, a gun, a big stick, whatever was available. Bluesman

Beale Street in Memphis, 1920. (Memphis Archives)

Johnny Shines told Paul and Beth Garon that he thought she once shot an old man's arm off in Mississippi: "Shot his arm off, or cut it off with a hatchet, something. Some say shot, some say cut. Minnie was a hell raiser."

Memphis Minnie was also a great musician. From the time she recorded her first record in 1929, she dominated the national blues scene. Throughout the 1930s and 1940s, along with her husband, Joe McCoy, she recorded an impressive string of over one hundred records, including classics such as "Bumble Bee" and "I'm Talking About You." Most of those recordings were made while she lived in Chicago, but when her luck ran out there and the records stopped selling and the money stopped flowing, she returned to Memphis, where she suffered a stroke and lived out the remainder of her life in a wheelchair, unable to play her guitar. She died in 1973 and was buried in a pauper's grave.

By the mid-1970s, not many people knew about Memphis Minnie. One of those who did was Bonnie Raitt, who figured that if Memphis Minnie could play the guitar, a man's instrument, then she, too, could play the guitar. "I would say that most of the music that I do and that has influenced me the most has come right out of Memphis or thereabouts," said Raitt. "Memphis Minnie...was the first woman I ever heard play blues guitar. If it weren't for the music that came out of that region, I probably wouldn't even be in the business."

◆　▲　◆　▲　◆

In 1945, Sam Phillips was twenty-two when he arrived in Memphis from Florence, Alabama, his head filled with dreams of making a difference in the world. He went to work at radio station WREC as an engineer, a behind-the-scenes position that did little to satisfy his yearning for recognition. The radio station was located in the basement of the Peabody Hotel, which William Faulkner once described as the starting point of the Mississippi Delta—a reference to the wealthy plantation owners who frequented the posh hotel during their overnight excursions to the city—and that put Phillips at the very center of Memphis' social scene. But Phillips, with his blunt Alabama ways, quickly learned that he didn't have the social skills or the personality to rally people to grand causes. He had a gift for gab, but he couldn't organize his thoughts into the short, punchy sentences required of radio. Those who came to know him well agreed that he would have made a wonderful hell-and-damnation preacher, especially for a church that had all-day services.

Lucky for Phillips, there was someone at WREC who possessed the social skills that he lacked: Marion Keisker, an energetic, socially skilled on-air personality that dazzled Memphians five days a week as the eternally perky Kitty Kelly, and then charmed them in the evenings as the announcer of "Treasury Bandstand," which was broadcast from the roof of the Peabody. At times, she wrote, directed, or produced as many as fourteen shows at a time for the radio station.

A divorcee with a young son, Keisker fell in love with Phillips, whom she once described as "beautiful beyond belief." She was especially impressed with his dream of one day having a recording studio where black musicians could come and express themselves. Soon, they became co-conspirators in that dream, despite the fact that Phillips was married. One day, while they were driving around town, Phillips spotted a vacant building at 706 Union Avenue, symbolically important because it is where Beale merges into Union, and began shouting, "That's it!"

In January 1950, with Keisker's help—she painted, laid the tile, and installed the bathroom—Phillips opened the Memphis Recording Service. It was his dream to attract black recording artists, but in the beginning he settled for what he could get—namely, recording wedding, bar mitzvah, and birthday greetings that he transferred from tape to actual records. At first, he tried to operate the studio while holding down his engineer's job at WREC, but after a year-and-a-half of trying to do two jobs, the stress got to

Sam Phillips in the studio. (Memphis Archives)

him, and he was hospitalized for a reported nervous breakdown and given electroshock therapy. As a result, he resigned from his position at WREC and devoted his full efforts to making the studio a success.

Keisker quit her job, too, so that she could be there for Sam. Her work title was secretary, but she was more of a business partner. She greeted the customers, most of whom felt honored to shake the hand of a woman that the newspapers had labeled "Miss Radio of Memphis." She also did the bookkeeping and the billing, and later she wrote up the contracts and made all the arrangements for record distribution.

For the first three years, Phillips focused almost entirely on recording African-American musicians: B.B. King, Howlin' Wolf, Joe Hill Louis, Walter Horton, Rufus Thomas, Doctor Ross, Ike Turner, and dozens of others who sang a song or two but never made it to the big time. Phillips' strategy was to record talented black performers and then lease or sell those recordings to record labels that specialized in black, or "race" music, as it was called in those days. He was very successful at that, from a producer's standpoint, but that success did not translate into dollars because the record labels paid him a flat fee, and his artists usually left him for the first producer who offered a bigger paycheck. That was the main reason that he decided to launch his own record label: Sun Records. If he distributed his artists' records, in addition to recording them in his own studio, with no middleman in the picture, he figured he would make money each time a record sold. He could also lose a great deal of money, which he did on a regular basis.

B.B. King wasn't one of Phillips discoveries, but he recorded in his studio after his record label made a deal with Phillips for studio time. King had come to Memphis in 1946 to visit his cousin, bluesman Bukka White, and he was impressed by what he saw. "Where I came from, they had only one nightclub," he later explained. "They had several on Beale. People seemed more into what was happening. Where I came from, you wore your work clothes to work, and you came home in them. On Beale you couldn't tell people were working. Everybody would be dressed up and looking neat in the evenings. They had places to go for socializing that we didn't have at home."

Two years later, King returned to Memphis, this time to stay. His first job was at the 16th Street Grill, across the river in West Memphis. At that time, the biggest thing going for blacks was radio. West Memphis radio station KWEM had hired both Sonny Boy Williamson and Howlin' Wolf to host radio shows, and across the river in Memphis, radio station WDIA had converted to an all-black format (the first in the nation). Early in 1949, King went into the radio station and asked for a job. He was given a ten-minute show that aired each day at 3:30 p.m. King called himself Beale Street Blues Boy, then shortened it to Blues Boy, and later decided to call himself B.B. King.

Encouraged by his success on radio, King recorded several songs in WDIA's Studio A for Bullet Records, but the Nashville company went out of business before the records could be released. King pushed ahead, recording a song titled "Three O'Clock Blues" on mobile equipment set up at the YMCA. The song, released in 1950, shortly after Sam Phillips started up his recording studio, made the national rhythm & blues charts, establishing King as the first Memphis radio personality to have a hit record. King's success was

the main reason that Phillips recruited DJs Howlin' Wolf and Rufus Thomas to record in his studio. Unlike the average Joes that came into the studio, fresh off the farm, radio DJs had a built-in platform from which to sell records.

B.B. King in the 1980s. (Steve Gardner)

B.B. King went on to bigger and better things, becoming one of the most important blues stylists of all time, but he never lost his sense of time and place, not even when those around him did. In the late 1960s, he was booked for a performance at an outdoor concert in Ann Arbor, Michigan—one of those massive affairs that mixed blues and rock acts—when an eighteen-year-old white girl sat beside him backstage. "I always dug what you did," she told him. "It's so awful that all those guys took all that stuff from you. You really started it, didn't you?" Before he could answer, the girl put her hand on his leg and asked, "Which motel you staying at?"

King never felt that anyone had stolen anything from him, at least not his music. He knew better, having grown up seeing the music evolve from field chants and hollers to his own style of sophisticated electric blues, always changing, just as the white and black cultures had changed and evolved into something else. Better than anyone else, King understood the relationship of time and space. "Time is one of the best doctors ever," King said in a 1986 interview. "Time makes you recognize mistakes. Time makes you search yourself. Time makes you grow up. Whenever I think of Indianola and how it was at that time, I think about how people, if given a chance, can change. That's the way I look at my hometown. I tell you, one of the greatest honors I have had in my career—and it means more to me than getting my first honorary doctorate degree or my Grammys—is the time, about three years ago, when a lady named Miss Jessie gave a party for me in Indianola. She seemed to have invited about 150 Archie Bunkers and 150 Fred Sanfords, knowing that. I felt all the whites would go in one corner and all the blacks would go in the other corner, but it wasn't like that. They mingled. A lot of them knew each other, but they didn't know where the others lived or how they lived. At this party, they talked and I believe, personally it was one of the first social gatherings of that kind in Indianola, and I was so proud. To me, that was one of the best things that ever happened to me in my life."

◆　▲　◆　▲　◆

One day in June 1954, Scotty Moore stopped by Memphis Recording Service to talk to Sam Phillips about releasing another record. Two months earlier, Phillips had released a song titled "My Kind of Carryin' On," recorded by Scotty, then twenty-two, and his band the Starlite Wranglers. The song hadn't done well and Scotty was eager for another chance. Sam wasn't convinced that another Starlite Wrangler release would do any better. Finally, Scotty asked him outright: "What exactly are you looking for?"

Sam looked at him, his eyes sparkling: "I don't know. I'll know when I hear it."

It was at that point that Marion Keisker joined in the conversation. "Sam, you remember that boy who came in to record that song for his mother's birthday about a year ago?"

"Yeah, a dark-haired boy."

"Well, you said you though he had a pretty good voice. Why don't you get him to come in and try it?"

"Yeah, I'll probably do that."

Several weeks later, when Scotty returned to the studio, the three of them—Sam, Marion, and Scotty—went next door to Taylor's Café for coffee. The cups had barely hit the table before Scotty asked Sam if he had contacted that dark-haired boy. Embarrassed that he hadn't, he asked Marion to give Scotty the boy's telephone number. When Scotty read the name next to the telephone number—Elvis Presley—he was taken aback. "What kind of name is this?" he asked.

"I don't know," Sam said. "It's his name. Give him a call. Ask him to come over to your house and see what you think."

Scotty called later that day, after dinner. Elvis wasn't there. His mother, Gladys, said that he had gone to a movie, but she promised he would call when he returned. That evening, when Scotty and Elvis spoke, they agreed to meet at Scotty's house the following morning, the Fourth of July. It was hot that day, the temperature soaring to one hundred degrees. Scotty's wife, Bobbie, happened to be looking out the window when Elvis started up the walk, wearing a white lacy shirt, pink pants with a black stripe down the legs, and white bucks. In his hand was a guitar. "He was still kind of a pimply faced kid, you know," Bobbie later recalled. "He had his ducktail hair pulled back. He was kind of odd for that time."

Scotty and Elvis sat in the living room for a while, running through songs they both knew, then Scotty asked Bobbie if she would go down the street to get Bill Black, the bassist in the Starlite Wranglers. When Bill arrived, the three of them began playing in earnest. Bobbie was surprised that all the songs that Elvis suggested had the word "because" in them: "I Love You Because," "Because of You," "Because You Think You're so Pretty." Scotty was impressed that Elvis knew so many songs. When they ran out of songs to play, they put their instruments aside and talked awhile. "I'll talk to Sam, and we'll probably be in touch," Scotty told Elvis." After Elvis left the house, Scotty asked Bill what he thought.

"Well, he didn't impress me too damned much," Bill answered. "What about you?"

"I thought he had good timing," Scotty said. "A good voice. Nothing different jumped out from the material he was doing."

Scotty and Bill agreed to give it a shot. Later in the day, Scotty called Sam and told him what had happened. Sam asked if he thought it would be worthwhile to audition Elvis in the studio, to which Scotty answered, "Sure."

The following day was a Monday. Scotty, Bill, and Elvis stopped by the studio after dinner. They did song after song, with Sam always asking what else they knew. Nothing seemed to click. Finally, around midnight, they took a break. They were sitting around in sort of a stupor, when Elvis jumped to his feet and started playing his acoustic guitar, really pounding it, as he sang "That's All right, Mama," a blues song that Arthur "Big Boy" Crudup had recorded in 1940. Bill, who was sitting on his bass when Elvis started, jumped to his feet, whirled his bass into position and joined in. Scotty followed, jamming his electric guitar into the rhythm and then branching out with delicious licks that really energized the song. Scotty loved uptempo music, and he had long ago worked up some licks that he hoped he would be able to use some day.

Elvis Presley with Scotty Moore (left) and Bill Black (rear) in May 1956 in Memphis. (Robert W. Dye)

When they finished the song, Sam stuck his head into the studio and asked, "What are ya'll doing?"

"Just foolin' around," Scotty said.

"Well, it didn't sound too bad. Try it again. Let me get in here and turn the mics on."

They played it through again, with Sam making suggestions for microphone placement, then they played it through with the tape rolling, with Sam saying afterward, "Man that's good. It's different."

"Yeah, what is it?" someone asked.

They all looked at each other, not certain how to answer the question.

Finally, Scotty said, "Well, you said you were looking for something different."

What they had done, not so much by accident as in desperation, was create a new type of music—part country, part blues, part something that had no name. It would later be named rock 'n' roll, but at the time no one was concerned about what to call it. Sam told them that they had a record and all that they needed to do now was come up with an idea for the flip side. Two days later, they returned to the studio and ran through a string of songs, including Billy Eckstine's 1949 hit, "Blue Moon," but nothing clicked.

Elvis at Overton Park Shell in Memphis. (Robert W. Dye)

"We were all below-average musicians," Scotty later recalled. "Elvis didn't know all that many chords, but he had a great sense of rhythm. Sam...treated Elvis as another instrument, and he kept his voice closer to the music than was the norm at that time...Elvis had great vocal control. He could do just about anything he wanted to. Sam mixed his voice closer to the music like it was an instrument."

Several days later, they returned to the studio and went through the same routine. They played song after song, and Sam never made a move to turn on the tape recorder. Then they got lucky again. This time it was Bill who got things rolling. During a break, he jumped to his feet and started slapping his bass, singing "Blue Moon of Kentucky," a song that Bill Monroe had recorded in 1946. Elvis and Scotty jumped in, with Elvis taking over the vocal. With "That's All right, Mama," they had taken a blues song and spun it white. With "Blue Moon of Kentucky," they took a white song and spun it black.

It is true that songs that preceded "That's All Right, Mama" had all the technical requirements of a rock 'n' roll song—"Rocket 88," for example, Ike Turner's flirtation with up-tempo rhythm & blues—but technicalities are not what the music is all about. The most accurate definition for rock 'n' roll is probably the simplest: Mojo music that white people outside the Triangle can relate to, and that is what Elvis, Scotty, and Bill gave the world.

What Elvis, Scotty, and Bill witnessed in the studio over the course of a few weeks was the same mysterious process that had shaped Mojo Triangle music for the past two hundred years, the main difference being that they concentrated that process into a single, desperate thought, gave it a violent shake, and then squeezed every ounce of passion they could into the resulting brew. They went on to record some of the most original music ever pressed onto discs, changing not just their own lives, but the culture of an entire nation.

◆　▲　◆　▲　◆

With Elvis Presley's explosive success, Sam Phillips felt that he had hit on the right formula to build a legitimate record label. The first raw talent that entered Sun Records in Elvis' wake was Carl Perkins, from Jackson, Tennessee, and he was soon followed by Johnny Cash from Arkansas, Jerry Lee Lewis from Louisiana, and Roy Orbison from Texas. With Elvis' success, it became clear that the future of Sun Records would be with hungry, young white artists, not the black artists who had helped get the label rolling. That wasn't a racist decision on Phillips' part. He had taken abuse from whites in Memphis for working with blacks in his studio, even to the point of being branded a "nigger lover"—the worst epithet you could slap on a white Southerner at that time—yet, he continued to work with blacks, without reservation. His decision to "go white" was strictly a business decision based on two factors: The lack of loyalty that black musicians such as Howlin' Wolf had shown, and the phenomenal sales among whites that he saw with Elvis' "new" music. With black artists, he had hoped to be a big fish in a small pond; with the new white music, he saw an opportunity to become a big fish in a big pond. Black musicians in Memphis were not happy about Phillips' new direction. Rufus Thomas said, "That is the only thing I dislike about the whole picture, Sam not carrying along the good black artists with the good white artists," but at that point in Phillips' life, following the electroshock treatments, the sleepless nights over an almost constant dire financial condition, Phillips wanted both security and peace of mind.

Carl Perkins had watched Elvis' meteoritic rise from Jackson. He had written a song titled "Blue Suede Shoes" while living in a housing project, and he thought it might fit in with the type of music that Elvis was recording. "I had been playing that music all my life, but I sure never got a contract," he said. "I sent tapes to record companies, and I would get them back with notes that they didn't know what it was."

Sam Phillips knew what it was, and he quickly signed Perkins to a recording contract. "Blue Suede Shoes" was released in early 1956 and immediately became a hit on three charts: Pop, country, and rhythm & blues. Phillips was convinced that Perkins was every bit as big a star as Elvis. (By that time, Phillips had sold Elvis' contract to RCA Records.) He watched with glee as "Blue Suede Shoes" moved up the charts faster than Elvis' "Heartbreak Hotel." In late March 1956, Perkins left a concert in Virginia to drive to New York City to appear on the Perry Como Show to accept his first Gold record, which represented verified sales of half a million records. Unfortunately, Perkins was involved

Carl Perkins, not long after he signed with Sun Records. (Courtesy of the Mississippi Valley Collection, University of Memphis)

in an automobile accident that nearly cost him his life. Not only did he miss the show, he suffered the indignity of watching, from his hospital bed, as "Heartbreak Hotel" overtook "Blue Suede Shoes" and topped off at number one.

When he recovered from his injuries, Perkins' released a new record, "Your True Love," but it stalled on the charts; he followed that up with "Pink Pedal Pushers," but it, too, bombed. Fame is all about timing. To his dying day, Perkins would blame the automobile accident for robbing him of the same level of stardom that Elvis achieved.

With Perkins in a downward spiral, Phillips focused his attention on Johnny Cash. He had signed Cash around the same time he signed Perkins, but he had put him on the back burner after "Blue Suede Shoes" was released so that he could devote his full efforts to promoting that record. By the time he called Cash into the studio, he was ready, with an impressive collection of self-penned songs, three of which—"I Walk the Line," "There You Go," and "So Doggone Lonesome"— quickly became Top 10 hits.

"Memphis is my roots," Cash reflected thirty years later. "Memphis and the Memphis sound and Sam Phillips' genius established the idea of me being a song stylist, having something of my own. I don't think it could have happened anywhere else."

Cash became Sun Records' biggest selling

Johnny Cash, circa 1994. (Andy Earl for American Recordings)

133

artist, with sales that surpassed Elvis' sales while he was with the record label. It was during that time that Roy Orbison entered the picture. Cash heard him perform in Texas and, in true Mojo Triangle tradition, encouraged him to send a demo tape to Sun Records. Eager for a record deal, Orbison sent a tape of "Ooby Dooby," an up-tempo tune written by some of his schoolmates. Phillips loved the song and gave him a call. The conversation went great until Orbison mentioned that Cash had suggested he send the song. Phillips lost his temper and snapped, "Johnny Cash doesn't run this studio," and then he hung up on Orbison. Later, once he cooled off, he called Orbison back and offered him a contract.

"Ooby Dooby" did well on the charts, but not as well as Phillips had hoped. Since the record needed a strong follow up, he assigned Orbison to the new engineer he hired, Jack Clement. At the time that Phillips hired him, he was working at a hardware store; he had no training as an engineer, but he had a knack for music, and when he took Phillips a recording that he had done in his garage, Phillips was impressed.

Clement turned out to be an ace engineer and producer, but Phillips had no way of knowing that at the time, so Clement's acquisition of Roy Orbison can only be viewed as an indication that Phillips was having second thoughts about the singer's potential. Clement recorded a number of songs with Orbison. "Rock House," "Sweet and Easy to Love," and "Mean Woman Blues" were the strongest cuts, but none of them reached hit status. Phillips asked Clement to push Orbison more in the direction of Johnny Cash and Carl Perkins, but Orbison bristled at that idea. He saw himself as more of a ballad singer.

In 1957, Orbison left Sun Records and moved to Nashville, where he focused on the type of songs that he wanted to record: "Oh, Pretty Woman," "Cryin'," and "Blue Bayou." Years later, interviewed about his experiences with Orbison, Clement was philosophical: "Musically, Roy was ahead of his time. He wanted to do things in the studio that were a little bit over our heads production-wise. Memphis wasn't quite ready for that. We didn't have organized vocal groups and strings. He was thinking orchestrally. He was wanting to cut what he ultimately did cut."

One day, Clement was working the studio when Marion Keisker stuck her head in and told him that there was a boy in the waiting room who claimed that he could play the piano like Chet Atkins played the guitar. Intrigued, he invited the boy into the studio. When he said his name, the boy spoke in a machinegun burst, running the words together, "JerryLeeLewis."

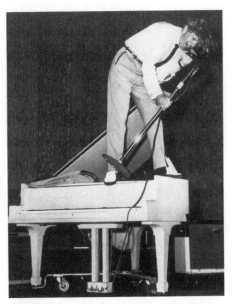

Jerry Lee Lewis. (Photofest)

Clement invited him to play the piano, and Lewis gave him his version of "Wildwood Flower," proving that he could indeed play like Chet Atkins. Then Clement asked if he could sing. All he said in response was "yeah," after which he banged out several George Jones songs, all of which Clement got on tape. Clement asked if he knew any rock 'n' roll, but Lewis said he didn't.

When he heard the tapes, Phillips told Clement to schedule a session for Lewis with studio musicians. It took place on a Friday, while Phillips was at a disc jockeys' convention in Nashville; otherwise, he would have been in the studio. They went through several songs that Lewis had written, but none of them hit the mark. Finally, Clement asked Lewis if he knew "Crazy Arms." Lewis said he knew enough to give it a shot

Afterward, Clement fell in love with Lewis' version of the song and played it for anyone who would listen. When Phillips returned to the studio on Monday, Clement started playing the tape for him, but before it even got past the introduction, Phillips reached over and stopped the tape.

"I can sell that," he said. "Just from the piano intro."

Lewis went on to record some of Sun Records most energetic hits. "Whole Lot of Shakin' Going On" and "Great Balls of Fire" both peaked at Number Two on the pop charts. Going into 1958, Lewis seemed unstoppable, but then he married his thirteen-year-old cousin, and the resulting publicity put his career into the deep freeze. He moved to Mississippi, where he patiently worked toward his comeback, despite a string of personal tragedies. This time, he was on the country charts with hits like "She Even Woke Me up to Say Goodbye" and "What Made Milwaukee Famous." In the mid-1980s, Lewis was asked how he wanted to be remembered. "I would like for them to remember me the way I am now," he said. "Just about the best talent they have around here... I've held my head up, and I've been my own man. Elvis sang a song, 'I Did It My Way.' No way! I did it *my* way! I think he did that song for me."

◆　▲　◆　▲　◆

Toward the end of the 1950s, three of Sam Phillips' session players—Ray Harris, Bill Cantrell, and Quinton Claunch—teamed with a group of Memphis investors, including Popular Tunes owner Joe Cuoghi, to start up a record label of their own. It seemed like a good marriage of talent and experience. Popular Tunes was one of the largest wholesale and retail record distributors in the South, and Harris, Cantrell, and Clauch were well known for their musical abilities. They named the label Hi Records.

Hi's first release was a remake of Jimmie Davis' "You Are My Sunshine," recorded by Jerry Lee Lewis' cousin, Carl McVoy. The record sold well enough, but Hi couldn't collect money fast enough from retailers to pay the pressing costs. With the view that a small part of a big thing was better than a big part of nothing, Hi sold the master tapes to Sam Phillips, who failed in his attempt to make the record a hit.

Hi took the money from the masters sale and used it to purchase an abandoned movie theater at 1320 South Lauderdale, which was located in a black neighborhood; the theater was then converted into a studio named Royal Recording. Once work on the studio was completed, they got serious about discovering new talent. They went through artist after artist—each one considered "can't miss" hit-makers—but none of them stuck. Finally, at a point when they were thinking about calling it quits, Bill Black, Elvis' bassist, stopped by the studio to talk to Cuoghi and Harris. Black and Scotty Moore had quit Elvis' band over money issues, and Black was desperate to find work.

At that time, Bill Justis had a hit single with an instrumental titled "Raunchy." The record was especially popular with jukebox operators, because it offered a solid dance beat. There were hundreds of thousands of jukeboxes in America, and their owners were easier to approach than radio programmers. If the label could record a series of jukebox instrumentals, they figured, they could bypass their distribution problems and have their share of hit records. They decided to put Black in a session band, led by guitarist Reggie Young, and name it the Bill Black Combo. Their first release, "Smokie," was a hit, especially with jukebox operators, and they quickly followed it with a long series of hits, eighteen in all.

Eager to build the record label's reputation as an instrumental hit-maker, they recruited a black trumpet player named Willie Mitchell and asked him to organize a second instrumental band. Mitchell, who had started out his career as a teen playing in B.B. King's band, put together a first-rate group that included Al Jackson on drums and Lewis Steinberg on bass. By 1964, they had a hit with "20-75." Mitchell's success convinced Hi that he should be put in charge of production.

Encouraged by the faith that Hi showed in him—at that time in Memphis, interracial mixing was not just frowned upon, it was illegal in many instances—Mitchell turned to the black community for talent. One of his first releases as production chief was "Don't Turn Your Back on Me," recorded by Don Bryant, the vocalist with Mitchell's old nightclub band. The song was a big hit in the South, but it didn't make the national charts. Mitchell then turned to a black female vocalist, Ann Peebles. Her first single, "Walk Away," did well on the rhythm & blues charts, but it didn't make a dent in the pop charts. Mitchell upheld his reputation by recording another instrumental, "Soul Serenade," which proved to be a solid hit.

It was while he was out touring Texas in support of "Soul Serenade" that he met a man who would change his life. "It was really hot that day, like a hundred and twelve degrees," Mitchell later recalled. "We pulled the bus up to the club in Midland. This guy runs up to me. He says his name is Al Green. He said, 'I'm stranded here. Can I work with you tonight so I can get back home?'"

Once they unloaded the bus, Mitchell allowed Green to come inside the nightclub to sit in on the rehearsal. He was so impressed by his voice that he invited him to return to Memphis with him. He told him that he thought he could make him into a star.

"How long would it take to do that?" Green asked.

"About eighteen months," Mitchell answered.

As it turned out, it was eighteen months, almost to the day, that their first recording, "Tired of Being Alone," went to Number Twelve on the pop charts and became a million-seller. At long last, Mitchell had the voice he had been searching for. Al Green was the perfect complement to his musical vision.

When they returned to the studio again, Green brought Mitchell a song titled "Let's Stay Together." Mitchell liked the song, but he knew it needed a little work before they could record it. With Al Jackson's help—he had a remarkable ability to find the groove in a song—they smoothed out the rough edges and recorded it. Within weeks, it was the Number One record in America.

For the next three years, Mitchell and Green recorded an amazing number of hits: "Look What You Done for Me," "I'm Still in Love With You," "You Ought to be with Me," and "L-O-V-E," songs that translated into eight Gold singles and six Gold albums. As Green's hits soared, Ann Peebles returned to the studio and scored a hit with "I Can't Stand the Rain." Hits with other artists followed: Sly Johnson with "Take Me to the River," and Otis Clay with "I Die a Little Each Day."

Rita Coolidge. (Courtesy of the Mississippi Valley Collection, University of Memphis)

As Willie Mitchell had hit after hit in the late 1960s, a Nashville-born woman named Rita Coolidge began hanging out at Royal Recording studio. Her parents had moved to Memphis while she was attending Florida State University, so when she left college, she went to live with her parents until she could figure out what she wanted to do with her life. The university had offered her an assistantship to work on her master's degree, but she wasn't certain she wanted an academic career. Drawn to music, she became a regular visitor to Mitchell's studio; it was scandalous behavior at the time, because it wasn't something that "nice" Memphis girls did. "She used to sit up all night with us," said Mitchell. "Just sit in the studio and watch what we were doing. I knew she was a singer, but we never did anything she wanted to sing at Hi."

Coolidge never recorded at Royal Recording, but she did jingles for a Memphis ad agency, and then recorded a couple of singles for American Studios, one of which was written by Memphian Donna Weiss, who went on to win a Grammy for a song titled "Bette Davis Eyes." It wasn't until she left Memphis and went to Los Angeles to join the Bonnie and Delaney tour that she began her recording career in earnest, doing a string of successful albums for A&M Records, including *The Lady's Not for Sale*.

Another woman who spent a lot of time in the Hi Records studio was Tina Turner, who recorded with Mitchell from 1965 until the mid-1970s, while she was part of the Ike and Tina Turner Revue. Born Annie Mae Bullock, just north of Memphis, she changed her name when she became Ike's lover and joined his band. Mitchell produced seventeen albums with her, but they were all rhythm & blues. It was not until the mid-1980s, after she had split with Ike, that she ventured into pop and became a superstar; but she never forgot her roots, returning to Memphis in 1983 for two Mitchell-produced songs that she wanted on her breakout album, *Private Dancer*. The two songs were Al Green's "Let's Stay Together" and Ann Peebles' "I Can't Stand the Rain."

Mitchell felt vindicated, for he had always felt that she was a major talent. "She was always there," he said, more than a year after the release of *Private Dancer*. "She always

Ike and Tina Turner in a 1967 publicity photo. (James L. Dickerson)

had the talent, the looks, everything...[Ever since then] people have been calling, wanting to know if I had any more songs like that."

Mitchell's major successes tapered off during the 1990s, but he never stopped trying to find that next big hit. Sadly, for most of his career, his contributions to Memphis music were largely ignored by the city, with a few exceptions. Not until 2004, after he had suffered a crippling stroke, did the city reach out to him by renaming that stretch of Lauderdale Street where his studio was located "Willie Mitchell Boulevard."

◆ ▲ ◆ ▲ ◆

In 1958, while Sun Records was soaring and the fledging Hi Records was making a lot of noise about making hits—and Memphis big-band singer Kay Starr had recorded "Rock and Roll Waltz," the first number one record to ever have the phrase "rock and roll" in the title—Estelle Axton, at forty, was working as a bookkeeper at Union Planters Bank in Memphis. Prior to that, she had spent years teaching grades one through eight in a one-room school just outside Memphis. Married, with two children, she was in a comfortable routine, thinking more about retirement than blazing new trails.

All that came to an end when her brother, Jim Stewart, approached her about starting up a record label. At the time, he was working in the bonds department of a rival bank. Estelle knew that he had an interest in music—he'd played fiddle in several swing bands and sometimes performed on local radio shows—but she was shocked that he wanted to enter the business end of music. His proposal was simple: He needed twenty-five hundred dollars to buy a recording machine, and if Estelle would mortgage her home and put up the money, she could be his business partner.

Jim and Estelle were not your typical music executives. Estelle was a strong-willed redhead, who could have taught the early feminists a thing or two about women's rights, and Jim was a dreamer in the best tradition of the Mojo Triangle—a mild-mannered visionary with an artist's sensibilities, who felt the power of the ancient pyramid rambling deep inside his soul, an intellectual who combined the raw talents of an Elvis Presley or Howlin'

Wolf, with the ponderous visions of William Faulkner and Eudora Welty. As a team, Jim and Estelle had a definite synergy. Estelle was the bean-counter, and the partner with an uncanny knack for recognizing records that would have commercial appeal, while Jim was the musical innovator who cared as much about the content of the music as he did its financial potential. Working together, they accomplished things never before done in America: They not only gave the country a new music, they provided a blueprint for racial healing.

The late Estelle Axton in Memphis, circa 1994. (James L. Dickerson)

Once Jim paid for the one-track Ampex recorder, they opened their studio in an abandoned grocery in a small town a few miles from Memphis. They named their company Satellite Productions, a reference to the national hysteria over Russia's launch of Sputnik, the world's first satellite. They spent a year searching for talent, often recording neighborhood children in the hopes of discovering the next Elvis, but it soon became clear to them that if they were going to have any hope of recovering Estelle's investment they would have to re-locate in Memphis.

During that first year, Jim worked with a young guitarist named Lincoln "Chips" Moman, a transplanted Georgian who dreamed of making it big in Memphis. Moman had seen what Hi Records had done with its movie theater, so he located a vacant theater that Jim and Estelle were able to rent for one hundred dollars a month. The price was low, because it was difficult to sell or lease the space as anything other than a movie theater, with its sloping floor and high ceiling.

Once they took possession, they ripped out the seats and put a partition down the middle of the theater to compact the sound. Then they put their recording machine up on the stage in front of the movie screen. In order to have income until they scored their first hit, Estelle opened a record store in an area of the building formerly occupied by a barber shop. Since she still had her day job, she couldn't keep the store open in the mornings and early afternoons, but she went to the store immediately after work and sold records well into the evening. It was a good thing: Their first recordings were not successful, and the record store kept the studio afloat.

Jim and Estelle's first break came when WDIA disc jockey Rufus Thomas stopped by the studio one day with his sixteen-year-old daughter, Carla. He pitched several songs he had written, but the one that caught their ear was the father-daughter duet, "Cause I Love You." They recorded the song in their new studio and released it as a single. It sold about fifteen thousand copies in the Memphis area, numbers that prompted Atlantic Records head Jerry Wexler to pay them one thousand dollars for the right to distribute it nationally. It sold thirty-five thousand copies nationwide, a respectable showing that earned Atlantic Records a profit many times over.

Later, Jim, Estelle, Rufus, and Carla were sitting around the studio, exchanging ideas, when Carla said she had written a song titled "Gee Whiz." "As soon as Jim and I heard that song, we knew it was a hit," Estelle later said. "It's funny; when you hear a song, you know if it's got something in it that will sell." They used the thousand dollars they had received from Atlantic for the first record and they took Carla to Nashville, where they recorded her song in a state-of-the art studio. When Wexler heard the record, he signed Carla to a five-year recording contract and released the song on Atlantic. Within weeks, "Gee Whiz" went to Number Thirteen on the pop charts, establishing Carla as a teenage sensation. For Carla, it was a "Twilight Zone" experience, in the sense that she was one of the most famous teens in the country, admired by thousands, yet in Memphis segregation laws made it

Rufus Thomas with his daughter, Carla, 1979. (Courtesy of the Mississippi Valley Collection, University of Memphis)

illegal for her to swim in a public pool, check a book out of the library, or eat in a white restaurant.

Encouraged by Carla's success, Jim and Estelle kept the tape reel spinning. Their next hit came from an unlikely source. Estelle's son Packy learned to play sax so that he could join a band named the Royal Spades, a rock 'n' roll group made of high school friends Steve Cropper on guitar and Donald "Duck" Dunn on bass. Cropper and Dunn brought Packy into the group because they were eager to hang out at his mother's studio.

One night, Moman was in a nightclub listening to a local band, when he got an idea for a three-chord instrumental riff. During intermission, he worked on it with keyboardist Smoochie Smith, then the next day he used some members from the Royal Spades to flesh it out. When Estelle heard the song, titled "Last Night," she loved it and encouraged Jim to release it as a record. Jim was against it at first, probably because he had a difficult time accepting his nephew as a professional musician, but he eventually relented and allowed it to be pressed into a record.

Satellite released "Last Night" in July 1961—by then the Royal Spades had become the Mar-Keys—and within two or three weeks, to everyone's surprise, it went to Number Two on the pop charts, becoming the best-selling record in Memphis music history. Not even Elvis' hits on Sun Records had done that well. To promote the record, Jim organized a touring band composed of Cropper on guitar, Dunn on bass, Smith on keyboards, Terry Johnson on drums, Packy on tenor sax, Wayne Jackson on trumpet, and Don Nix on baritone sax. "It was a high school band that lucked into a hit record—just seven people trying to have a good time," Nix recalled. "It was the big time to us. At that time, guys our age doing that was really crazy."

As word of the record spread, Jim and Estelle were threatened with a lawsuit if they did not change the name of their company. Unknown to them, there was already a record company doing business as Satellite Records. They avoided a lawsuit by changing the name of their company to Stax Records, the "Stax" coming from the first two letters of their last names. As a result, some copies of "Last Night" were sold with a Satellite label, and other copies were sold with a Stax label.

By late 1961, Jim, Estelle, and Moman felt they were on the right track. The next hit, "You Don't Miss Your Water," was written and recorded by a black nightclub singer named William Bell. The record was a hit in the South and made the national charts, but before they could capitalize on the record's initial success, Bell was drafted into the Army. The record was important because it gave Stax Records an identifiable sound.

Not long after that, Jim booked several musicians—Cropper on guitar, Booker T. Jones on keyboards, Al Jackson on drums, and Lewis Steinberg on bass—for a session with a country singer. When the singer failed to show up, the musicians started jamming on an instrumental titled "Behave Yourself" that Jim had heard Booker and Steve play in a nightclub. It sounded so tight that Jim decided to record it. Feeling he might have a hit, he asked them to come up with another idea for the flip side.

"[Steve and I] had this idea for 'Green Onions,'" Booker recalled. "We had been fooling around with it on the piano a couple of weeks before...Something just caused me to play it on the organ this time. It sounded a lot better on the organ than it did on the piano. That was a thrill for us to see that come together by accident."

"Green Onions" peaked at Number Seven on the pop charts, and the house band morphed into Booker T. and the MGs, providing Stax not only with a hit record, but with a new sound. Today, it doesn't sound like such a big deal—two white guys, two black guys together in a studio working together—but when you consider the times, it was a huge moment in music history. At that time, blacks had access to recording studios all over the country, but when it came to whites and blacks working together as equals, the racial climate in New York and Los Angeles was not much better than it was in Memphis, where it was actually illegal for whites and blacks to sleep or dine together. It took enormous courage for Jim and Chips Moman to do what they did—either that or an overwhelming desire to achieve success at any cost.

From that moment on, Jones, Cropper, Jackson, and Steinberg became Stax's house band (though Steinberg was soon replaced with Duck Dunn). Moman had a flare-up with Jim around that time and left to start up a studio of his own, American Recording Studio, but the two men and Estelle had already set something in motion that would prove to be unstoppable: A belief that music was important enough to override the old stereotypes associated with blacks. It wasn't intentional, but they did more to integrate America than all the politicians and social scientists combined.

"For us, music had no color," Cropper said. "What went on politically, we were not involved with....There were a couple of instances on the road

Otis Redding in a 1960s publicity photo. (Courtesy of the Mississippi Valley Collection, University of Memphis)

later when we ended up leaving in the middle of the something, but that only happened a couple of times....If we went to a place and played in a town where things were segregated, we just stayed on the outskirts of town. We didn't worry about it."

For the next several years, Stax put together an incredible collection of artists, beginning with Otis Redding, who traveled to Memphis from Macon, Georgia, in the hopes of impressing someone at Stax—first, with an original composition, "These Arms of Mine," and then with a soulful voice that could tear at the heartstrings with effortless shifts of vocal emphasis. "These Arms of Mine" wasn't a hit, but it did enter the national charts, setting the stage for other hits, including ""Mr. Pitiful," "Respect," and "I've Been Loving You Too Long (To Stop Now)."

Ironically, it was not until after Redding died in a plane crash in 1967 that he had a Number One record. He had recorded "(Sittin' On) The Dock of the Bay" three days before his death, with Steve Cropper serving as co-writer and co-producer. Three months later, it topped the charts, giving Stax its first Number One record. Redding never heard the finished record, but he and Cropper had a good feeling about the song. "The day we cut [it], Otis and I looked at each other and said 'this is a hit!'" Cropper recalled. "Not everyone in the studio agreed with us, but we knew in our own minds that this would be his biggest record. It was just an electric thing."

Stax went on to introduce an incredible array of talent, including Sam and Dave, with their hits, "Soul Man" and "Hold on, I'm Coming"; Rufus Thomas, who scored the hit he had always dreamed about, with "Walking the Dog," a song that Thomas later argued was the first rap song; guitarist Albert King; songwriters David Porter and Isaac Hayes, who found success as an artist in 1971 with a number one hit titled "Theme from Shaft"; black comedian Richard Pryor, who scored a hit with his album, *That Nigger's Crazy*; and many others, most of whom shared the Stax approach to music that critics latter named Sweet Soul.

Of course, sweet soul was not so much a musical product as it was the result of white and black musicians working together as equals. Sweet soul is a metaphor for the type of racial harmony that can occur when people give love a chance. Jim Stewart's genius was that he understood it and harnessed its power to produce music, the likes of which the world had never before seen. His luck was that he devised a makeshift way of replacing human vocals with a sax and a trumpet. It is that distinctive sound in the background of all Stax's major hits that most people identify with the record label. Sometimes there would be an additional sax or trombone in the mix, but for the most part it consisted of Wayne Jackson on trumpet and Andrew Love on sax. The two men became so famous for their unique horn parts that they named themselves the Memphis Horns; at live events, they typically baffled audiences when they walked out on stage, because the sound was so large that most people expected an entire orchestra.

Stax Records continued to dominate soul music until 1976, when it closed its doors amid a string of scandals (none of which involved Jim or Estelle), but the essence of the music was dealt a fatal blow long before the studio doors were locked shut. Stax's demise actually began on April 4, 1968, the day civil rights leader Martin Luther King was shot to death by an assassin at the Loraine Motel, in Memphis. In the days that followed, blacks rioted in more than eighty cities, resulting in the deaths of twenty-nine people.

Memphis exploded, along with other major American cities, requiring the deployment of bayonet-toting national guard troops, whose job it was to patrol the streets and enforce a 7:00 p.m. curfew. Duck Dunn and Don Nix were standing in front of the Stax studio when the rioting began. They weren't overly concerned, because Stax was located in a black neighborhood and they felt that afforded them a degree of protection. "We went back inside, and Isaac [Hayes] said, 'Man, ya'll better go home,'" Nix recalled. "He said, 'Let me carry you and Duck home.' We said no. By then you could see smoke on the horizon."

Jim and Estelle locked the doors, out of respect for Martin Luther King, and loaded all their master tapes into their cars and took them home, where they hoped they would be safe. About a week later, when the rioting had stopped, they took the tapes back to the studio and opened the doors for business. Unfortunately, it was not business as usual—and would never again reach the old heights. "I thought that was when the music started dying," Nix said. "After that, you couldn't go back out on the street."

For blacks in the Mojo Triangle, the King assassination was the equivalent of Meriwether Lewis' death. It was as if the wheel had turned full circle. April 4, 1968, was the day that sweet soul turned rancid. What was there about the pyramid that allowed such violence to take place at such an important time

The aftermath of the Martin Luther King assassination near Memphis' Beale Street. (Courtesy of the Mississippi Valley Collection, University of Memphis)

in the region's troubled history? How long would the assassination plague the region—ten years, a hundred years, a thousand years? The assassination was as important, historically, as any of the earthquakes, floods, or plagues that had given the region its unique wellspring of talent. In what direction would

Mourners view the body of Martin Luther King in 1968. (Courtesy of the Mississippi Valley Collection, University of Memphis)

this latest catastrophe send the talent of future generations?

Stax produced only two Number One records after the assassination: Isaac Hayes' "Theme From Shaft" in 1971, and the Staple Singers' "I'll Take You There" in 1972, neither of which could be classified as sweet soul. Estelle sold her shares in the company long before it went under, but she had the last word in 1976, with the last

Number One record to ever come out of Memphis, Rick Dees' mind-numbing, anti-sweet-soul anthem, "Disco Duck." Upon Estelle's death in 2004, Isaac Hayes attributed the racial harmony at Stax to her, telling reporters, "You didn't feel any back-off from her, no differentiation that you were black and she was white....She was like a mother to us all."

◆ ▲ ◆ ▲ ◆

After leaving Stax, Chips opened his own studio, American Recording Studios, choosing a location in a rundown black neighborhood on the north end of town on 827 Thomas Street. He wasted no time putting together a first-rate house band, which soon became known as the 827 Thomas Street

Band: Guitarist Reggie Young left Hi Records when he was drafted into the Army and never returned. Bobby Wood (piano) had a hit record of his own, "If I'm a Fool For Loving You," but he was in a bad car wreck that cost him an eye and split his head open; when he was released from the hospital he went to work for Chips. Drummer Gene Chrisman had played out on the road with Jerry Lee Lewis just prior to joining the staff at American; a very religious man, he was known to do a little preaching on the side. Bobby Emmons was the former organist for the Bill Black Combo; he was fifteen and still in high school when he first started playing with Chips. And Mike Leech, who played bass, had been a music major at Northwest Junior College; he joined Chips' band, then had second thoughts and left ("before I knew it he had Tommy Cogbill in there on bass, and they were cutting hits and I got jealous and went back"). All the members of the 827 Thomas Street Band were born in Memphis, with the exception of Reggie Young, who was born across the river in Arkansas.

Chips had an exceptionally strong relationship with all the band members, to the point where they all became an extended family. Years later, Chips got into trouble with the Internal Revenue Service. "[The IRS] was fixing to take what I had to pay the tax," Chips said. "Bobby Emmons was the first one down there. 'I just heard about it,' he said. 'The bank told me they would let me have eighty thousand dollars and I'll have it for you by this afternoon.' Reggie came in and said, 'Hey, man, I'm gonna borrow some money on my farm. I can let you have one hundred thousand dollars.' Bobby Wood called. They all came to bail my ass out. I said, 'I don't want you to do that. Let me see if I can't take care of it myself,' and I did take care of it myself. But do you know what kind of an honor it is to have your friends offer to do that for you? These are special people. Whatever I got, it's theirs if they want it. That's the kind of relationship we got."

American's first hit was an up-tempo rock song that peaked at number four on the pop charts: "Keep On Dancing," recorded in 1965 by a group of white Memphis teens who called themselves the Gentrys. The next hit, "Born a Woman," came in 1966 from the studio receptionist, Sandy Posey. In the early years at American, Chips seldom left the studio in an effort to make ends meet. "I wouldn't turn anything down," Chips recalled. "There was a ten-year period in which I might have averaged three hours of sleep a night. I recorded one time for nine days without going home. I would fall unconscious behind the board, and people would pick me up and shake me and say, 'Can you do one more mix?'—when they should have taken me straight to a hospital."

In 1967, Chips and his studio band received an unusual assignment. Jerry Wexler had signed a Memphis-born artist named Aretha Franklin to Atlantic. His first thought was to record her at Stax, but Jim Stewart turned down Wexler's offer because it was not financially advantageous for Stax. Wexler was a talented studio executive and producer, but many people in the Mojo Triangle felt that he was sucking the life out of the Triangle's talent and not leaving much in the way of a tip. Stewart had reached a point where he felt no deal was better than a bad deal. To get back at Stewart, Wexler asked Chips and one of his producers, Dan Penn—who had left Fame Studio in Muscle Shoals, Alabama, to work at American—to participate in the session, which he booked at Fame. They recorded one complete song, "I Never Loved a Man," and put down a track for a second song written by Chips and Dan, "Do Right Woman." Then Wexler returned to New York. "I Never Loved a Man," peaked at Number Nine of the pop charts, making an overnight star out of Aretha Franklin. Anxious to get an entire album out at breakneck speed, Wexler sent for the 827 Thomas Street Band. They flew to New York and completed the album in one week, recording several more hits—"Natural Woman," "Chain of Fools," and "Respect."

It was around that time that Penn started working with a group of white Memphis teens—Danny Smythe on drums, Gary Talley on guitar, Bill Cunningham on bass, John Evans on keyboards, and a sixteen-year-old singer named Alex Chilton. Chips was scheduled to produce the session, but at the last minute something came up and he asked Penn to take over production duties. "We didn't know what to think," said Evans. "Dan was primarily a writer, but he worked as an engineer. Dan thinks, 'Uh-huh, here's my chance to do something.' I think it was the first tune he ever produced."

Evans showed the band the chord progression for a song, "The Letter," that Penn earlier had asked him to work up, and then Penn suggested to Chilton that he pronounce the word "ae-ro-plane" in three syllables. It took them thirty-three takes to get it right, but the song that emerged was unlike anything else ever produced in Memphis. Once they nailed the song, they chose a name for the band—the Box Tops.

"The Letter" was released on Mala, a New York-based label that specialized in black music; none of the mainstream labels could figure out whether the song was pop, or rhythm & blues, or something that didn't even have a name, so they all passed. In September 1967, "The Letter," peaked at Number One on the pop charts, giving Memphis its first ever chart topper.

Chips was elated that the city's first Number One record had come from his studio, but his absence from the project made him determined never to miss another session. In time, that determination would pay off. Over the next few years, he produced a string of more than 120 hits at American, a feat unrivaled by any other producer, with the possible exception of Quincy Jones in Los Angeles. Some of the more memorable hits include "Cry Like a Baby" (the Gentrys), "Son of a Preacher Man" (Dusty Springfield), "Hooked on a Feeling" and "Eyes of a New York Woman" (B. J. Thomas), "Sweet Caroline" and "Holly Holy" (Neil Diamond), "Lost That Lovin' Feeling" (Dionne Warwick), "Goodnight Sweet Dreams" (Petula Clark), "Hold on to What You've Got" (Joe Tex), "Fly Me to the Moon" (Bobby Womack), *Goin' to Memphis* (Paul Revere and the Raiders), *Memphis Underground* (Herbie Mann), and "Land of a Thousand Dances" (Wilson Pickett).

"Some of those people are singers, and some of them are artists—there's a big difference," Chips said. "Take B. J. Thomas. When I recorded him, he was never a problem in the studio. He was a singer. He had no idea which song was good and which song was bad. It didn't make him no difference. He would sing his heart out on a trashy song, just like he would on a great song. But you had to make sure you got him to do what you wanted him to do. But then there's people like Neil Diamond. He's written some great songs, and he's got a lot of input. Lots of times, it's helpful. Lots of times, it is a hindrance. Sometimes I will cut something that I absolutely hate, waiting to get to something that I know is great, knowing that if I don't make this come off, it'll blow getting this good song. So, I might have to work real hard on a piece of trash. But sometimes those trashy things I didn't like turned out to be something I absolutely loved."

Sometimes things got downright confusing in the studio. Once, Jerry Wexler brought Wilson Pickett in for a session, along with Bobby Womack, a songwriter and guitarist who had played on some of Pickett's previous sessions. Pickett was first to record, and Womack, who was eager to help, gave him all his songs. "Every time he asked for another [song], I gave it to him," Womack recalled. "I was so happy. He got his whole album down, and then they said, 'Bobby, you're next.'" Once Pickett left the studio, they looked at

Womack and asked him what he wanted to record first. "I didn't have a damn song left. I tried my best to write something. Chips came in and said, 'Hi Bobby, how's it going? I didn't tell him I had given Pickett every song I had. I started playing 'Fly Me to the Moon,' and Chips said, 'Speed it up—that's a smash. Let's cut it.' It was about two o'clock in the morning. He never knew that 'Midnight Mover' and the others were on the Pickett album. They'd have really shit in their pants if they had known that."

In January 1969, Moman began a recording session with someone he never thought would be in his studio: Elvis Presley. By that time, Elvis had a baby girl, Lisa Marie, and he still was very much in demand as a movie actor, but his record sales had plummeted, due to the changing nature of pop music, affected greatly by an influx of British groups onto the charts. The previous year, Elvis had invited Scotty Moore and D.J. Fontana to Hollywood to participate in a pre-recorded television special for NBC. Bill Black had died of a brain tumor in 1965, and Elvis had not had much contact with Scotty and D. J. in recent years. The program, which featured Elvis sitting on a stage with Scotty and D.J., surrounded by the audience, was a huge success. A *New York Times* writer noted that 'There is something magical about watching a man who has lost himself find his way home," and convinced Elvis that it was time to return to his old Memphis roots for a new album. His manager, Colonel Tom Parker, spoke to Chips about Elvis recording at American, but when Parker insisted on a cut of the publishing, Chips balked. Parker then tried to book the session in Nashville. When Elvis would not agree to that, Parker went back to Chips and worked out a deal. Scotty and D. J. were hopeful that they would be asked to play on the session, but Chips had a longstanding rule about using only the 827 Thomas Street Band. Years later, Chips said that it was a mistake not to invite Scotty: "If I had it to do all over again, he would be invited to that session."

When the time came to start the session, Elvis paraded into American studio with his full entourage, a gesture that did not endear him to Chips and the band. Once they began work, it was obvious to Chips that Elvis needed help. "He obviously hadn't had any direction in a great while," said Chips. "If he had, I don't think he would have cut all those junk records he cut. When I told him he was off pitch, his entourage would come up and say, 'Oh, don't tell him that.'"

Chips realized that he would not be able to go on the speaker and talk to Elvis from the control room. Instead, each time he had suggestions for Elvis, he walked out into the studio and over to the vocal booth where he could talk to Elvis without his entourage overhearing their conversation. "He took direction great, but I'm sure [he] wouldn't have taken direction over the monitors where fifty people could hear me say he was flat. That would blow things out of proportion. But if you did it quietly, one on one, it was no problem at all."

Soon it became obvious to Chips that Elvis had good days and bad days. On a bad day, it was better to send him home so that he could come back refreshed the next day. In his absence, the band laid down the tracks so that when Elvis returned to sing, he sang with a recorded track instead of a live band. "A lot of people didn't understand how I could get him to do so many takes. I would have him sing a song twenty or thirty times, over and over. Back up and fix little lines that he would miss. He went through it without a problem. He wasn't the world's greatest singer, but he had a sound. I worked with people who were more talented, but nobody bigger."

Chips recorded enough material for two albums. Among the songs recorded were "Kentucky Rain," "In the Ghetto" (which gave Elvis his first Top 10 hit since "Crying in the Chapel"), "Gentle on My Mind," "Any Day Now," and "Suspicious Minds," which went to Number One in November 1969. (It would prove to be Elvis' last Number One record.) Elvis' return visit to a Memphis studio—he had not recorded in Memphis since 1955—gave him an album that critics said contained his best material since his early days at Sun Records with Scotty and Bill.

Because of his work on the songs, Chips was named Producer of the Year at the annual Bill Gavan Radio Program Conference held in Atlanta. The award meant a lot to Chips, because he was feeling increasingly isolated in Memphis as a result of the rivalries among the various studios. By 1970, events were set in motion that would forever change his life. It was the year that a young songwriter named Toni Wine flew to Memphis to hand-deliver a song for a Brenda Lee session. She had already penned hits for the Mindbenders ("A Groovy Kind of Love"), the Shirelles ("Black Pearl" and "Candida"), and themes for the film *To Sir with Love* and Dick Clark's television show "American Bandstand."

When Chips and Toni met, it was love at first sight, although Chips was married at the time. Chips and Toni were radically different; she was a

Northern Jew, educated at Juilliard School of Music for nine years, opinionated and quick to speak her mind, and he was a Southern boy, through and through, a musical genius, uneducated but overflowing with street smarts. When Chips' marriage fell apart, he and Toni were married and started a partnership that produced not only great music, but a son named Casey. They were an animated couple, and no one who spent time with the two of them together ever walked away unimpressed.

By 1973, Chips was suffering from burnout, not so much over the music as over the politics involved with making music in Memphis. That year, Elvis booked time at Stax Studios to record a new album and hired Chips' studio musicians to lay down the tracks. That was fine with Chips, who never stood in the way of them making money elsewhere if he didn't need them in the studio. The session fell apart when CBS News went to Memphis to do a segment on Isaac Hayes, who was working in another part of the studio. Elvis was incensed that CBS would travel to the studio and not ask to interview him. As a result, he left his session and sent the 827 Thomas Street band home. He returned to the studio later in the year for another session, but he was unable to book the 827 Thomas Street Band because they had left town, and after a few miserable days in the studio, Elvis went home, never again to record in Memphis

Following the Isaac Hayes incident, which Chips resented because of the inconsiderate way that his boys were treated, he was irritated further by a local awards show that totally ignored the 827 Thomas Street Band. Chips became so angry that he closed his studio and moved to Atlanta, and then later to Nashville, where he opened a new studio. The studio band followed, and helped Chips create a fresh new sound for country music. The final song they worked on at American was Billy Lee Riley's "I Got a Thing About You, Babe."

◆ ▲ ◆ ▲ ◆

Chips Moman's departure from Memphis left an ominous void in the musical landscape, but that was only part of the picture. The doors at Stax were padlocked by federal marshals when the company declared bankruptcy. Hi Records had shut down years ago. In 1976, the only major studio still left standing in Memphis was Ardent Recording Studio, located in midtown. It was founded in 1966 by John Fry, who earlier had tried to start a record label in his grandmother's sewing room, with the help of two high school friends—John King and Fred Smith (Smith later started up an air freight company named Federal Express, the Mojo Triangle's most significant contribution to interstate commerce).

Jim Dickinson (left) and Alex Chilton at Ardent Stuido in Memphis. (Courtesy of the Mississippi Valley Collection, University of Memphis)

Fry's burning desire to own a studio was complicated by the fact that he didn't possess any musical abilities of his own. His talents were more business-oriented. Luckily, Fry was able to attract people who had the skills he lacked. One of the first was Jim Dickinson, a Mississippi piano player who had skills as a producer; he had worked as a sideman at Stax and American, and had performed for six months with the Miami-based rock band, Dixie Flyers.

One of Ardent's first albums was by a group named Big Star. The band's front man was Alex Chilton, who had walked away from the Box Tops in 1969 during a performance. Titled *#1 Record*, the Big Star album was filled with Beatles-style harmonies and should have generated a hit or two. When it didn't, Fry tried a second album, *Radio City*, an album that received glowing reviews, but no public support. Fry was mystified. Chilton was a proven hit-maker, and the band had a contemporary sound. He began to wonder if perhaps he was the problem. (He had engineered and produced the first two albums himself.) For the group's third album, he asked Dickinson to step in as producer. The resulting album, *The Third*, was exceptional, but Fry declined to release it, holding it until 1980, when it, again, received great praise from critics while being ignored by the record-buying public. Big Star disbanded, and Fry and Dickinson moved on.

It was not until 1974 that Ardent formed a relationship with a successful recording group. That year, the Texas-based rock band ZZ Top came to Memphis to perform at the Memphis Blues Show. While in town, they stopped by Ardent to discuss studio rates with chief engineer, Terry Manning. They liked what they heard and recorded their next album in Memphis— and the next, and the next, and the next. Throughout the 1970s and 1980s, it remained a well-kept secret that almost all of ZZ Top's so-called "Texas" albums were cut in Memphis.

"I would like to be able to tell you that what we offer them is so unique they could not get it elsewhere," said Fry. "We offer them good facilities and do a good job for them, but there are other people who could do the same thing....Frankly, to be really honest with you, those records could be made at the north pole and still be popular. There is a factor of the chemistry of the people working together, but I cannot paint a picture that would say ZZ Top could not live without Memphis."

Primarily because of ZZ Top, Ardent quickly got a reputation among music insiders as a great place to record. Part of that was due to creative producers and engineers like Manning and Dickinson, but the label's success was due, to no small degree, to Fry's desire to own one of the most technically advanced studios in the country. He ordered the best equipment that money could buy, and he operated his studio with a type of button-down-collar professionalism that many artists found appealing.

By the 1980s, Ardent was attracting a wide variety of talent to its studios. Dickinson produced an album with the Replacements, and R.E.M. traveled to the city to record its *Green* album at Ardent. And two more Texas-based groups, The Fabulous Thunderbirds, and Stevie Ray Vaughan and Double Trouble made Memphis their second home, attracted to the city's reputation as a mystical place in which to record.

T-Birds' guitarist Jimmie Vaughan was instrumental in the band's decision to go to Memphis. "I had never recorded here, and we had done it in London, in Los Angeles, in New York, and in Austin and Dallas," he explained, adding, "It's magic here."

T-Birds' producer Dave Edmunds noted that the only other musicians that the band wanted on their album were the Memphis Horns. "I always thought the horns on the old Stax records sounded so unique, and I wondered how they did it," he said. "Now I've worked with them, and I still don't know."

Lead singer Kim Wilson marveled at how two men could create such a full sound. "With a horn player, you can't settle for anything less than the best, and those guys just blew me away," Wilson explained. "It was entertaining to watch them work. I just sat there, drank beer, and watched them play. I told myself, 'You'd better keep your mouth shut—anything you can think of, they probably thought of years ago."

The Fabulous Thunderbirds recorded two albums at Ardent: *Powerful Stuff* in 1989, with Terry Manning as producer, and *Hot Number* in 1987, with Edmunds as producer. The same year that the T-Birds recorded *Powerful Stuff*,

Stevie Ray Vaughan went to Memphis to record what turned out to be his last solo album, *In Step*. It was not recorded at Ardent, but rather at a new studio named Kiva.

While in town making the album, Stevie Ray had occasion to travel across town with this author to record an interview for a syndicated radio show. As he glanced out the window, the guitarist marveled at the city's reputation for music. "The Memphis thing—I can feel it all around me," he said. "It just comes up out of the ground or something. There's just *something* about the place." Puffing on a cigarette, he glanced out the window at the passing landscape. "It's out there—you can't see it, maybe, but it's there."

Later, Stevie Ray and his brother Jimmie returned to Memphis to record the only album they ever did together, *Family Style*. It was done at Ardent, with John Hampton doing the engineering duties. "[Stevie] was chewing tons of Nicoret gum," recalled Hampton, which had to do with the guitarist's recent alcohol and cocaine recovery. "We'd be in the middle of a guitar part and if Stevie got frustrated, he would turn everything off and say 'Let's go to a [AA] meeting.... I think Jimmie was starting to clean up then. Everyone was off the drugs and booze, and if there was any weirdness there, it was just the frustration of [making a record]."

After the session ended, Stevie and Jimmie felt reinvigorated, not exhausted, the way they usually felt after wrapping up a project. "We've probably gotten closer making this record than we have been since we were little kids at home," Stevie told VH1. "And, uh, I needed it, you know? I can honestly say I needed it." Jimmie echoed his brother's sentiments, adding that "It was like we had gotten back together, and it was almost like we were at home." It wasn't long after Stevie made those comments that he was killed in a helicopter crash. The event led to Jimmie's decision to leave the T-Birds and begin a career as a solo artist. He returned to Ardent to make his first solo albums, but then he drifted away, not so much away from Memphis as from music itself.

In the years that followed, Ardent continued to draw big-time recording artists to its studios, but it never really recovered from losing its Texas connection, for it was in Stevie and Jimmie's enthusiasm for the city's music heritage—and their understanding of the power of the Mojo Triangle—that the studio was able to most clearly define itself.

More and more, the history of Memphis music became the specter of closing doors, as one artist, producer, and songwriter after another moved on, the most lingering sentiment being, "Will the last one to leave, please turn out the lights!" If that sounds like a dismissive obituary, it is not: Memphis mojo will rise again, simply because the Mojo Triangle, after generations of musical innovation, has mandated a future based on the past.

6 NEW ORLEANS
▼ A Gumbo That Keeps on Giving

Four years after the French set up a trading post in Natchez, Jean Baptiste Le Moyne, Sieur de Bienville, traveled further south in 1718 to establish a settlement on the camping grounds of the Choctaw and Natchez Indians. The settlement, which was built on the east bank of the Mississippi River, ninety miles from the river's mouth but only a few miles from the Gulf of Mexico, was named Nouvelle Orleans (New Orleans) after the Duke of Orleans. Built on mosquito-infested swampland, it possessed a high water table that made it impossible to build basements or dig graves. As a result, all burials had to take place above ground in stone vaults.

For the first eighty-five years of its existence, the settlement went through a series of changes, with ownership transferred for a brief time to Spain, and then back again to France, which sold it to the United States as part of the Louisiana Purchase in 1803. By then it had become an important port, with ships arriving from all over the world. Despite the change in ownership, the French influence remained strong; today, the French Quarter runs from Canal Street to Esplanade, covering an area of approximately 130 square blocks, a showplace of architecture that dates back almost to the beginning, when French builders strived to duplicate the triumphs of Paris.

New Orleans quickly became a major center for the slave trade, at one time boasting more than two-dozen slave auction houses. Ironically, the city possessed one of the largest populations of people of color in the South, due largely to the sexual experimentation that took place between whites, Native Americans, and black slaves. In time, these people of mixed color began calling themselves Creoles. By going into professions such as cigar making and bricklaying, they built a solid middle class that became the foundation of French Quarter society. They dressed well, spent their money freely— especially on entertainment—and they sometimes sent their children to France to be educated in the best schools.

New Orleans was also unique in its liberality toward women's roles, whether they were prostitutes, musicians, homemakers, or politicians. During the Civil war the women of New Orleans reacted violently to

Union occupation. They wore emblems on their dresses that announced their support of the Confederacy and, on occasion, they verbally abused Union soldiers and hurled objects at them. Union forces tolerated that behavior until the day an irate woman emptied her chamber pot from her balcony onto the head of Admiral Farragut, prompting the military to issue "Order Number 28," which vowed to henceforth treat New Orleans women as women "of the town plying their trade." There was a worldwide reaction to the order, but the military refused to rescind it, noting that it dramatically reduced the number of insults that soldiers had to endure.

It was into this freewheeling atmosphere that music made its appearance in the city, primarily as an emotional reaction to the flooding, yellow fever epidemics, constant wars, and periodic racial conflicts that battered the population. Throughout the 1800s, the most popular music was associated with blackface minstrel shows and marching bands, though the city did boast two symphony orchestras that served the cultural cravings of the city's elite. Essentially, New Orleans, despite its melting pot reputation, listened to the same music that was heard in other American cities.

The seeds of new music were planted in the 1890s with ragtime, an up-tempo take on popular songs that had evolved in the North with the help of black musicians who wanted to breathe some life into the staid marches and waltzes that they were always asked to play at social functions. Ragtime wasn't a new type of music; it was merely a new style of playing old music, but it made people realize that music didn't always have to be played exactly as it was written, and that was an important intellectual leap for musicians of that era to make. Music is meant to be felt, not viewed in the mind's eye, but its forward progress is always dependent on the individual's ability to visualize where it might go, given the right send off. Great musicians can see, as well as hear, their music.

Three pioneers aided the transition from ragtime to jazz. Trumpet player Charles "Buddy" Bolden, whose five- to seven-piece band, made up of horns, a guitar, a bass, and drums, was considered the best in the city. (His second cornet player once remarked, "Buddy could not read a note, but he surely played a good stiff lead.") Jack "Papa" Laine, the leader of the Reliance Brass Band and Jack Laine's Ragtime Band, set the standard for white Dixieland music. And last but not least, there was pianist Ferdinand "Jelly Roll" Morton, who once claimed to be the sole inventor of jazz.

Jelly Roll's boast may have been extravagant, but he was a pivotal figure in the development of jazz. Born in 1890 of Creole ancestry—his birth name was Ferdinand Joseph Lamothe—he was playing in bands by the age of seven, first on the guitar and then on piano. By the time he was in his teens, he was drawn to Storyville, a district the city had designated for prostitution in the hopes that preemptive isolation would prevent it from spreading to other parts of the city.

Jelly Roll found work playing piano in the whorehouses, where drunken men on the prowl would sometimes dole out twenty- and fifty-dollar tips to piano players in exchange for playing a song that pulled the heart strings of their "dates." He later claimed that any night that he made less than one hundred dollars was a "bad night." With lots of money to spend, Jelly Roll invested in his image—nice suits and hats, big rings, all creating a presence that made him one of the most dapper musicians in the city.

After hours, Jelly Roll frequented the more traditional nightclubs, where he traded stories and piano licks with other musicians. Soon he began writing songs—"The Wolverine Blues," "Jelly Roll Blues," and "King Porter Stomp," to name a few. Ten to fifteen years into the new century, the blues—as defined by W.C. Handy—became New Orleans' favorite new music. Horn players hadn't had new music since ragtime, so they embraced it, re-creating Handy's precise structure note for note. That suited Jelly Roll just fine, because he was a stickler for detail; everything he did in life, whether it pertained to his dress or his music, had to be perfect.

Handy's blues were written for orchestras, but Jelly Roll had no problem distilling the essence of the music and adapting it for the piano. The blues seemed especially suited to Storyville, where, he wrote, "Hundreds of men were passing through the streets day and night. The chippies in their little-girl dresses were standing in the crib doors singing the blues...Lights of all colors were glittering and glaring. Music was pouring into the streets from every house."

With time, Jelly Roll started putting his own touches to the blues— nothing drastic, just flourishes that caught the attention of other musicians who began to question whether music had to be played exactly as written, particularly after they heard Jelly Roll make up dirty rhymes that fit the music. Two of the first New Orleans musicians to open the door on the improvisation that Jelly Roll winked at in his lyrics were Creole cornetist Freddie Keppard and his Olympia Orchestra, and Joe "King" Oliver, the top cornet player in New Orleans. Between 1912 and 1915, these two band-leaders followed separate but parallel musical paths, generating some of the most exciting music the city ever heard.

At the core of their music was the belief that they didn't have to follow Handy's blues, note for note. Rather, they used the blues as a starting point from which to begin a musical journey, the effect being to smother the song's lyrics with instrumental artistry that highlighted each player's skills. It was at that point that Handy's blues morphed into jazz. There is no one person responsible for completing the transformation, only dozens of musicians who each contributed their own piece to the puzzle.

As an art form, jazz is instinctive in nature, relying on musicians' genetic and cultural history for expression. The hot wiring that took place in the brains of Jelly Roll, Keppard, and Oliver—and all the other musicians who invented jazz—occurred at a subconscious level beyond the edge of reason, in that dark and melancholy place where the history of the Mojo Triangle rests, until it is unleashed through genes that carry the imprint of centuries of travail and spiritual wandering. Not convinced? Then consider what psychologists call flight response. A person sees rising water, or feels a tremble, or hears a sound in the dark, and he or she instinctively knows to respond, the result of thousand of years of genetic imprinting.

The original music and literature that emanate from the Mojo Triangle are based on the same principle—namely, that the experiences of the region can be passed from generation to generation genetically, inhabiting the subconscious of the chosen few until summoned like a muse, by events or spiritual necessity.

Of all the original music created in the Mojo Triangle, jazz is the most instinctive, and the music most likely—by virtue of its passion and power—to unite the millions of lost, wandering souls that have preceded it through the long night.

◆　▲　◆　▲　◆

Louis Armstrong was born August 4, 1901, in a bleak and foreboding section of New Orleans called Jane Alley. His mother, Mayann, was only fifteen, and his father, William Armstrong, abandoned him shortly after his birth, leaving Louis and his mother to fend for themselves in a shanty neighborhood that reeked with poverty and despair.

African-American men had few opportunities for advancement in New Orleans at the turn of the century, unlike African-American women, who could take their pick from three categories of always-in-demand jobs: Cook, maid, or prostitute. Too young to have learned how to cook, and too inexperienced to know how to be a cleaning woman, Mayann put Louis in the care of his grandmother, Josephine, and went to Storyville to work as a prostitute.

Within two years, Mayann had another child, a girl she named Beatrice. Apparently, she kept her daughter at her Storyville apartment, because she was there when Louis left his grandmother around the age of seven to live with his mother. Making good money as a prostitute, Mayann was able to enroll Louis in a boys' school. As many black children did at that time, he got an after-school job with a Jewish ragman. Morris Karnofsky hired him to ride in his wagon with him while he made his rounds of the whorehouses, collecting bottles and rags, and delivering coal.

Louis got an eyeful as they went from crib to crib, the prostitutes often standing in the doorways half naked, calling out to men on the street to entice them to spend their money. He quickly formed a strong bond with the entire Karnofsky family, and he basked in the warmth of their acceptance, which was often expressed by allowing him to sing Russian folk songs with them.

"The Karnofsky family kept reminding me that I had talent—perfect tonation [sic] when I would sing," Louis later wrote. "One day, I was on the wagon with Morris Karnofsky—we were on Rampart and Perdido Streets—and we passed a pawn shop which had in its window an old tarnished, beat-up B-flat cornet. It only cost five dollars. Morris advanced me two dollars on my salary. Then I put aside fifty cents each week from my small pay—finally the cornet was paid for in full. Boy was I a happy kid."

When Louis was eleven, the Karnofskys bought a home in the white section of town and Morris found a new occupation, which meant that he could no longer provide Louis with a job. Devastated, Louis dropped out of the third grade and joined hundreds of other kids on the street, all supporting themselves by hustling scams of one kind or another. Louis had several confrontations with the police and once was arrested for firing a pistol. The judge sentenced him to an indeterminate term in the Colored Waif's Home, where he often lay awake at night thinking about his horn. On occasion, he could hear Freddie Keppard's band performing at nearby lawn parties. The sound of Keppard's horn stirred his soul like nothing else ever had. He decided then that what he wanted more than anything else was to become a musician.

By the time thirteen-year-old Louis was released—and invited to move back into the home with his mother and sister—Handy's orchestrated blues had made its way to New Orleans, and the city was jumping with hot bands experimenting with their own versions of the blues: Jazz. Louis wasn't good enough yet to play with a band, but he continued to play at every opportunity, when he wasn't earning a living by unloading banana boats or selling coal on the streets.

Within four or five years, Louis was good enough on his cornet to perform regularly in the dives that couldn't afford to book top players like Keppard or King Oliver, who took an interest in Louis and advised him on his playing. When Oliver left New Orleans in 1918 and moved to Chicago, Louis took his place in Kid Ory's Band. He was only seventeen, but he quickly made a name for himself.

Because Kid Ory's Band did not perform seven days a week, Louis picked up work in out-of-the-way places like gambling halls and brothels. It was while he was performing at a brothel called Brick House that he leased the services of twenty-one-year-old prostitute Daisy Parker. She was a light-skinned black woman with a slender build and an attractive face. She had a violent temper—and she was extremely jealous of the other women in the brothel—but that set off no alarms in Louis' mind. After several weeks of paid sex, Louis was so smitten by her that he asked her to marry him.

A short time after they were married, Louis was awakened one morning by a frightening incident. "Daisy had a big bread knife on my throat, with tears dropping from her eyes, saying, 'You black son-of-a-bitch I ought to cut your goddamn throat," Louis later recalled. "That's why I always said the Lord was with me. Many times she and I went to jail from fighting in the streets, and my boss would have to come get me out."

Soon Louis realized why King Oliver had left town: New Orleans musicians were headed for tough times because the city was cracking down on prostitution and alcohol sales. Neither activity stopped, of course, but new rules meant that gin joints and whorehouses could not use noisy bands to advertise their products. Louis did what all the other musicians did and looked for work outside the city, finally taking a job on a riverboat that made runs during the spring and summer from New Orleans to St. Paul, Minnesota. His first excursion put him in the company of bandleader Fate Marable, who played piano, along with George "Pops" Foster on bass, and

Johnny and Baby Dodds on clarinet and drums, respectively.

The riverboat gig was good for Louis in many respects. It kept him away from his hot-tempered wife and her butcher knife; it put him in the company of older, more experienced musicians—and helped him develop social graces by exposing him to people of different races and social standings.

Louis played the riverboat for three years, returning to New Orleans in 1921 to discover that Daisy had taken up with another man, a cornet player who had stolen Louis' old gigs as well as his wife. Louis separated from Daisy and moved in with another woman. For the next ten months, he played at various clubs around town, pessimistic about his future as both a musician and a husband.

One day, Louis returned home from performing in a funeral procession to find a telegram from his mentor and idol, King Oliver, who urged him to take the next train to Chicago, so that he could join his band. That was all it took. All the fears and self doubts that Louis had about himself and his playing evaporated with that telegram. He made up his mind that very day to leave New Orleans. He packed everything he owned into two cardboard suitcases and, with a fish sandwich that his mother made for him (blacks were not allowed to eat in the dining car with whites), he set out on a glorious adventure.

Louis Armstrong. (Photofest)

When Louis stepped off the train in Chicago, he expected Oliver to be waiting there for him. He was not. Louis looked around the busy train station for a friendly face but saw only strangers. Finally, a redcap approached him and asked if he was Mr. Armstrong. It frightened him at first, to hear a stranger call out his name, but once the redcap explained that Oliver had made arrangements for him to be taken by taxicab directly to the nightclub where he was performing, he went with the flow, arriving at the nightclub at a moment when Oliver's band was revved to full throttle, overflowing the nightclub into the street. Louis went inside, astonished at how good the band was. Once the set ended, Louis approached the bandstand, where he was warmly greeted by Oliver. After the intermission, Oliver asked Louis to join them on the bandstand. "I was so happy I did not know what to do," Louis later recalled. "I had hit the big time."

In 1922, King Oliver's Creole Jazz Band was the top jazz group in Chicago, although it wasn't the first to arrive from New Orleans; white Dixieland musicians had preceded them by several years and built a following for jazz. Louis was asked to play second cornet, behind Oliver, but he didn't mind because he figured that playing second in the world's greatest band was better than playing first in the type of no-name bands he was used to in New Orleans.

Not long after he arrived, Oliver asked Louis to accompany him to another club to meet his former piano player, Lil Hardin, who had left him to work at a popular nightspot called Dreamland. Long before Oliver ever sent him an invitation to join him in Chicago, he had written Louis letters about Lil— about how good she was on piano, about what a sweet person she was, but mainly about how good-looking she was. (He once included a photograph of Lil to prove his point.) Because of the way King Oliver had built her up, Louis was already in love with Lil before they met that night. Oliver had hoped that fireworks would occur between Lil and Louis—but, while Louis reacted entirely as expected, Lil did not. "I wasn't impressed at all," she later confided. "I was very disappointed; I didn't like anything about him." She especially disliked the fact that he weighed 226 pounds and dressed in shabby, second-hand suits. Besides, she was married and not looking for a new man.

Several days later, Lil left the Dreamland and rejoined Oliver's band. She never gave Louis another thought, at least not in a romantic way, until Oliver confided in her one night that Louis was the better horn player. After that, Lil listened more closely, and what she heard dazzled her—so much so that she fell in love.

Louis and Lil tried to keep their romance a secret from the other band members, but they fooled no one. They both filed for divorce, Louis' being a little trickier, because his knife-toting, former prostitute of a wife was reluctant to divorce a man that was making good money, even if he lived halfway across the country. Eventually, their divorces went through, and they were married in 1924, making them Chicago's reigning Power Jazz Couple.

King Oliver was pretty proud of himself—that is, until it became obvious that his matchmaking scheme had backfired on him. Lil, whose stage name was the "Hot Miss Lil," didn't like seeing her husband play second cornet behind Oliver, so one day, she told Louis that he was going to have to choose between her or Oliver, meaning she wanted him to quit the band and go with a band that needed a first cornet.

"I can't quit Mr. Joe," Louis protested. "Mr. Joe sent for me, and I can't quit him."

"Well, it's Mr. Joe or me!"

Louis quit the band and began a journey that took him to greatness. As Lil predicted, he had no problem landing a first cornet position, first in Chicago and then in New York, when he was asked to join Fletcher Henderson's Black Swan Troubadours at Roseland, one of New York's more popular dance halls. As Louis' fame spread, Lil searched for even bigger opportunities for her husband. Almost by accident, she learned that Okeh Records was looking for a band to record a few jazz sides, so she booked Louis for the session, put together a band she named Louis Armstrong and the Hot Fives, and wrote three songs for the session, including "My Heart" and "My Heart Will Always Lead Me Back to You." They also recorded one of Louis' compositions, "Gut Bucket Blues." When they finished the session, they collected their fifty dollars each, with no thought given to the significance of the music they had recorded.

Historians would later regard the songs laid down during that session as the first true jazz recordings—not the ragtime records that some people mistakenly called jazz, but the real thing. It was a perfect musical marriage: Louis, from the southernmost point of the Mojo Triangle, with his incredible talent for making his trumpet or cornet do things that no one had ever before heard; and Lil, representing the largest angle in the triangle at Memphis, with her talent for songwriting and organization.

The Hot Fives were a studio band only—their only concert was at the Chicago Coliseum, where they drew ten thousand fans—but almost overnight, they became the hottest jazz band in America. One of their early songs, "Heebie Jeebies," sold more than forty thousand copies within weeks of its release (fantastic numbers in those days). Other songs, such as "Cornet Chop Suey," "Skid-Dat-De-Dat," and Lil's masterpiece, "Struttin' With Some Barbecue" became classics that set a high bar for future jazz musicians.

Ironically, Louis and Lil never considered themselves as doing anything that would be remembered. "We had no idea in the beginning that jazz was going to be that important, that someday people would want to know how we started," Lil later admitted in a recorded interview. "It's amusing to read in books people tell why we did this. I'm glad they know, because we didn't."

◆　▲　◆　▲　◆

By 1928, when Antoine "Fats" Domino was born in New Orleans, Louis Armstrong was the hottest musician in America, but the city that had nurtured him was headed for hard times, both musically and economically. Most of the hot jazz players had left New Orleans for Chicago, New York, or Los Angeles, and those that stayed behind quickly fell into an easy groove of jazz that was little more than a caricature of its former self. In addition, big bands such as those led by Duke Ellington and Benny Goodman found favor during and immediately after the Great Depression, which affected New Orleans more than any event since the Civil War.

Prohibition, and then the Great Depression, greatly reduced the number of jazz clubs in the city. (Liquor sales continued, but without live music in most instances.) This made it difficult for bands to find work. Pianists who worked solo were the exception. They could always slip into a bar and bang out a few tunes on the house piano without creating a lot of attention. No one in the clubs cared whether the piano players could sing or not, but if they could sing, that was a plus, always good for extra tips.

In the 1930s, New Orleans was a musical wasteland: There was plenty of music, but it came primarily from piano bars, white Dixieland performers that were booked in the posh venues, big bands that traveled in and out of the city, and down-on-their-luck jazz players who had day jobs when the sun was up and low-paying gigs when the streetlights came on. Among those hit hard by the bad times was Henry Roeland Byrd, later known as Professor Longhair. Born in 1918 in Bogalusa and raised in New Orleans, he started working for tips at an early age as a street performer. He learned to play the piano, guitar, and drums, and spent the late 1920s and early 1930s moving in and out of bands, working with pretty much any group that would hire him.

When the going got tough during the Depression, he quit playing music and worked as a cook, making money on the side as a professional gambler. It wasn't until the late 1940s, following army service during World War II, that he started playing music again. Because jazz had fallen out of favor in the black community, replaced by rhythm & blues, he formed a group named Professor Longhair and His Shuffling Hungarians, and released his first record in 1949. The following year, he formed a new group called the Blues Jumpers and released his second record—"Bald Head," a song that went to number five on the rhythm & blues charts.

That was the musical world that Fats Domino entered in 1948, when he was hired as a pianist at the Hideaway Club. As a child he had been taught to play the piano by Harrison Verrett, a respected musician who had performed with numerous jazz notables in the 1920s. Verrett had married Fats' sister when Fats was four, and that had opened the door to Fats tagging along with him on his gigs. Verrett taught Fats to play by writing the names of the black keys on white tape and the names of the white keys on the keys themselves, which probably didn't make the owners of the pianos very happy.

About one year after Fats started at the Hideaway, he was approached by producer Dave Bartholomew about making a record. There was something different about Fats. He played a standard boogie and R&B run on the piano, nothing that really stood out; but his singing had a country flavor to it, a down-home twang that complemented his 224-pound shape, making him seem like the avuncular neighbor who was always asking you over for barbecue.

Bartholomew recorded eight songs during their first session, including their first release, "The Fat Man," a song that stayed in the Top 10 for three weeks, eventually earning Fats a Gold record and sales of over a million units. Fats couldn't believe his good fortune. One day he was a nobody, playing in a local dive and feeling lucky to have the job, and the next day he had a hit record. He came down hard from that high, though, when the next three releases from the session flopped.

Fats went out on the road to capitalize on his fame, and it was during that time that he developed the style, first appearing in the 1950s hit, "Every Night About This Time," that would stay with him for the rest of his career. Between 1956 and 1960, he recorded a series of hit singles—including "Blueberry Hill," "Walkin' to New Orleans," and "I Want to Walk You Home"—that established him as a star with rock 'n' roll audiences, even though the music he played wasn't, strictly speaking, rock 'n' roll.

What is interesting about Fats' career is the way he blended rhythm & blues with country to develop a distinct sound. Elvis Presley did the same thing, albeit with different results. In fact, Elvis may have had more in common with Fats than any of the other entertainers that preceded him. According to Fats, Elvis once visited him early in his career. "I liked him," he told *USA Today*. "I liked to hear him sing. He was just starting out, almost. He wasn't dressing up. Matter of fact, he had plain boots on. He wasn't wearing all those fancy clothes. He told me he flopped the first time he

Fats Domino early in his career. (Photofest)

came to Las Vegas. I loved his music. He could sing anything. And he was a nice fellow, shy. His face was so pretty, so soft."

Fats didn't have another hit after 1960, but he inspired another New Orleans piano player who did—Mac Rebennac, better known as Dr. John. Born in New Orleans in 1940, he was booked for his first gig when he was one year of age, when he was asked to appear in an Ivory Snow advertisement with his mother. When he was older, his father pointed him in the direction of music. His first memories of music occurred when he was "a little biddy child," when his father, who sold records for a living, invited people to their home to jam on the piano. "My father would give me all these 78s as a little child—the bebop, race records, also hillbilly records," he said. "I had a real mixture of music I grew up with. They asked me when I was a very young child to name my favorite songs, and I said, 'Gimmie [sic] That Old Time Religion,' and 'Blueberry Hill.'"

Later, when he was a teenager, he became friendly with Fats' guitarist Walter Nelson, who gave him advice on his guitar playing. He became skilled enough on guitar that he was able to get a job with the house band at Lincoln Beach, where all the top blues acts performed. That led to an offer to work as a sideman with Professor Longhair on the 1957 recording of "Mardi Gras in New Orleans."

During the 1960s, Dr. John toured with various bands and recorded several regional hits, but he didn't start making a name for himself until he moved to the West Coast and started working as a session musician with Phil Spector and Sonny and Cher. It was then that he recorded his first album, *Gris-Gris*, a mixture of voodoo blues and psychedelic attitude. For that album, he billed himself as Dr. John, The Day Tripper—a reference to the past (Professor Longhair), and a very popular Beatles' song ("Day Tripper"). He recorded a second album under that "West Coast" persona, but then decided to return to New Orleans to get back in touch with his roots. He dropped the "Day Tripper" addendum, shedding it the way he shed the psychedelic scene, and he immersed himself in his native rhythm & blues.

Dr. John began the 1970s by working with legendary New Orleans producer Allen Toussaint, a New Orleans native who, in addition to producing tracks for Irma Thomas and Art and Aaron Neville, had proved himself to be

a great composer and songwriter, especially on instrumentals such as "Java" and "Whipped Cream." It was around that time that Dr. John decided to front his band from behind a piano instead of a guitar. He was a student of music history, and he knew that New Orleans' biggest musical successes had played the trumpet or the piano. Under Toussaint's guidance,

Dr. John. *(Andy Earl for Virgin Records)*

he recorded a funky version of "Iko Iko," a New Orleans street chant, that was his first single to chart. He followed that success with several hits, including his biggest hit of all, "Right Place, Wrong Time."

Over the years, Dr. John has given a lot of thought to the way that New Orleans music compares to the other music of the Mojo Triangle, especially the heralded Memphis groove. "New Orleans relates to Memphis a lot in the way of funky, down-home music," he said. "But it also has a little Caribbean flavor because there is a lot of connection with Cuba or Jamaica or Brazil or whatever music has come out of the Caribbean, and that has been mixed with the parade music and funeral music and marching band music in such a way that a funkified version of that came out of it."

◆ ▲ ◆ ▲ ◆

The most perplexing thing about New Orleans music is that, while elements of country music have worked their way into the city's rhythm & blues, and even its jazz, New Orleans has not made a major contribution to country music. This is in spite of the fact that the State of Louisiana has managed to produce a number of country stars, including former Governor Jimmie Davis, famous for writing and recording the classic, "You Are My Sunshine;" Faron Young; Tim McGraw; and Hank Williams Jr., all of whom were born beyond the sacred perimeters of the Mojo Triangle. Despite their success— and their individual talents—none of them were music innovators, the quality that most distinguishes residents of the Triangle.

The only country music artist from New Orleans who has ever made a splash in Nashville is Lisa Angelle, a beautiful, dark-haired singer/songwriter who first went to Nashville in the early 1980s, while she was still a pre-law student at Southern University. She went door to door, literally, introducing herself to strangers who had made names for themselves in the music business. Mostly, they smiled and sent her somewhere else.

Things weren't going very well when she ducked into an anonymous office to use the telephone. Unknown to her, it was the headquarters for producer Tom Collins, who had major success with Barbara Mandrell and Ronnie Milsap. "He heard me and told them to show me in," she later recalled. "My first impression was that he was an ice-cream pusher because he had on bright green Izod pants and shirt. I didn't like his cigars, but we started talking and he was warm and very sweet and he talked to me for about an hour, explaining how Nashville worked. I left very confused because the way he looked very much contradicted the way he was."

When she returned to New Orleans, she felt discouraged, not so much because of her door-to-door failure, but because of her talk with Collins, a conversation that left her with a sinking feeling about the music industry. She resumed her classes and modeled part-time to make extra money, but she couldn't shake that burning desire to make music. "If you have music in you, if you wake up every morning singing and thinking of new songs, everything else goes out the window. If it is a burning thing inside you, you can't put it out."

One of the things that Collins had told her was that country music rarely made stars of singers who hadn't paid their dues. Not sure how to go about that—she was so straight that she neither smoked nor drank alcohol—she put together a mini-tour of the redneck joints along the Gulf coast, sitting in with country bands that played behind wire screens erected to keep the patrons' beer bottles from crashing into them.

When she returned to New Orleans, she wrote song after song, sending them off to publishers as soon as they were finished, usually getting negative responses by return mail. One of her songs landed on Tom Collins' desk. He remembered their conversation and gave her a call. He was impressed enough by her song that he signed her to a songwriting contract and got her a deal with EMI-America as a recording artist.

Lisa moved to Nashville filled with hope. Her first single, "Love—It's the Pitts," was released in 1985 (*Billboard* called it a "scorching debut"), followed by a second single titled, "Bring Back Love." Unfortunately, neither song was a hit, and EMI-America put plans for an album on the back burner until they felt they had a hit single, a decision that disappointed Lisa but did not discourage her. "I don't want to be a fad," she said at the time. "I may take longer developing because I don't want to fizzle. I want to be around for a lot of years."

Lisa wrote more songs and then packed up her bags and went to Muscle Shoals, where she recorded an album's worth of new material, not all of it country. One song, "Sex Jag," was a deep-groove rhythm & blues number that showed she was struggling with her puritanical upbringing. (Her father was a famous New Orleans DJ and a part-time preacher.) She gave EMI-America the country songs and went home to wait for their answer. She waited...and waited...and waited. They liked the album very much, but they didn't hear a hit single, so they postponed making a decision so long that her contract eventually ran out and she packed up and moved to Los Angeles.

Frustrated by her inability to get her career off the ground, she started writing songs for other established artists. She wrote "I Saw the Light" for Wynonna, a Number One hit; and followed that with other hits for Trisha Yearwood, Kathy Mattea, and Tanya Tucker. A successful songwriter, she returned to Nashville to give her own career a second chance. She signed with DreamWorks Records and re-invented herself as a more worldly woman, someone who understood the valleys and peaks of life.

Titled *Twisted*, the album was filled with songs she wrote herself or co-wrote with renowned guitarist/producer Andrew Gold. The first release, "I Wear Your Love," was a taunting swamp song that injected her New Orleans roots into a traditional country framework. The accompanying video had her seductively walking through a marsh, at one point holding a rather large snake. When he saw the video, a writer for the Nashville Tennessean playfully dubbed Lisa "Shania with snakes."

Lisa Angelle, circa 1999.
(Tony Baker for DreamWorks)

Unfortunately, "I Wear Your Love" faltered on the charts, delaying the release of the album. By the time it was released, the promotions department seemed to run out of energy, throwing Lisa back into the same familiar dark hole. The problem with the album, some critics felt, was that it was too innovative, giving country audiences more than they could digest in a single sitting.

Lisa was not discouraged. She had been there, done that, and she had no intention of backing down from doing it yet again. "No matter what happens, I'm not going anywhere," she told *Country Weekly*. "I'll stick it out, because, like my grandmother told me, 'God doesn't make junk.' If he puts a gift in you, you don't quit.'"

◆ ▲ ◆ ▲ ◆

The success that Fats Domino had in the 1950s with rhythm & blues had a profound impact on African-American jazz musicians, for it convinced them that the glory days of jazz were over. They abandoned the genre in droves, allowing the white Dixieland groups to dominate the New Orleans jazz scene with a more sanitized version of jazz that put a focus on new arrangements of old standards, such as "When the Saints Come Marching In," W.C. Handy's "Beale Street Blues," and Kid Ory's "Muskrat Ramble."

One of the most successful white groups was The Dukes of Dixieland, which sometimes featured a clarinetist named Pete Fountain. Improvisation was not the group's forte; rather, it excelled at playing high-energy versions of music that was already popular. In the late 1950s, Fountain left New Orleans to join Lawrence Welk's television band, a move that made him an instant celebrity. When he returned to New Orleans in 1959, city officials declared "Pete Fountain Day," a celebration that ended with a concert at Municipal Auditorium. The performance was later released as an album titled *Pete Fountain Day: In New Orleans*.

Fountain opened a jazz club in the French Quarter and continued to perform into the new century, thus providing New Orleans with an internationally known venue for Dixieland. Complementing Fountain's efforts was a trumpet man named Al Hirt, who at six-foot-six and over three hundred pounds, gave the music a larger-than-life image. Like Fountain, Hirt was born in New Orleans. His father was a police officer who encouraged his son to learn to play the trumpet. Hirt attended the Cincinnati Conservatory of Music from 1940 to 1943, then landed jobs with a succession of big bands, including those fronted by Tommy Dorsey and Benny Goodman. In 1950, he returned to New Orleans, where he started his own band and performed in a combo with Fountain.

Hirt's big break came in 1960, when he signed a recording contract with RCA Records. Throughout the 1960s, he released a series of albums—*Greatest Horn, Bourbon Street*, and *He's the King*—that made him a popular television guest, dazzling viewers with his extraordinary technical skill on the trumpet. Jazz purists often derided him for not performing improvisational jazz, but Miles Davis, not known for complimenting other horn players, came to Hirt's defense in a *Playboy* interview, saying, "Hell, that cat down in New Orleans, Al Hirt, he blows his ass off, too!" Improvisational jazz was simply not what Hirt wanted to play.

Hirt had several pop hits in the 1960s, including "Cotton Candy" and "Java," which earned him a Grammy, and he went on to record more than fifty albums. Throughout it all, the debate raged over whether he was a jazz or pop musician. Hirt resolved the debate in 1984 with an interview with the *New York Times*: "I'm a pop commercial musician. "I'm not a jazz trumpet, and never was a jazz trumpet. When I played in big bands for Tommy Dorsey and Jimmy Dorsey and Ray McKinley and Horace Heidt, I played first trumpet. I led the trumpet section. I never played jazz or improvised." Like Fountain, Hirt opened a popular nightclub in the French Quarter, which he continued to run until 1983, defining New Orleans Dixieland with his friend Fountain. Hirt died in 1999 of liver failure

New Orleans jazz, improvisational or otherwise, might have died in the 1980s if it were not for the Ellis Marsalis family. Ellis, a respected jazz pianist and teacher, fathered three sons who made it their life's work to recover and then promote the type of improvisational jazz that had largely vanished from the city that invented it. Of the three sons—Delfeo, Branford (best known for his stint as the bandleader for television's "The Tonight Show with Jay Leno"), and Wynton—it was Wynton who had the greatest impact. Born in New Orleans in 1971, he did not study music seriously until he was twelve years of age, despite having received his first trumpet at the age of six—a gift from Al Hirt, with whom his father sometimes performed—but once he got started, Wynton proved himself to be a talented instrumentalist.

While still a teenager, he joined Art Blakey's Jazz Messengers, and by age nineteen, he had signed a contract with CBS Records, beginning a recording career in both jazz and classical music that allowed him to become the first recording artist to ever receive Grammys for both classical and jazz recordings in the same year. His recordings include concert music for trumpet from the Classical and Romantic periods, and jazz recordings, the depth of which can be gleaned from their titles: *Soul Gestures in Southern Blue* (a three-volume set that includes *Levee Low Moan, Uptown Ruler,* and *Thick in the South*), *The Resolution of Romance* and *Intimacy Calling.*

Like Al Hirt, Wynton Marsalis is a virtuoso performer who has amazing dexterity with his instrument, but, unlike Hirt, Wynton revels in improvisation and celebrates the history of jazz. This dedication earned him the Pulitzer Prize for Music in 1997, for his oratorio, *Blood in the Fields*, making him the first jazz musician to win the award. The award put Wynton in the same artistic category as Eudora Welty and Tennessee Williams, and one of his heroes, William Faulkner. "I really like William Faulkner," Wynton once told an interviewer. "He's from the South; just the poetry of his language and the type of people he is describing—it's like people that I knew. I like his writing, and I like [Ernest] Hemingway, too, for the short sentences. Just the style. It's like the Lester Young style in jazz, whereas William Faulkner, that style is more like Art Tatum, or Coltrane, like real virtuosic runs, or just long two-hour sentences."

Like Faulkner, Welty, Tennessee Williams, Elvis Presley, Louis Armstrong, Robert Johnson, and the other innovators from the Mojo Triangle, Wynton's genius lies in his ability to understand his history, and his willingness to feel the power of the land, attributes that have made him the target of small-minded critics outside the Triangle. Perplexed by his genius, critics have called him pompous, a pseudo intellectual—a musician who thinks too much for his own good. That annoys Wynton, but it hasn't stopped him from studying music as a complicated, historical force that has significance beyond its popular, regional appeal for dancing and socialization.

"History is the playing field," Wynton said in an interview for *Jazz: A History of America's Music*. "That's true in all the arts. Shakespeare's dealing with themes that existed long before Shakespeare. Picasso used to say he could bring to life forms of art that had been dead for years—Sumerian art, Etruscan art. He could take these forms and bring them back to life and give them another flavor or feeling. That's the question of art; that's the fun of it. Do you want to play with the whole history of humanity? Or do you just want to play with the last ten years?"

Wynton's understanding of the history of music, mythical as well as actual, has been crucial to the development of his art. More so than any artist before him, he has come to terms with the power that is inherent in music, especially as it relates to past events. Triangles have been associated with mysterious power since ancient times, and it is no different with the Mojo Triangle, for it is the source of America's greatest music and literature. And although Wynton has never had access to the theories present in this book, he has sensed them, anticipated them the way a great musician anticipates an upcoming time or key change. He is guided by instinct, which is the thesis of this book—that great art comes from a mixture of genetics and shared past, an accumulation of wisdom that is trans-generational. It is what Wynton meant when he said, "The feeling of jazz is like the feeling you get going into your favorite grandmother's house. You know there's all kind of things in there that you might not recognize, but it's accumulated wisdom. The whole feeling of the house is warm. And it's a familiar place. You've been there before, and then when you sit down to that table to eat—well, everything is laid out for you." That's a sentiment that Faulkner, Elvis, Jimmie Rodgers, Howlin' Wolf, Muddy Waters, B.B. King, Welty, Louis and Lil Armstrong—all the great ones—would understand without explanation.

◆ ▲ ◆ ▲ ◆

Overlapping the success of the Marsalis family in the 1980s and 1990s was another New Orleans African-American family, the Neville Brothers: Arthur, Charles, Aaron, and Cyri. Before the brothers joined forces as an official group in 1977, Aaron had two hits as a solo artist, "Over You" (1960) and "Tell It Like It Is" (1966), and Art recorded several regional hits. Working together, the brothers recorded a series of successful albums, beginning with *The Neville Brothers* and continuing into the 1990s with *Yellow Moon, Brothers' Keeper,* and *Family Groove.*

At the same time that the Neville Brothers were establishing themselves as a group, Aaron pursued a solo career, beginning with a 1989 country duet with Linda Ronstadt titled "Don't Know Much," which won a Grammy in 1990. Incredibly, the Neville Brothers also won a Grammy that night in the Best Pop Instrumental category, for "Healing Chant."

As a result of their success with "Don't' Know Much," Ronstadt produced a solo album of Aaron's vocals titled *Warm Your Heart*—and they recorded a second duet, "All My Life," which won a Grammy the following year. Aaron's second Ronstadt-produced album, *The Grand Tour,* was also nominated for a Grammy. Aaron tried to stay true to his brothers—and to their soulful brand of rhythm and blues—but the opportunities for solo work kept coming his way. Ironically, the further Aaron went into a solo career, the further he went into country music.

In 1993, MCA Records put together a concept album titled *Rhythm Country & Blues,* which combined the talents of country and rhythm & blues stars. Aaron sang a duet with Trisha Yearwood, "I Fall to Pieces," which became a bestseller, and in 1994 the song was nominated for Vocal Event of the Year by the Country Music Association. By the end of the 1990s, it became apparent to Aaron that he couldn't live in both worlds, but by then it was too late for him to be a star in either world, causing him to recede in the public consciousness to the point where neither world existed. Music is a gambler's game—Aaron rolled the dice and lost.

By 2000, New Orleans music was headed in other directions with the "new" music aimed more toward white pop audiences. Harry Connick, Jr. came into the world with a certain amount of public recognition, for when he was born in 1967 in New Orleans his father, Harry, was the District Attorney for New Orleans, and his mother, Anita, was a respected judge. In addition to their law careers, Harry and Anita owned a record store and filled young Harry's life with music, so much so that by the age of three, he was playing piano and performing publicly at the age of six.

When Harry was thirteen, his mother died of ovarian cancer, an event that sent him even deeper into music. Soon he was performing in the French Quarter and recording with local jazz bands. Encouraged by his father, he attended the New Orleans Center for the Creative Arts, where he learned from Ellis Marsalis and others. That led him to New York's Hunter College and the Manhattan School of Music. By the age of twenty, he had a recording contract with Columbia Records; the label execs were impressed by his mature, big-band-era sound and piano style. A self-titled instrumental album was released in 1987, and that was quickly followed by a vocal album, *20*, which displayed his skills as a crooner.

Hollywood movie producer Rob Reiner was so taken by his retro sound that he signed twenty-year-old Harry to compose a soundtrack for *When Harry Met Sally*, a romantic comedy starring Meg Ryan and Billy Crystal. The movie was a box-office success, and the soundtrack went double Platinum with songs such as "It Had to Be You." As a result, Harry became a star while still in his early twenties.

When he was twenty-two, he landed an acting role in 1990's World War II film, *Memphis Belle*, and he has since appeared in a series of films, including *Hope Floats* (with Sandra Bullock), and a thriller, *Copycat*. Throughout the 1990s, he continued to perform at sold-out jazz venues and to make million-selling albums, but by the 2000s he had cooled somewhat, focusing more on movies and television—where he had a recurring role on the sitcom "Will & Grace"—than on breaking new ground in his music career.

By the end of the 1990s, it was clear that the New Millennium belonged to teen sensation Britney Spears, a pop vocalist who displayed the most charisma and audience appeal of any performer since Louis Armstrong and Elvis Presley. Born in Kentwood, Louisiana, just north of New Orleans—and educated, in part, in McComb, Mississippi—Britney began her career by going to New York to study at the Off-Broadway Dance Center and at the Professional Arts School. While in New York, she landed a job as the understudy for Laura Bundy in *Ruthless*, a play based on the film *The Bad Seed*. After a year of being the understudy, she was given the role, at age eleven, when Bundy left the production to pursue other interests. Britney's promotion meant that the understudy's job had to be filled by another actor, Natalie Portman, who went on to fame as Queen Amidala in the *Star Wars* trilogy.

Britney later dropped out of the play when she learned she had been accepted by the "Mickey Mouse Club," a major ambition at that point in her life. After two years as a Mouseketeer, she made an effort to land a recording contract. The seventeen-year-old was signed by Jive Records, which paired her with Swedish producer Max Martin, who previously had scored hits with the Backstreet Boys and Ace of Base. The album that resulted from that collaboration was *Baby One More Time*, released in 1999 just weeks before Britney's eighteenth birthday. Britney appeared in the video as a much younger girl, wearing a Catholic-school mini-skirt and an unbuttoned white shirt over a black bra. The song was an instant hit, propelling the album to sales of over ten million units.

In 2000, Britney released her second album, *Oops!...I Did It Again*. By then, she was the undisputed Queen of American Pop—a feat she managed by falling back on the vehicle that gave Elvis his start, sex appeal. She pushed the envelope with her videos, making each new release more daring than the last, and she posed for a series of provocative photographs in *Rolling Stone*, all designed to focus attention on her physical attributes. An *Entertainment Weekly* writer compared her to Mick Jagger, then qualified that by writing, "Before enraged Stones fans write in, it should be stated that Spears is not the modern equivalent of Mick and Co. But her barely hidden lasciviousness is; she's akin to the first girl in elementary school to wear makeup and flirt.

That demeanor is heard in her horny grunts in 'Satsifaction'...and throughout the best parts of *Oops!...I Did It Again* [and] amounts to nothing so much as a jailbait manifesto, with Spears admitting to leading a boy on and confessing she's 'not that innocent.'"

As if to prove that her sexuality was not merely a video creation, Britney began a very public affair with Memphis-born Justin Timberlake and then broke it off, to the horror of her fans. By 2003—critics called it her "wild year—she seemed desperate to cast off her teen image and redefine herself as an adult. She posed for more provocative photographs for *Rolling Stone*, and she startled viewers of the Video Music Awards by kissing 1980s star Madonna on the mouth.

Britney Spears at the 2002 American Music Awards. (Photofest)

Toward the end of 2003, Britney released her fourth album, *In the Zone*. It sold 609,000 units the first week and debuted at Number One on the pop charts, but by the start of 2004 she seemed more intent on self-destructing than in promoting her album. Early on the morning of January 3, 2004, while in Las Vegas, Britney and her childhood friend Jason Allen Alexander decided to get married after watching *The Texas Chainsaw Massacre* in their ten-thousand-dollar-a-night suite at the Palms Casino Hotel. Two days later, they asked a judge to annul the marriage on the grounds that they did not "know each other's likes and dislikes."

By 2004, Britney's fans had a difficult time separating the thrills of her music from the frills of her private life—and so, apparently, did Britney, who sometimes seemed to go out of her way to focus attention away from her music (being photographed in a tattoo parlor getting needle work done "down there" is an example). The criticism she has received for her off-stage antics may be justified, but it is helpful to remember that Louis Armstrong and Elvis Presley went through the same sort of fiery media baptism. Their music was often relegated to the back burner when they generated scandalous headlines exposing their sexual exploits and illegal drug use. Whatever else she does with her life, Britney has earned, by virtue of her enormous popularity and her willingness to ignore her critics—especially those that suggest that she should act more like a "lady,"—a memorable place in Mojo Triangle history.

7 MUSCLE SHOALS
▼ When a Man Loves a Woman

Roughly only six miles apart, Muscle Shoals (population 9,611), Florence (population 36,426) and Sheffield (population 10,380) form a tightly knit community on the banks of the Tennessee River in a picturesque area in the northwest corner of Alabama. They are an hour's drive from the nearest interstate highway, but only a twenty-minute drive from the Natchez Trace, which slices through the western tip of Alabama. Taken together, the three towns are known to the international musical community simply as Muscle Shoals.

The first white settlement in that area was at Colbert's Ferry, where Trace travelers crossed the Tennessee River by ferry. (Today there is an expansive concrete bridge that seems to go on forever.) George Colbert secured the crossing in the early 1800s, when the territory belonged to the Chickasaw. The fact that his mother was a Chickasaw worked to his advantage with tribal leaders, who allowed him to live there and operate a ferry across the river for all travelers, white and Indian.

A crafty negotiator, Colbert persuaded the United States Army to construct buildings for his private use, including stables and a kitchen, at no cost to him, and to build him a new ferryboat, all of which appealed to the Army because troops crossed the river regularly on trips from Nashville to New Orleans. His stand, as inns were then called, charged exorbitant rates (a quart of whisky that sold for a quarter in Natchez sold for one dollar at the crossing) and made him an unpopular figure on the frontier. R. J. Meigs visited the stand in 1806 and later wrote about Colbert, describing him as "extremely mercenary," a man who "miscalculates his importance, and when not awed by the presence of the officers of the government takes upon himself airs." That assessment of Colbert was incorrect in at least one aspect: He reportedly once charged Andrew Jackson seventy-five thousand dollars to ferry his troops across the river, a price that reflected more disdain than awe. Colbert was a hard-nosed capitalist, and his business tactics set a standard for free enterprise that spread to the rest of the country and exists to this day, especially in financial dealings involving the government.

Later, Colbert was instrumental in negotiating treaties with the

Chickasaw. In the beginning, the treaties involved small tracts of land that could be opened up for white settlement. Later, it involved the acquisition of more than five million acres of land in Tennessee. The Chickasaw trusted Colbert because of his mother. The government trusted him to say or do whatever it took to get the Indians off their land. In the end, the government got the land, the Chickasaw were relocated across the Mississippi River, and Colbert got forty-five hundred dollars cash and a tract of land north of the Tennessee River that was his to keep or sell for profit.

White settlers poured into the area after that, some of them drifting east to the Muscle Shoals area, where they farmed and built businesses that catered to travelers on the Tennessee River. There were never any plantations there that matched those of the Mississippi Delta, simply because the land was not as fertile, but a small number of black slaves were imported, presumably to help clear the land and erect permanent buildings.

After the Civil War, during Reconstruction, many of the blacks left, though some remained to try their hand at farming. Muscle Shoals differs from the other key areas of the Mojo Triangle in that the statistics on race are reversed. Where many of the towns in the Mississippi Delta were 70% to 80% black, the Muscle Shoals area was 80% to 90% white, a distinction that perhaps contributed to the rise of nearby Tuscumbia as a national headquarters for the Ku Klux Klan. The KKK rarely established a visible presence in highly populated black areas, presumably because klansmen would have been so outnumbered by blacks.

"Where the Tennessee River, like a silver snake, winds her way through the red clay hills of Alabama, sits high on these hills my home town, Florence," W.C. Handy wrote in his autobiography. "Here I came into the world, as my parents often told, 'squalling for six months straight' from the six-months colic. They used to place the date of some particular event as 'so many years before, or so many years after surrender.' This, of course, referred to Lee's surrender to Grant, which resulted in the emancipation of my race. I began exercising my vocal organs 'eight years after surrender;' to be exact, November 16, 1873." It is incredible to think that the "Father of the Blues," the same man who revolutionized Twentieth Century American pop culture—and provided blacks with a vehicle that contributed more to racial integration than all the laws and Supreme Court judgments combined—was born in a humble log cabin only eight years after the Civil War, the son of former slaves.

Handy's grandfather, William Wise Handy, wound up in the Muscle Shoals area after he and his two brothers made a break for freedom from their slave masters in the East. One brother made it to safety in Canada, and the other brother found safe refuge elsewhere. Only William was captured and re-sold into slavery to Alabama landowners. After the Civil War, he became a methodist minister and built the first African-American church in Florence, making him the first black landowner in town.

Handy's father, Charles B. Handy, like his father before him, was also a pastor, a calling that placed him in frequent contact with persons of both races. One day, he was conversing with a local banker who had recently traveled to Nashville, where he came into contact with blacks of wealth and culture. Perplexed, he asked Handy why that was not the case in their small community. "In a community of cultured white folks, there will be found a similar group of colored people," Handy answered. "But in any place where backward whites predominate, there will always be found a group of backward and uncultured colored people." It was an astute observation: Another way of saying, in language peculiar to the post-war generation, that uneducated blacks were the sole creation of ignorant, white rednecks and not part of God's plan.

Growing up in Florence, W.C. Handy worked at a variety of jobs—picking berries, working as a water boy at a rock quarry, chopping and picking cotton, operating a printing press—but it was not until he was hired by the sheriff to work in the courthouse that he began to save enough money to buy the things that he needed. That two-dollar-a-day job was supplemented by a second job in another section of the courthouse, where the white Baptists met to hold services. Handy was hired by the church as their janitor.

While working for the Baptists, he heard a traveling trumpet player from Birmingham who regularly went to Florence to perform with the choir. It was then that Handy decided that what he wanted most in life was a trumpet, a feeling he later described as being "like falling in love." As the weeks went by, he realized that he would never save enough money to buy a trumpet. Like many a jilted lover, he decided to pursue his second choice—a guitar. Once he purchased the instrument, he ran home to show it to his parents, overflowing with excitement. Their reaction was not what he had expected. Outraged that he had purchased the "devil's plaything," they ordered him to return it to the store and exchange it for a dictionary, which he did. His father told him that he would rather see him dead than waste his life being a musician.

One day, toward the end of his term at the Florence District School for Negroes, where he sang in a choral group, he met a fiddle player from Memphis, who had stopped off in Florence to organize an orchestra. The man filled Handy's head with stories about Beale Street, tales that made him even more determined to purchase a trumpet. When the opportunity arose, he purchased a musical instrument—not the trumpet he desired, but the cornet that was available at the right price. He hid the instrument from his parents and took lessons from a circus bandleader, who taught at a local barbershop while the circus was temporarily stranded in town. Handy used what he learned from the bandleader and applied it to his experience in the choir, so that by the time he left school, he played his cornet well enough to join a traveling minstrel show.

Handy never returned to Florence to live, but he never forgot the life lessons that he learned there, the most important of which was that his past was commingled with the whites' past, shaped by the strongest force of all, the land itself. Handy saw much to admire in both white and black cultures, and he saw no reason why the best of both cultures should not be combined for better effect. It is the very sentiment that became the foundation for all the great innovations that have emerged from the Mojo Triangle.

◆　▲　◆　▲　◆

In 1923, about thirty years after W.C. Handy left Florence to find his way in the world, another music pioneer was born on the banks of the Tennessee River. Sam Phillips didn't have a lot in common with Handy—Phillips was white, and slavery had no meaning in his life whatsoever—but they walked the same streets, experienced the same cultural challenges, dreamed the same dream, and possessed the same vision that had been transplanted from Colbert's Ferry: Namely, that big things happen to people who take big chances.

Small Southern communities like Florence are propelled from decade to decade, not by news of the nation's greatest triumph, but by remembrances of events that took place on the land they inhabit. In the 1920s, Florence was insulated from the rest of the world; its history was not written onto the sides of pottery, as the Chickasaw had done, but passed by word of mouth, from generation to generation. George Colbert was a living force in Florence, long after his death. People who grew up there used his legend as a measure of their own accomplishment, and they repeated the stories of marauding Union troops as reminders of what could happen at the hands of strangers.

Sam was the youngest of eight children, and he was raised on a farm at a bend of the Tennessee River, where he worked in the cotton fields with his brothers and sisters, and whatever black laborers the family could afford to hire. "I never did see white people singing a lot when they were chopping cotton," he told Robert Palmer. "But the odd part about it is, I never heard a black man that couldn't sing *good*. Even off key, it had a spontaneity about it that would grab my ear."

As a youngster, Sam was quite taken by a blind black man named Silas Paine, who lived on their farm. At the time, Paine was dying of syphilis, but he did what work he could do around the farm and he spent time with Sam, singing folk songs to him. One song in particular stuck in Sam's memory, a song about a cow.

Perhaps because of that, Sam developed a love of black music. One day, on his way home from a Baptist church (his family was Methodist, but Sam liked the Baptist sermons better), he passed by a black church and heard the uplifting music, joyful and full of promise, that overflowed from the church onto the road, and he wondered why the music in his church did not reach such heights. Two of the most potent remembrances he carried from childhood were Silas' songs and the sound of the Baptist music he heard on the way home from the Methodist church.

Sam attended school during the Great Depression. Education in a small farming community like Florence is a tug-of-war, in the best of times, between a family's needs and the community's need to produce successful citizens, but during hard times schools tended to give families lots of slack. Teachers were expected to teach their students reading, writing, and arith-metic, but not fill their heads with impossible dreams, because the short-term survival of the community depended on the survival of the farms.

Sam dreamed anyway, not so much about attaining wealth as about music—and even then it wasn't about making music so much as it was about being around it. When he entered Coffee High School, he joined the marching band, playing first drums and then sousaphone, and demonstrated enough organizational ability to become band captain. Later, he started up a dance band and talked the band director into allowing him to conduct a benefit concert where parents were asked to contribute money for musical instruments for some of the poorer students.

Everything that Sam did as a teen suggested that he might want to pursue a career in music. However, the dream that pulled at him the hardest was actually a recurring fantasy that he would become a crusading lawyer, someone who would correct all the ills of the world. That dream—and his participation in the high school band—came to an abrupt end during his senior year with the sudden death of his father, a tragedy that made it necessary for the children to support their mother and their deaf-mute aunt. Although there were eight siblings, the oldest brother had joined the Marines, so Sam had no choice but to quit school and help work the family farm.

Sam soon realized that he could help the family more by getting an outside job, so he applied for work at Muscle Shoals radio station WLAY. The station manager hired him, based on his recollections of the way Sam had announced songs for his high school band. With no experience—and very little training to speak of—Sam started work as a DJ, spinning gospel and country records. He really didn't have the voice for it, and he displayed a tendency to ramble when he spoke between records, but he more than made up for those shortcomings with wide-eyed enthusiasm.

Two years after his father's death, in 1942, he married a local girl named Rebecca Burns, and soon began a family with her. After his stint at WLAY, he moved to a radio station in Decatur, Alabama, and from there to radio station WLAC in Nashville, where he stayed until 1945, at which point he packed up his wife and infant son and moved to Memphis, where he started work at radio station WREC.

Sam's timing could not have been better, proof of the old adage that success often depends on being in the right place at the right time. The best thing that post-World War II Memphis had going for it was a lively radio market. Big bands performed regularly at the top floor of the Peabody Hotel, where WREC was located, and Sam's first assignment was to engineer live broadcasts of those performances. From the time that Sam arrived in Memphis, until the time he left WREC to open Memphis Recording Service—a period of five years—the city's radio scene exploded.

In 1957, the owners of radio station WDIA, two white men named Bert Ferguson and John Pepper, converted a general-format radio station that targeted white listeners to an all-black format. What did they have to lose? WDIA was losing money in a city where half the potential listeners were not being served. If they had done that and nothing more, they would have radically changed Memphis, but they didn't stop there; they decided to staff the radio station entirely with black personnel—something that no radio station had ever done. They ended up radically changing American broadcasting.

Memphis blacks were amazed that white owners would turn a radio station over to them, and they repaid that gesture by supporting the station's sponsors with their shopping dollars. Equally amazed were the people who worked at the station. "Bert Ferguson had rules that were different from any other place I had ever gone," said B.B. King. "At the station, you gave honor to whom honor was due. You didn't have to say 'yes sir' or 'yes ma'am,' simply because a person was white....You felt like you were at home. That's the way I felt at WDIA. It wasn't intimidating—it was like a college of learning for me."

Sam Phillips was mesmerized by the station. It took him back to the days when, growing up near Florence, he listened to black music in the fields and in the churches. The music didn't have to be broadcast to be heard. It rose up from the earth: One only had to stand in the right place at the right time to catch an earful. When the time came for Sam to start up his recording studio, it made sense that two of his first clients were B.B. King and Rufus Thomas, two very popular WDIA announcers.

Incredibly, at the same time that WDIA was making music history, so was radio station WHBQ, which hired an announcer named Dewey Phillips (no relation to Sam). Dewey had no radio experience—his claim to fame at that point was taking over the intercom in Grant's dime store so that he could play records for startled customers—but he had a natural exuberance that emanated from him like radiation. WHBQ turned its most popular program, "Red, Hot and Blue," over to him, primarily because of his personality, but mostly because that was the only way they could stop him from pestering them. The show became even more popular with Dewey at the helm, and it was expanded from fifteen minutes a day to three hours a day. It was the only radio show in Memphis that attracted equal numbers of white and black listeners, and that was because neither race could really tell what color skin he had (he was white). By the time Sam Phillips started up Sun Records, Dewey was Memphis' equivalent of Howard Stern, which is to say that he was one of the first "shock jocks" in America.

When Sam wasn't engineering a show for WREC, he listened to Dewey Phillips, B.B. King, Howlin' Wolf, Rufus Thomas, Sonny Boy Williamson, and others, an astonishing collection of DJs that kept the streets of Memphis sizzling. He was 150 miles away from Florence, but the tingle he got from Memphis radio was the same tingle he felt walking past black churches as a youth.

◆ ▲ ◆ ▲ ◆

By the time Sam Phillips left the Muscle Shoals area, the economy had already begun to change, beginning with the 1941 arrival of a massive Reynolds Aluminum plant that offered residents, for the first time in their history, an alternative to farming and river-related occupations. Industry changed the economy, but it didn't change the social fabric of the community. The two counties in which Muscle Shoals, Sheffield, and Florence were located, Lauderdale and Colbert, continued to wave a Bible Belt banner, which meant that they remained "dry" when it came to the sale of alcohol.

It would be historically gratifying to say that Sam Phillips left an entertainment void in Muscle Shoals when he departed that was never filled, but that would be inaccurate, because he never had a major influence on the community until after he created a national sensation by discovering Elvis Presley. However, it would be correct to say that there was an entertainment void before and after Sam Phillips, simply because there are few entertainment opportunities in dry counties.

The first musical group that anyone can remember coming out of Muscle Shoals was the Johnson Brothers, a country-western duet made up of Ray and Dexter Johnson. These brothers worked as full-time musicians, beginning in the late 1930s and continuing through the 1950s. Playing the type of music that Bob Wills and Gene Autry made popular—"Back in the Saddle Again," for example—they built up a radio network of about ten stations, offering a regularly scheduled, half-hour program during which they played requests that were mailed in to them.

Ray Johnson's son, Jimmy Johnson, was born in 1943, during the heyday of the Johnson Brothers, but it wasn't until he was five or six years old that he realized that his father was a professional guitarist. That was partly because his mother also played guitar, and he naturally assumed that all parents sat around the house playing guitars. As Jimmy grew older, he became interested in the trumpet, and he joined the junior high band so that he could learn to play. However, he soon tired of the trumpet and dropped out of the band when he entered high school, choosing instead to play football (students in those days were typically divided into two groups—those who went out for sports and those who played in the band—and it was seldom that anyone dared doing both).

It was not until 1958, when Chuck Berry's rousing hit "Johnny B. Goode" reached the airwaves, that fifteen-year-old Jimmy decided he wanted to play guitar. "I was dead-serious about the guitar when I started, but I never had any idea that it would be my life," said Johnson. "Pretty soon, it was the most important thing in my life. I was listening to Jimmy Reed, Bo Diddley, Chuck Berry—and the Ventures, when they first came on the scene...and then Ricky Nelson and James Burton."

Johnson's mention of Ricky Nelson revives the memory that there was an intense rivalry between Ricky and Elvis in the late 1950s...well, not so much a rivalry between the two singers as between their fans. It was culturally unacceptable in the South to be fans of both singers, so classrooms, Boy Scout troops, and Sunday school classes were all divided along Ricky-Elvis lines. The singer you chose determined your friends, affected your relationships with the opposite sex, and, in some instances, influenced your choice of a profession—silly stuff, but very important at a time when everyone was worried about nuclear annihilation and collecting suitable records for their bomb shelters. *I want to hear Elvis when the bombs start falling...no I want to hear Ricky!*

So, Jimmy chose Ricky and followed the "Be Bop Baby" road, one that eventually made a full circle, symbolically passing through Hollywood along the way, and led him back to the Mojo Triangle, to music that was right under his nose all along. "I loved the music that the black people were making," he explained. "Then some of them came to town at the community center. Bo Diddley came. As a matter of fact, Elvis came three times. For some reason, my parents allowed me to see Bo Diddley, but they kept me from going to see Elvis. They weren't into rock 'n' roll."

Jimmy's Uncle Dexter, the other half of the Johnson Brothers, lived up the street from him and often invited him to go with him to the National Guard armory, where square dances were held on weekends. Dexter played bass with various bands at the dances, and Jimmy took pride in his uncle's dexterity with his instrument. His interest in his uncle increased even more in 1951, when Dexter opened the first recording studio in Muscle Shoals. At that point, the entire Muscle Shoals music industry consisted of Dexter's studio and a music-publishing house named Spar Music, established by Tom Stafford, whose family owned the City Drugstore in Florence.

By 1956, Muscle Shoals had a second recording studio set up by James Joiner, who owned the local bus line (he cut his first recordings in the rear of the Florence bus station). Incredibly, he recorded a song called "A Fallen Star" with a local man, then watched with amazement as it made the Top 100, after being covered by Ferlin Husky. When word of that got out, song-writers flocked to Muscle Shoals in the hopes of selling their songs. Two of the first to arrive were Rick Hall from Hamilton, and Billy Sherrill from Campbell, Alabama, who rode into town on a bus. Joiner eventually signed them and placed their songs with artists such as Brenda Lee and Roy Orbison, establishing Hall and Sherrill as mainstream songwriters.

By the summer of 1959, Hall and Sherrill decided that they should end their relationship with Joiner and go into business for themselves. That was facilitated by Stafford, who invited them to join him at Spar Music; he put up the money for a recording studio that operated out of the room up over Stafford's parents' drugstore. They soundproofed their makeshift studio the best they could, using carpet pulled up from an abandoned movie theater and heavy drapes, and they started writing songs and recording demos for other songwriters and bands that dreamed of putting out a record.

By that time, Jimmy Johnson's uncle had shut down his studio, and Jimmy had joined a rock 'n' roll band named the Del Rays, a four-piece group that also included Norbert Putnam, Jimmy Ray Hunter, and Roger Hawkins, who liked to hang out at Spar to watch Hall while he worked. As a result, Hawkins arranged for the Del Rays to cut a record at Spar. "It wasn't something that we sold," said Jimmy, "but we had copies made and we played it ourselves."

By 1962, the relationship between Hall, Sherrill, and Stafford had soured, so Hall broke away and built a studio of his own, a twenty-by-seventy-foot cinderblock building that he named Fame Studio. The name wasn't hubris on Hall's part, but rather an acronym for Florence Alabama Music Enterprises. Jimmy Johnson was his first employee. "I got paid for working as Rick Hall's assistant," said Jimmy, who did everything from helping out with the engineering to typing to sweeping out the studio. "I didn't know then that I was going to do it forever. I was going to the University of North Alabama, so I don't think I planned on being a musician."

When he wasn't working at Fame, he was performing with the Del Rays. They were booked all over Alabama and Mississippi, but their best bookings were at the University of Mississippi in Oxford. Ole Miss had twenty-five fraternities and sororities at that time, and most booked bands at least once a week, while some fraternities such as Sigma Alpha Epsilon and Delta Kappa Epsilon booked bands twice a week. In the early Sixties, Ole Miss was one of the largest venues for bands in the country. Rufus Thomas once told this author that he and other rhythm & blues artists could not have survived without the bookings that came their way from the university. On any given night, Rufus Thomas might be at one fraternity and Booker T. and the MGs at another, or perhaps even jazz stylist Julie London, who once spent a memorable weekend at the Deke house. On weekends, students would wander from frat house to frat house, drinks in hand, sampling the best music that America had to offer. This author recalls that scene well, having played in three Ole Miss-based bands during that era: The Dynamics, the Strokers, and the Roadrunners.

The Del Rays performed at Ole Miss on a regular basis, partly because they knew every rhythm & blues song ever recorded, and partly because Jimmy Johnson was friends with an Ole Miss Pike, Tommy Couch, who was in charge of booking his fraternity's entertainment. Couch was from Tuscumbia, Alabama, a few miles from Muscle Shoals, so they spoke the same language. "When he paid me at the end of the night," Jimmy recalled, "I said, 'By the way Tommy if you ever want to make some extra money, I'd be glad for you to book us down here for ten percent.' And I could tell it set a little light off, but he didn't say too much. A few weeks later, I get this letter in the mail that said, 'Campus Attractions, Oxford, Mississippi.' I opened it up, and it went 'Hey Jimmy, I took your advice. By the way, do you know any good black bands up your way?' I hooked him up with James Richards and the Esquires—the lead singer was the undiscovered Percy Sledge. Pretty wild."

Rick Hall's Fame studio attracted a house band that was not so much a band as it was a collection of ships passing in the night—Dan Penn, a sixteen-year-old singer-songwriter-guitarist from Vernon, Alabama; Spooner Oldham, a piano player who started out with Hall at Spar, where he occasionally stood in as engineer; bassist Norbert Putnam, another veteran from Spar; and drummer Donnie Fritts, the self-styled rebel of the group, who cared more about writing songs than playing on sessions—all of them young, white, and hungry for something none of them could quite articulate.

The first hit out of Fame was Jimmy Hughes' "Steal Away," a gospel-tinged rhythm & blues number that Rick Hall released himself after every major record label turned it down. To promote it, Hall went on the road and visited every radio station in the South that could possibly be interested in playing the record. By the time he returned to Muscle Shoals the record was in the Top 20, an unqualified success.

Other successful records followed, including Joe Tex's "Hold What You've Got," but the type of monster hit that Hall needed to ensure his long-term success eluded him. Hall's obsession with success meant that he worked long days and nights, running one would-be superstar after another through his studio. This business approach meant that he didn't have time for the more mundane work assignments that studios take on—commercial jingles and demos for songwriters.

Watching Hall turn away clients was Quin Ivy, a popular local deejay at WLAY who had written songs for Hall ever since the days up over the drugstore. He suggested to Hall that it might be a good idea if he opened a studio to handle the overflow. That was fine with Hall since it would mean fewer annoying telephone calls to field; he graciously offered the services of guitarist Marlin Greene, who had been working with him at Fame in various capacities. Ivy, who was born in Oxford, Mississippi, had a good feel for music, so piecing together the studio he named Quinivy from used remnants, beginning with a console he purchased from his own station, was a labor of love for him. Of course, Ivy didn't just take referrals from Fame; he actively looked for new talent.

One of the first people he recorded was Percy Sledge, a hospital orderly by day at Colbert County Hospital and the lead singer of the Esquires on weekends. It was one of those situations in which everyone in town knew that Sledge sang in a band—those who didn't know and were unfortunate enough to be admitted to the hospital heard him sing in the hallways while he mopped the floor—but no one saw any potential in him to be a major star. It's not clear if Ivy thought he was a star, or simply someone fresh to work with, but he took him into his fledging studio and recorded a demo of a song called "When a Man Loves a Woman."

Muscle Shoals musicians and would-be record moguls were good students of the profession. They studied Nashville, and they especially studied Memphis, and they learned from Stax and American that making records was vastly different from playing in a nightclub, that the best way to record hit records was to put together a house band and require the singer to check his or her band at the door. That's the way it happened with Percy Sledge—he was invited into the studio, but not his band.

Jimmy Johnson was asked to engineer the session, which consisted of Spooner Oldham on organ (because the studio didn't have a piano), Roger Hawkins on drums, Junior Lowe on bass, and Marlin Greene on guitar. They brought in four people to sing background around the lead microphone and a horn section that was asked to play only whole notes. "A lot of the sound was accidental," Jimmy recalled. "We cut the tracks first with drums, bass, and organ. We had only one condenser microphone in the building, and that was the one we had on Percy. The drums had no booth, just a baffle. The first pass was just those three instruments and Percy, so I was using four inputs of the five on the console. I had to get the vocal on this big rotary knob as big as a hand, and you had to anticipate when he would hit hard notes because if you went one iota past zero, you were into distortion. It was like going ninety miles an hour around a curve in a jalopy and never getting out of the curve. We didn't know any better."

When they finished the session, they felt pretty good about it, though they didn't think it would prove to be the hit record they had hoped for. "I thought the record we did was pretty good, but I didn't think it would be the monster hit that it became," said Jimmy. "I don't think that many of the people that played on it realized how great it was."

When the session ended, Ivy took the tape to Rick Hall and played it for him. Hall asked him what he planned to do with it, and he said he thought he would send it to Atlantic Records' Jerry Wexler, primarily because of his success with black artists at Stax Records. Since Hall had already established contact with Wexler, he offered to send the tape to him, and that was fine with Ivy, who figured he needed all the help he could get.

Jerry Wexler was the stereotypical Northern Jew, at least in the minds of Southerners who seldom encountered Jews that did not look like them and think like them, as was the case with southern-born Jews. He was brash, prone to talking too loud—and supremely confident of his abilities. He was also a very good salesman, whether his pitch was directed toward wholesalers, retailers, studio owners, or would-be stars from the back roads of Alabama, Tennessee, and Louisiana. Of course, none of that would have mattered if he hadn't possessed a unique talent for sniffing out new talent. He was one of those guys who knew a hit record when he heard it; he wasn't interested in having someone convince him that it was a hit record—he had to feel it for himself.

When Wexler listened to "When a Man Loves a Woman," he knew that it was a hit, and for the same reasons that records from other black Atlantic artists such as Ray Charles were hits: It appealed to white, middle America. "Music can be funny sometimes," he told Joe Smith. "The things you think are black can actually be rooted in country. Chuck Berry is a good example of that. 'Maybellene' is really an update of an old country tune, 'Ida Red.' Listen to Chuck Berry sing. There's nothing black about his songs. He sounds like an American country person...His songs aren't black, they're mid-American country."

What Wexler heard in "When a Man Loves a Woman" was a song that fit his format for success. He called Rick Hall and told him so, then he called Ivy and worked out a deal in which Hall received a finders fee, payable in "points" (a percentage), and Ivy and Sledge received an advance and royalties on records sold (more points). It was then that the Cinderella story turned a bit wacky. Wexler told Ivy that he wanted him to re-do the horn parts because they sounded flat to him. He suggested that Ivy hire the Memphis Horns, who had made an art form out of playing accent notes. Happy to do that, Ivy re-cut the horn parts with the Memphis Horns and sent the new tape to Wexler. Incredibly, the old tape and the new tape were mishandled at Atlantic, and the old tape with the flat horns was sent to the pressing plant. That was the record that everyone heard on the radio, and the record that went to Number One in May 1966, giving Muscle Shoals its long-awaited, first monster hit. Everyone was embarrassed about the mistake, but record-buyers and critics were so enthralled by the song that no one ever mentioned the horns.

Jimmy Johnson had a blow-up with Quin Ivy around that time and left, partly because his name was left off the credits as engineer, an oversight that it took him twenty years to correct.

◆ ▲ ◆ ▲ ◆

One of the white bands that Jimmy Johnson told Campus Attractions about was the Mystics, a rhythm & blues group that quickly found favor with white college audiences in the South. Campus Attractions booked them all over Mississippi, but especially at Ole Miss. "It was the most fun I ever had," said bassist David Hood. "Prior to that, I was just a nerd. I worked in my father's tire store and went to school. I wasn't an athlete or a great student or popular. Jimmy was playing in the Del Rays, and I loved that, so I bought a guitar and never turned back."

Growing up in Sheffield, David had little contact with blacks or black music, at least not that he was aware of. His family lived on a lake about ten miles from town, so he didn't hang out with a lot of town people, and the music he listened to came from a radio station that played all types of music. "I listened to black music growing up, but I didn't know a lot of it was black," he said. "I never knew what was black and what was white. It was the new rock 'n' roll that my daddy hated and we loved. My daddy called it 'nigger music.' Back then, nigger was a word. I don't use it myself, other than in the context I'm using it now—and I would never allow that word to be used in my home—but back then, it was just a name that my daddy and others used [to identity anything black]."

When David was graduated from high school, one of the first things that he did was get married, a "crazy, dumb-ass thing to do, since I was eighteen and she was sixteen." That fall, he started college and joined the Mystics, while holding down a part-time job at his father's tire store. "We made a hundred dollars a man, every night on the weekends, and that was more money than I was making at the tire store. Back then, in the early 1960s, you were lucky if you made a hundred dollars a week."

David's run with the Mystics ended on May 14, 1966, at a nightclub in Tuscaloosa, when the band played its final gig. The following day, he reported to Quinivy Studio to work on his first recording session at union scale—the follow-up to Percy Sledge's "When a Man Loves a Woman." Junior Lowe, the original bassist, had decided that he wanted to switch to horn, and that left an opening for a bass player. "The reason I wanted to do it was so that I could stay in town and make music, and be there with my wife and child and work part-time at the tire store," David said. "I wasn't all that good, but I was eager.

I drove home from Tuscaloosa, and the next day did that session."

By that time, Percy Sledge had been making personal appearances and raking in more money that he had ever before seen. "When Percy came back, he had bright-colored suits and a Cadillac," David recalled. "We loved seeing it. We were touched by stardom. He never big-timed anybody. He's still a nice guy."

The song that Atlantic chose for a follow-up to "When a Man Loves a Woman," was "Warm and Tender Love." Unfortunately for everyone involved, the song never made the Top 20 and made Sledge look like a one-hit wonder. He rebounded two years later with "Take Time to Know Her," which peaked at Number Twelve on the national charts. Sledge never had another hit, but he did go on to have a successful career as a nightclub and concert performer, all based on that one monster hit.

It was not long after the Percy Sledge hit that Stax turned down Jerry Wexler's offer to record Aretha Franklin, and he took her to Muscle Shoals to record at Fame with Rick Hall. David Hood was invited to the session, but not as a bass player; he was asked to play trombone, an instrument he had played in his high school band. "They were going to get the Memphis Horns to play on it, but the guys were all busy and couldn't play on it, so Rick had to put together a horn section at the last minute," David said. "I was so thrilled. I was probably the only guy in town who knew who Aretha was. What I remember about it is sitting back with the horn guys, while they were cutting tracks, trying to work up parts. I remember Aretha sitting at the piano, playing and singing. I remember thinking, 'That's wonderful!'"

That night, after the first session had wrapped, Aretha, Jerry Wexler, Rick Hall, and Aretha's then-husband and manager, Ted White, went to the hotel to have a few drinks. Unknown to Hall, White was unhappy about the lack of black faces at the session. One thing led to another, and words were exchanged, escalating into an argument that ended in a fight between Hall and White. "Rick was kind of a smart ass, and back when he used to drink, he was a white redneck," recalled David Hood. "He worked with a lot of black people and never had problems, but this uppity black guy from Detroit wasn't having any of it...Nobody could tell you exactly what happened, because they probably were all drunk. But that was it—Aretha decided she wasn't going to record in Alabama, so they moved the session to New York. I thought that was going to be the end of my career. It was two or three years before I got to work with her again, this time playing bass."

Fame rebounded from the Aretha Franklin fiasco, and began a run of hits as impressive as anything coming out of Memphis or Nashville. Rick Hall had already scored big hits with Wilson Pickett—"Land of 1,000 Dances" and "Mustang Sally"—and he went on to record Clarence Carter's "Slip Away," but his studio personnel situation was in constant flux, with Dan Penn and Spooner Oldham going to Memphis to work with Chips Moman. Through trial and error, he finally put together a house band that he thought would stick for the duration: Jimmy Johnson on rhythm guitar, David Hood on bass, Roger Hawkins on drums, and Barry Beckett on keyboards. The lead guitarists changed with the artists being recorded; guitarist Eddie Hinton played on some sessions and Junior Lowe on others. An occasional lead picker was Duane Allman, who once persuaded Wilson Pickett to record his own version of the Beatles' "Hey Jude," which also was a big hit. Allman also worked on albums with Arthur Conley (*More Sweet Soul*) and Clarence Carter (*The Dynamic Clarence Carter*). When word spread about Allman's guitar technique, an offer came from Wexler and Phil Walden, who had managed Otis Redding until his death, to buy Allman's contract. Hall caved; he was not certain what to do with Allman, anyway, because Allman played a grittier style of guitar than he envisioned for Fame.

Not long after Allman left, Hall started negotiating with Capitol Records for a long-term recording deal. He felt he had the strongest rhythm section of any studio in the South, and he wanted to use the band as leverage with Capitol. Unknown to Hall, his house band was investigating other opportunities as his talks with Capitol continued.

"Rick had had quite a bit of success, and we had had a lot of success as a rhythm section on things that he really didn't have anything to do with," said David Hood. "He wanted to have a label deal with Capitol, and he wanted us to work exclusively on his projects, and he wants us to do it for $20,000 a year, guaranteed. By that time, we were making more money than that playing with other people, and enjoying playing with other people more than we enjoyed playing with him. So, when he wanted us to go exclusive, Jimmy [Johnson] and Roger [Hawkins] had been talking to Fred Beavis in Sheffield who had this little studio he wanted to get out of because he didn't know what to do with it. Jimmy and Roger had been doing this longer than Barry and I had, and they had a little money saved, so they said, 'Let's buy a studio and go into business for ourselves.' I remember the night they called. I didn't have any money. I was married and had a car payment. I said I wanted to do it, but I couldn't invest as much as they did. They invested like ten thousand each, and I invested a couple of thousand. Barry did the same, and we decided to buy the studio."

After they closed the deal, they went straight to Hall's office. He was glad to see them. The Capitol executive was there, eager to ink the deal. "Rick wanted us to sign, but we told him we weren't and that we had bought our own studio," said David Hood. "Boy, it was like we hit him with a pie full of shit or something. He said, 'Well, you'll never make it.' He was pissed off big time, and it was embarrassing to have it happen in front of the Capitol executive that he had been grooming."

Once that bit of unpleasantness was over, the new studio owners talked over possible names for their studio. "As a joke I said why don't we name it the Muscle Shoals Sound Studio?" said David. "Everyone laughed because no one had ever used that term. It was the Motown sound, the Memphis sound, whatever, but no one had ever said Muscle Shoals Sound, and it was a joke. To the people that live in Sheffield, Muscle Shoals is another town, just as Florence is another town. It was a joke and a jab at Rick because his studio is in Muscle Shoals. After we laughed at it, we decided it wasn't such a bad idea, so we named the studio Muscle Shoals Sound, and we became the Muscle Shoals Rhythm Section."

◆　▲　◆　▲　◆

The first major artist to come to Muscle Shoals Sound was, culturally speaking, both the most unlikely and the most likely: Cher. She was an unlikely artist to go to Muscle Shoals, where patriotism is equated with conservatism, because she had the reputation for being a 1960s hippie chick from the Left Coast, where conservatism is akin to satanic ritual. And she was a likely artist to visit Muscle Shoals because of her Native American heritage. Cher maintains that she is of Cherokee descent on her mother's side of the family; her genetic foundation would make her feel right at home on the ancient Chickasaw land upon which the studio was built.

If Cher was shocked when she saw the studio, she never let on, not even to ask why a studio named Muscle Shoals Sound was actually in Sheffield. Located

Cher outside Muscle Shoals Sound's original studio with David Hood (left, white shirt), Sonny Bono, and Jerry Wexler (center). Also in the photo: Jimmy Johnson, Tom Dowd, Roger Hawkins, and Barry Beckett. (David Hood)

at 3614 Jackson Highway, it was an ultra-plain, box-like building that bore no identification as to its purpose; it was the type of structure that farmers routinely build to house their equipment. "Everyone thinks that Atlantic Records bankrolled us," explained David Hood. "They didn't; they gave us the money to buy the eight-track tape player. Rick just had a four-track, and they said we needed the eight-track and they lent us the money to upgrade our equipment. But we paid them back by giving them a reduced rate. Union sessions are supposed to last three hours. We worked eight hours for the same rate. That was how we paid them back. They didn't bankroll us at all."

Jerry Wexler chose most of the songs for the session, which included a remake of the Otis Redding hit "(Sittin' on the) Dock of the Bay," written by Redding and Steve Cropper; and the Aretha Franklin hit, "Do Right Woman, Do Right Man," written by Chips Moman and Dan Penn. As if he were mixing some sort of illegal mojo hooch, to be savored in the dead of night under a full moon, Wexler also tossed in two country-leaning songs: "Just Enough to Keep Me Hangin' On" and "Please Don't Tell Me." Just to keep it interesting, he included Bob Dylan's "Lay Lady Lay." It's dangerous business to try to explain what Jerry Wexler was thinking at any given point in time, but the idea behind the album seems to have been to pair proven hits by other artists with an artist who had recorded hits, though not recently (her last solo Top 20 hit was 1966's "Bang Bang").

Never mind all that, though; the session went splendidly. "Cher was great; she was like a hippie, but rich," recalled David Hood. "Sonny was sort of a smart-ass, so we didn't care for him so much. I took Cher riding on my motorcycle. She was very easygoing, really easy to work with. We took about a week-and-a-half to record the album. I think Wexler got sick with walking pneumonia and had to go to a hospital, so it seems like we recorded in parts of two different weeks."

At the end of the session, Cher posed with the band for a photograph in front of the studio. Later, when the album was released, the band had two surprises. The first was that Atlantic used the photo on the album cover, and had titled the album *3614 Jackson Highway*. The second surprise was that an artist had placed type across the top of the building pictured in the photo that read "3614 Jackson Highway," thus insinuating that the address was plastered across the studio. When the studio owners saw the impressive album cover, they decided to have a sign made that looked exactly like the album jacket.

Cher's album didn't sell well, but the publicity that accompanied the album gave the studio invaluable exposure. Later that year, in December, Wexler knocked on the door with yet another surprise: The Rolling Stones, the rock world's elite. He didn't want to record the entire album at Muscle Shoals Sound, just enough songs to get things rolling. "They had no visa, no record, and they really wanted to record, and they were afraid to try it in New York, so no one knew whether they would be here for two days or more," said Jimmy Johnson. "They stayed at the Holiday Inn. During the day, Atlantic had their attorneys here, and the Stones had their attorneys. That's why Wexler was there and why he brought Ahmet Ertegun [head of Atlantic Records]. This was Atlantic's first release with the Stones."

The Stones decided to affiliate with Atlantic after their contract with British Decca had expired. The idea was to record under their own label, Rolling Stones Records, and have Atlantic be the distributor. In addition to the Stones and the lawyers and the Atlantic Records honchos from New York City, all checked into the Holiday Inn, there were two musical stowaways: Writer Stanley Booth, who was touring with the Stones in order to write a book about them (later published as *The True Adventures of the Rolling Stones*); and his friend Jim Dickinson, from Memphis.

When they arrived at the Muscle Shoals airport, the entourage was greeted by local fans who had gathered to give the band a proper welcome. "Just to start things off right in Alabama," Booth wrote, "Mick walked up in full view of the watching rednecks and kissed Keith sweetly on the cheek. 'How are you babe?'" to which Keith, who had arrived earlier, answered: 'All right. We been drivin' around lookin' at the woods this mornin', it's beautiful around here.'"

At the time the Stones arrived, the studio had two different sessions booked. During the day, from ten until five, they recorded an album with a black singer named R. B. Greeves; then from six o'clock on, they worked with the Rolling Stones, who lived up to their reputation in one sense (musically), but not in another. "They were stone sober, and I didn't expect that—and I was highly impressed," said Jimmy. "It would start off each day, just kind of bedlam, and then move from there to Keith coming up with the guitar riff. Jagger pretty much had the hook, and everything else was done. Jagger was an incredibly gifted lyricist and melody writer. Brian [Jones] had just died the year before, and they had gone for a year without recording. They brought in Mick Taylor [to replace Brian], and he was as nervous as a cat on a hot tin roof. I don't think I heard him say three words the entire time he was there. He was just working from the shoulders down, you know, and just happy to be there. But he played well. Most all of the hit licks were by Keith."

Mick Jagger recording "Brown Sugar" at Muscle Shoals Sound. (David Hood)

The Stones planned to record two songs, "Brown Sugar" and "Wild Horses," just enough to fire all the album's cylinders, and then move on to New York. To hear the participants talk, there were many memorable moments at what turned out to be a three-day session, but one of the best was a serendipitous event that gave Jim Dickinson a start on what turned out to be a fine music career, and gave the album a sound that is still talked about today. "Dickinson came to just hang out, which was fine," recalled Jimmy. "Very few people got to come and hang out, but he got to be there because he was with Stanley Booth. He was just sitting in the control room most of the time. By the second night, he could move around the studio a little and not alarm anybody. They would take four to five hours to work up a song. About two-thirds of the way through arranging 'Wild Horses,' Dickinson went to the back of the building and started playing along on a piano that had tacks on the hammers. He was just playing along, when Keith walked in and said, 'This is great, listen to this.' Jagger said to get him to play, so I had to get a mic and mic the piano." Jimmy laughed. "All of a sudden, his career was launched."

Jim Dickinson's career wasn't the only one that was launched at the session. When the album, titled *Sticky Fingers*, was released, it went to the top of the charts, and "Brown Sugar," a song that some critics thought had racist and sexist overtones, became a Number One hit. From that point on, everyone who was anyone in rock wanted to record at Muscle Shoals Sound to gather up that "sticky finger" magic.

The artists who came in the 1970s reads like a who's who of American music, and the songs they recorded at Muscle Shoals Sound formed the bedrock for an entire decade: Aretha Franklin returned for a long string of memorable songs, including "Lady Soul," "Think," and "Call Me"; Paul Simon recorded "Loves Me Like a Rock"; Rod Stewart with "Tonight's the Night"; Art Garfunkel made "Crying in My Sleep"; Bob Seger with "Old Time Rock and Roll" (written by a Memphis songwriter) and *Night Moves*; the Staple Singers' "Respect Yourself"; Millie Jackson's "Hurts So Good"; James Brown with "People"; Dire Straits with *Communique*; Dr. Hook's "When You're in Love With a Beautiful Woman" and "Sharing the Night Together"; Canned Heat's *One More River to Cross*; Kim Carnes' *Sailin'*; Lynyrd Skynyrd's *Platinum and Gold*, *Street Survivors* and "Down South Jukin.'" And so it went, day after day, year after year.

◆ ▲ ◆ ▲ ◆

Muscle Shoals was a three-hour drive from Memphis, but it was such a pleasant drive, through virgin (almost) forests and farmland fat with cotton and corn, not to mention a constant stream of sharecroppers' shanties that made travelers sometimes feel that they were going back in time. Don Nix had started out at Stax playing baritone sax in the Mar-Keys, but as the years went by he had ventured into production, when he wasn't organizing rock 'n' roll bands of his own. One day, Nix and Duck Dunn were driving Joe Cocker to Muscle Shoals Sound for a session, when Cocker urged them to pull over off the road, somewhere near Iuka, Mississippi. Cocker had spotted an outhouse from the highway and insisted that Nix take his picture standing next to it. Once that touching interlude passed, they drove on to Muscle Shoals Sound, where they recorded "Black-eyed Blues" and "High Time We Went."

One day, Nix received a telephone call from Booker T. and the MG's drummer Al Jackson, who had been asked to produce an album with guitarist Albert King. Jackson pleaded with Nix to produce the album because King was driving him crazy. Nix had known King for four years, and during the time he was around him he never once felt like going crazy, so he agreed to take over the project. That's when things started getting a little strange. Jim Stewart asked him to produce a live album, so Nix put together an all-star band in San Francisco to back King at the famed Fillmore West.

The practice session began smoothly enough, but Nix noticed that King was stalling, doing everything he could to keep from joining the band, including devoting fifteen minutes to tuning his guitar. He didn't want to be there. Finally, King got motivated enough to join the band, only to storm out of the rehearsal room after playing only a couple of songs. Nix followed King out of the room, doing everything he could to calm him down. King told him that he just didn't like the band. Frustrated, Nix left the rehearsal room, went to the hotel and checked out of his room and returned to Memphis.

Two weeks later, King telephoned Nix and apologized. They made plans to start over on the album, only with a different band this time, and in a different part of the country. Nix booked Muscle Shoals Sound for a week, but instead of doing a live album he did one that contained songs he wrote just for the session, except for one cover, King's version of the Rolling Stones' "Honky Tonk Woman."

"I would get a line, a guitar line—back then they all had one that they repeated—and you just write a song on top of it," Nix explained. "When you get that down, you start putting things on top of it. I'd just show the players a couple of simple lines." King didn't mind working that way, according to Nix. "Albert was an artist—just show me what to do. Show me where to stand. Tell me what you want me to do. He had done that stuff for so long, his attitude was, 'Get me in, get me out.'"

Nix figured out that King was difficult to work with sometimes because he couldn't read or write, and he felt it put him at a disadvantage with other musicians. He felt comfortable in Muscle Shoals, because the band members were all down-home, Alabama-bred boys that understood that it wasn't unusual for black men to grow up without learning to read or write. One night, Nix challenged him on it. "While we sat in his hotel room going over some lyrics he was to overdub the next day, I told him, 'Albert, I know you can't read, but if I could play guitar like you I wouldn't care if I could read or not,'" Nix wrote in his memoir. "He sat there looking at me for a long while. I thought for a minute he was going to pull that big old army issue .45 out of his britches and shoot me. A big broad grin came across his face, and he stuck out his hand. 'I like you Don. You alright.' I will never forget it."

That Muscle Shoals session produced King's critically acclaimed *Lovejoy* album, which included memorable songs such as "Everybody Wants to Go to Heaven," "Bay Area Blues," and "Like a Road Leading Home."

Albert King could be temperamental at times, a personality trait that was amplified by the fact that he did, indeed, keep a loaded .45 in his belt, out of sight under his jacket, but Nix generally found blacks much easier to work with in the studio. "Leon Russell always told me to go in there and, whether you know or not, act like you know what you're doing," Nix said in a 1989 interview. "Like, I'd do string sessions and I'd have an arranger, and I'd go in there, 'Hey, Albert—how you doing?' If he said that the music didn't sound right, then I'd call out, 'Who's doing that?' I did fifty-one albums. Nobody ever said, 'Do you know what you're doing?' I'd always say, 'Did anyone make any mistakes?' That was fun. It isn't fun now."

◆ ▲ ◆ ▲ ◆

As Muscle Shoals Sound churned out hit after hit, Rick Hall remained competitive at Fame, although he found that more and more of his clients were doing records for country music labels. One of the hot new songwriter/producers there was Walt Aldridge, who got his first producer's job when Bruce Springsteen's producer Chuck Plotkin backed out of producing Lacy J. Dalton's album, *Highway Diner*. Journey keyboardist Jonathan Cain volunteered to produce the album, but his budget was turned down by Dalton's record label. Dalton was desperate for a producer.

"Jonathan said 'You're always talking about Walt Aldridge, why don't you call him?'" Dalton recalled. "So I did, and though this is not a style he was familiar with, he took the project." *Highway Diner* took ten days to record, with Aldridge doing some of his work from a hospital bed, but he put everything he had into the project. His dedication didn't pay off with the album, because it wasn't a big seller, but it benefited him in other ways. About six months after he finished *Highway Diner*, Aldridge and his songwriting partner, Gary Baker, submitted some songs to CBS, Dalton's label, for a T. G. Sheppard album that was under way at Fame. CBS head Rick Blackburn passed on the songs, but he asked for tapes from Aldridge and Baker, the end result being that Blackburn signed them as part of a Muscle Shoals "super group" named The Shooters, a group that also included Barry Billings, Chalmers Davis, and Mike Dillon.

Aldridge attributed his good fortune to the mojo that practically oozed up from the ground at Muscle Shoals. "There is a real heritage factor here," Aldridge explained. "If you sit down in the studio where Duane Allman sat playing on a Wilson Pickett record, you're going to be influenced by—I don't know, you can call them vibes or whatever voodoo name you'd like to give it, but there's just a real feeling of heritage and a desire to continue it."

Aldridge's comments were echoed by T. Graham Brown, who recorded a number of country hits at Fame's chief competitor, Muscle Shoals Sound. "I mean, I got the original drummer and bass player who did all those hits...twenty years go," he said in a 1987 interview. "And these are white guys. *White* guys. It's real cool. I sing a version of 'Too Weak to Fight,' with a little bit of 'Slip Away' [Clarence Carter's hit]. So, one day I thought, well, we're gonna record this. I took the tape down there, just how we did it on the Kenny Rogers show, and played it for them. It was everything they could do to keep from laughing in my face. They said, 'Brown, you know we played on the original.' Oooo, it was embarrassing."

◆ ▲ ◆ ▲ ◆

In 1985, Malaco Records of Jackson, Mississippi, purchased the Muscle Shoals Sound studio, putting to an end one of the most successful runs in music history. The studio owners didn't exactly sell to strangers: Malaco, which had started up in 1967, was owned by Tommy Couch, who had a relationship with Jimmy Johnson, David Hood, Roger Hawkins, and Barry Beckett that went back for almost three-and-a-half decades. Malaco had experienced great success with artists such as bluesman Mississippi Fred McDowell, and Anita Ward, whose song "Ring My Bell" went to Number Two, selling an estimated ten million copies.

Two years before purchasing Muscle Shoals Sound, Malaco signed Bobby "Blue" Bland and enjoyed immediate success with his albums. The Muscle Shoals studio was earmarked for rhythm & blues artists like Bland and for the company's emerging gospel label. "When you talk about the Memphis sound, the Muscle Shoals sound, I don't think that they really exist anymore," Couch said in a 1988 interview. "The publicity was built around a group of musicians. We could talk about the Memphis sound—would that be a ZZ Top, or would it be...We could name ten groups that have recorded in Memphis in the last year. They're probably all different, and the sound is all different. And the same is true of Muscle Shoals. We do everything from country to blues to gospel to rock 'n' roll. So the Muscle Shoals sound has grown into a lot of things." Couch said he had no plans to change anything at the Muscle Shoals studio. "There is still a very good pool of musicians there that do have a certain personality in them, a certain expertise. Just located where it is—there is a legacy in that area for making records."

Twenty years after the sale, Jimmy Johnson and David Hood are still there, still making music—sometimes at their old studio, where they sometimes help put down tracks for Bobby "Blue" Bland; sometimes in Nashville, where the music community always had a soft spot for Muscle Shoals musicians and songwriters. They've changed since the 1960s, when they began, but then so has everyone else. The market itself has changed. Rhythm & blues, or sweet soul music as it is called when it is especially mellow, was once a raging fire that seared the charts. All that changed in the 1980s, when rhythm & blues artists, and the bands that recorded with them, were re-categorized as blues artists, a kiss of death since it implied that they were no longer economically viable as recording artists. In the 1970s, it was not unusual for Bobby "Blue" Bland's albums to sell half a million copies; by 2000, he was lucky to sell one hundred thousand copies. Muscle Shoals, as a recording center, has followed a similar track: The wheel still turns, making music where none existed before, though perhaps not with the same youthful, wide-eyed passion that characterized it in the early years.

8 NASHVILLE
▼ Workin' On the Next Big Thing

Nashville is not the oldest city in America, but it is one of the oldest in the South, which counts for something in a region that reveres the past. Founded around 1780, Nashville was the terminus for the Natchez Trace hundreds of years before white settlers ever set foot there. The Natchez Trace Parkway was not completed at the Nashville end until the mid-1990s, when a 1,648-foot-long bridge was built at the roadway's scenic terminus. Rising more than 150 feet over Highway 96, it is the largest segmented, arched span in the United States, an engineering marvel—a fact that, no doubt, influenced the bridge's first suicide leaper in 2000. (It is one thing to leap from a bridge into water, but quite another thing to leap onto a busy highway.)

Nashville was a good place to settle, primarily because of its location on the Cumberland River, offering travelers a gateway to the Mississippi River to the west, and to the Ohio River to the northeast. The first inhabitants were Shawnee Indians, who lived there in quiet seclusion until a French trader came and opened a trading post. In the beginning, there was an attempt to name the settlement Nashborough, after Francis Nash, a Revolutionary War soldier, but new arrivals to the settlement who wanted to sever all links with England thought the name took on British airs, so it was changed to Nashville to make it sound more "American." Because the city is situated roughly in the center of the state—about two hundred miles from Memphis to the southwest and about two hundred miles from Knoxville to the east—it was named the state capital in 1843, which gave the city less than two decades to establish a respectable skyline before it was ravaged by federal troops during the Civil War. It was the site of some of the bloodiest fighting of the war, which left hard feelings that exist to this day.

Not long after the first settlers arrived, Andrew Jackson was sent to Nashville to serve as the area's first prosecutor. His success with evildoers gave him the foundation for a successful law practice, which led to a life of public service as a judge, congressman (he was generally opposed to anything that President George Washington wanted to do), respected general, and, finally, president. More so than any other person, Jackson, or "Old Hickory" as he was sometimes called, shaped Nashville's outlook and character.

As the years went by, Nashville became a cultural buffer between the almost entirely white, Republican part of the state to the east, represented by Knoxville, and the majority black, Democratic part to the west, represented by Memphis. The state's racial balance has remained reasonably consistent over the years (80 percent white, 16 percent black). Nashville, with a population that is 66 percent white and 27 percent nt black, is viewed by black Memphians traveling east as the last outpost they will pass before entering one of the "whitest" regions in America.

Culturally, Nashville is vastly different from Memphis, which rightfully should be an extension of the Mississippi Delta. In Memphis, both white and black residents think like Mississippians. The only cultural ties that Nashville has to the Delta are those that African Americans have brought to the city and nurtured over the years. Their migration was encouraged by the establishment of Fisk University, which was founded in 1865 for the purpose of providing the sons and daughters of former slaves with a Christian education that was strong both spiritually and academically. It was through Fisk that the city's music tradition began. When the school fell on hard times, school officials put together a group of students named the Jubilee Singers for a tour of the North, in an effort to raise money for the school. Singing spiritual or "slave songs" as they were called at the time, the Jubilee Singers became enormously popular all over the country, at one point performing for President Ulysses S. Grant at the White House.

For nearly half a century, the singers were Nashville's only major connection to America's music scene. That started changing in 1925 when radio station WSM, an NBC affiliate, went on the air. Before that, Nashville had served as an anchor to the Mojo Triangle by only the slimmest of technicalities—because that is where the Trace ended. WSM was built because Edwin W. Craig, the son of the president of National Life and Accident Insurance Company, heard a show broadcast out of Atlanta called the "National Barn Dance." The insurance company's slogan was "We shield millions," and Craig told his father that if they built a station in Nashville and used the call letters WSM, they would be able to sell lots of insurance. His father agreed, and gave him the go-ahead.

For the premier broadcast, Craig invited the announcer of the "National Barn Dance," a former journalist from Memphis named George D. Hay. Things went so well that Craig offered Hay the program director's job. NBC was set up in such a way that it sent programming from New York to its affiliates in exchange for local programming that it could distribute to its nationwide chain of radio stations. NBC's big Saturday offering was its "Music Appreciation Hour," which featured classical music and opera. At the end of that program, WSM was free to offer its own program.

Hay didn't think too much of what he felt was pretentious music, so he created a tongue-in-cheek antidote that he named "Barn Dance." With Hay as announcer—he called himself the "Solemn Ol' Judge"—WSM countered the opera and classical music with a program that presented live music from an old-time fiddler named Uncle Jimmy Thompson. That went over so well that Hay brought in other musicians, including Dr. Humphrey Bate, a physician who had put together a string band. At that time, country music was simply folk music that had sifted down from the hills of Kentucky and the mountains of eastern Tennessee, and up from Mississippi, where Jimmie Rodgers had breathed life into a bluesy form of white folk music.

"Barn Dance" prospered, as Craig had predicted, and sold lots of life insurance to people who had never before had life insurance. Nashville's elite were not sold on the show, feeling that it presented the city in a bad light. Among that group, the preferred entertainment was orchestra music. There were no country music bars or nightclubs in Nashville at that time; the only place in the city that you could hear country music was on "Barn Dance." Why, the socialites wondered, should a city be identified with a type of music that, for all practical purposes, did not exist anywhere in the city, except on the radio.

WSM ignored the complaints, and pushed ahead with Hay's common-man vision for the radio station. And why shouldn't they? "Barn Dance's" audience grew from week to week, with Hay playing the role of a likeable country bumpkin who was smarter than his citified critics. Six years into the show, after hearing the NBC Symphony Orchestra one time too many, Hay told his audience, "From here on out folks, it will be nothing but realism...You've been up in the clouds with grand opera, now get down to earth with...the 'Grand Ole Opry.'" The name stuck, and when WSM later increased its broadcasting power from 1,000 watts to 50,000 watts, the "Grand Ole Opry" could be heard in homes all across the country. Before long, the program outgrew the facilities at the radio station. WSM tried out several locations, including the War Memorial Building, but finally settled on the Ryman Auditorium in downtown Nashville.

Because the "Grand Ole Opry" was based on live entertainment, Nashville soon attracted fiddle, guitar, and mandolin players from all over the South. The program eventually became the elitists' worst nightmare, as trucks filled with raw-boned pickers and dreamers from Oklahoma, Kentucky, North Carolina, Georgia, and Mississippi poured into the city, all hoping to earn their moment of glory on the Opry.

Critics around the nation who hated country music wasted no time labeling it as "hillbilly" music, a derisive term that was as offensive to white musicians as the term "nigger" music was to blacks. WSM played a leadership role in fighting the hillbilly label, with Hay once writing, "We never use the word [hillbilly], because it was coined in derision...Country people have a definite dignity of their own and a native shrewdness which enable them to hold their own in any company."

Nashville became America's country music capital, not because it is where the music originated, because clearly it had no more country pickers than any other Southern city—Nashville was and still is a reservoir of rhythm & blues talent—but because WSM provided country music lovers with a beacon that they simply could not ignore.

◆ ▲ ◆ ▲ ◆

Despite the success of WSM, country music did not appear overnight in Nashville, and other than the leadership that WSM took in spreading the word, there were no leaders who stepped forward to say, "This is how it will be." First came the people, the dreamers, the ambitious, the pickers whose souls were on fire; then came the song publishers, who sought to profit from the dreamers, the ambitious, the pickers whose souls were on fire. Slowly, one by one, publishers set up offices in Nashville during the 1930s and 1940s. These businesses encouraged the dream-starved to bring them their songs, and if the songs weren't quite up to standards, they would encourage them to go home and try again. Record labels began to send representatives to Nashville to scout new talent, both artists and songwriters, but from the time that WSM first went on the air, it would be three decades before record labels would start opening offices in Nashville.

There was confusion over what to call the music. The hillbilly label that Northerners liked to use did nothing in the South but create hard feelings.

Those who played the music preferred "folk," but that seemed to confuse people on the East coast who associated folk with songs from Ireland and Scotland. Then they tried "western," but that created problems because the music had originated in the South. Finally, "country and western" evolved (RCA Victor was the first record label to use that term), and it soon morphed into simply "country," although artists from the West thought that leaving out "western" slighted them in some way. Ironically, the man who helped start it all, Jimmie Rodgers, never heard the word "country" applied to his music, because he died long before people started fighting over what to call it.

Still, they came to Nashville—sometimes to live, other times to perform on the Grand Ole Opry. The Carter Sisters & Mother Maybelle came from Virginia, making more than 270 recordings between 1927 and 1942. Kitty Wells, one of a very few country artists actually born in Nashville, started singing in the 1930s at WSM's competition, WSIX, and made history in 1952 by becoming the first woman to have a solo Number One hit, "It Wasn't God Who Made Honky Tonk Angels." Early on, before she had any success, Wells married Johnny Wright, from nearby Mt. Juliet, Tennessee, and while she worked in a garment factory and he worked in a furniture factory, they formed a trio: Johnny Wright and the Harmony Girls (the second "girl" was his sister Louise).

During the 1930s and 1940s, hundreds, perhaps thousands, of country artists operated out of Nashville, but it wasn't until the 1950s that anything approaching an industry began to take shape, and that was due, in part, to the pre-1950s success of artists such as Lester Flatt and Earl Scruggs, the Louvin Brothers, Hank Williams, who only lived long enough to have a six-year career as a recording artist, but who became one of the most beloved country singers of all time, and Bill and Charlie Monroe. These were artists who used the Grand Ole Opry to build nationwide audiences.

In the 1950s, the rising stars of country music were Hank Snow, who had eight Number One songs in a twenty-five-year chart career; Webb Pierce, who had thirty-four Top 10 records in the 1950s; Patsy Cline, who mesmerized audiences with songs such as "Crazy" and "I Fall to Pieces"; and Eddy Arnold, who had 150 charted singles from the mid-1940s to the mid-1980s, and gave country music its first crossover superstar. Despite thirty years of success with country music, the record labels were still hesitant to open permanent offices in Nashville.

The problem with country music, after thirty years of success, was that it had not produced a single individual who could energize the boardrooms of the New York record labels to the point where they wanted to attach their corporate logos to buildings in Nashville. It was much easier for them to simply send producers, along with recording equipment, to Nashville, get what they needed, and then return to New York.

The person who changed all that was Elvis Presley. His relationship with Nashville began in October 1954, when he and Scotty and Bill—collectively billed as the Blue Moon Boys—appeared on the Grand Ole Opry. Jim Denny, manager of the Opry, had heard Elvis' version of "Blue Moon of Kentucky" and felt that the trio would be a good fit for the show. The night of their performance, the audience was polite, but not wildly enthusiastic. After the show, Denny reportedly told Elvis, "You'd better keep driving the truck."

Fifteen months later, after Sam Phillips had sold Elvis' contract to RCA Records, Elvis returned to Nashville as the record company's most promising new artist. RCA had no recording history in Memphis, so New York executives decided to record Elvis in Nashville, where they had a long track record. Memphis and Nashville were in the same state, so the executives didn't think there could possibly be any difference in the music. The previous year, RCA staff producer Steve Sholes had rented space from the Methodist Television Radio and Film Commission and set up a studio. Because Sholes lived in New York and only traveled to Nashville when recording sessions were booked, he needed someone to run their new office there. He chose Chet Atkins, who by that time had his own show on WSM, and a recording contract with RCA. In 1954, RCA released his first album, *Chet Atkins' Gallopin' Guitar,* in 1955 he had two hit singles, "Mr. Sandman" and a guitar duet with Hank Snow titled "Silver Bell."

Uncertain of how to categorize Elvis' music, Sholes figured that whatever it was, it would be easier to market him to country music radio stations than to stations that played popular music, so he put Atkins in charge of the session, even though Atkins had told him that he didn't think Elvis had much of a future.

The session came as a shock to Elvis and his band members, Scotty and Bill. In Memphis, they were used to a relaxed studio setting, with the engineer sticking his head into the studio from time to time to give them suggestions. In Nashville, they had a seasoned engineer who called out take numbers in a businesslike manner. Over a two-day period, they recorded five songs: Ray Charles' "I've Got a Woman," "I Was the One," "Money Honey, "I'm

Counting on You," and "Heartbreak Hotel," on which Atkins played guitar. Scotty was amused by the lengths to which the engineer and Atkins went to copy the echo effect that Sam Phillips had captured in his Memphis studio. For "Heartbreak Hotel," they added slapback—or delay as it is called today—to Elvis' vocal, then recorded the song in a hallway of the studio. "They had a speaker set up at one end of this long hallway and a microphone at the other end," Scotty recalled. "They had a sign on the door that said, 'Don't open the door when the red light is on.'"

After the session, Elvis and the band went on the road, while Sholes took the tapes back to New York to play for his bosses at RCA. To his horror, they hated the recordings. They ordered him to return to Nashville to record new tracks that sounded like what Elvis had recorded in Memphis. Sholes didn't think that returning to Nashville would help, so he suggested that the new songs be recorded in New York when Elvis arrived later that month to appear on the nationally broadcast television show, "Stage Show." Everyone was agreeable, so new sessions were scheduled in New York without Atkins. As they worked on new recordings, Elvis' first RCA release, "Heartbreak Hotel," soared to the Top 20 on the pop charts.

As it turned out, even though Sholes got more great recordings from Elvis in New York, the singer just wasn't that comfortable recording there, primarily because it was so far away from home. The success of "Heartbreak Hotel" made Nashville—and Chet Atkins—look good, so it wasn't long before RCA's competitors started opening branch offices in the city. Atkins became a hero to the recording industry, but he never really wanted that kind of fame. "I remember when they made me a vice president," Atkins recalled. "I wanted to be known as a guitarist, and I know, too, that they give you titles like that in lieu of money." Atkins laughed, not so much at RCA as at himself. "So, beware when they want to make you vice president. The paycheck would be better [if they didn't]."

When Nashville needed someone to sell country music on the radio, the job fell to Memphian George Hay. When the city needed someone to boost its fledging music industry to the next level, it was Elvis. Nashville is an important part of the Mojo Triangle, but it has always had to draw on the deeper soul of the triangle for the inspiration behind its own music successes. Elvis ended up recording almost all of his early hit songs in Nashville, a fact that was not lost on an industry that is always searching for the next Big Thing. Within seven years after "Heartbreak Hotel," Nashville could boast twenty-six record companies, two hundred and sixty-five publishing houses, ten recording studios, four record pressing plants, and more than seven hundred songwriters.

◆　▲　◆　▲　◆

Elvis wasn't the only Memphis artist to look eastward to Nashville. Unhappy with the way his career was progressing at Sun Records, Johnny Cash signed with Columbia Records and moved to Nashville. Sun engineer Jack Clement said that he thought Cash left because he got his feelings hurt: "One day Johnny dropped by and wanted to talk to Sam or have lunch or something and Sam was too busy. He was doing something with Jerry Lee. I think John felt slighted. I think that's what started it."

When Phillips learned that Cash had signed with Columbia, he sent him a curt letter than demanded that he complete the recordings agreed to in their contract. Later, Cash recalled: "I did every song that Jack asked me to do. I really don't think I would have done it for anyone else in the world. I could have played off sick or pulled this or that excuse. Jack said after we got to working, 'I don't like this any better than you do.' I said, 'Well, I'm really kind of enjoying it.' I recorded everything he asked me to do." The session with Clement was so productive that Phillips was given enough Johnny Cash singles to release long after the "Man in Black" had begun releasing singles on Columbia.

The following year, in 1959, Sam Phillips and Jack Clement had a falling out that resulted in Clement following Cash to Nashville. Clement recalled it this way: "We'd been recording all day. There was this guy named Cliff who was one of Elvis' entourage. He hit another member of Elvis' entourage over the head with a tennis racket, and Elvis threw him out of the house. For some reason, Cliff was staying with me...It got into the evening and Bill Justis had been having a few cocktails, and Sam came in and he had a few cocktails. Cliff also had a few cocktails. I wanted to go home because it was snowing, and I wanted to get across the bridge before it froze up. So, somehow I worked in the control room, and Sam was there telling jokes, and they were having a big party. I said, 'Cliff, we need to go.' Sam interpreted that as meaning 'You don't want to stay here and talk to this idiot.' In the meantime, he and Justis had been arguing. I just wanted to go home." Clement did go home, but when he returned to the studio the next day there was an envelope there for him. "Sam had fired me," said Clement in a 1995 interview. "I saw another envelope there for Justis. He fired him, too. The next day I think he was sorry about it and we probably could have reconciled, but I was ready to go. Sam still don't know to this day why he fired me. We still argue about it."

Once he relocated in Nashville, Clement began a career as a producer, beginning with Johnny Cash's new records for Columbia. That producer-artist pairing was more than symbolic, it was indicative of a new trend in country music. Clement also worked with Waylon Jennings, and it was Clement who talked Chet Atkins into taking a chance on Charley Pride, and who then went on to produce more than a dozen Gold albums with the singer. Beginning in the late 1950s and continuing to the mid-1980s, country music was shaped by transplanted Memphians who gave the music more of an edge, the result of blues and rock influences from the Mississippi Delta and Memphis. Almost everyone who started out at Sun Records—Elvis, Cash, Roy Orbison, Carl Perkins, Jerry Lee Lewis—ended up in Nashville, not because they changed their music, but because Nashville had finally come around to their way of thinking. Even Sun Records itself ended up in Nashville, when Sam Phillips sold the record label in the late 1960s to Shelby Singleton, a former Mercury Records executive.

Scotty Moore, who had helped put Memphis on the map as the birthplace of rock 'n' roll, also moved to Nashville. After leaving Elvis' band, Scotty had enjoyed success as the co-owner of Fernwood Records, a Memphis company that had a million-selling hit with Thomas Wayne's "Tragedy." Scotty had produced the record, using himself and Bill Black as the only musicians. Unfortunately, the money collected for "Tragedy" quickly dissipated for expenses, and Fernwood went out of business. Scotty continued to record with Elvis in Nashville, but that didn't bring in enough money to live on, especially

Jack Clement in a backyard swing outside his Nashville office, circa 1994. (James L. Dickerson)

for a man with a family to support, so in the summer of 1960, he asked Sam Phillips for a job and was offered an engineering position in Phillips' new studio, Sam Phillips' Recording Service. That went well for a while, with Scotty engineering several Jerry Lee Lewis records, but as time went by, the work environment deteriorated, with Sam often getting into arguments with his employees. By then, Sam had opened a studio in Nashville, so Scotty made excuses to go there to escape the bickering taking place in the Memphis studio. It was there that he met Billy Sherrill, fresh up from Muscle Shoals. Sherrill didn't work for Sam long before Epic Records hired him as a producer. One day, Sherrill asked Scotty why he hadn't recorded an album of instrumentals. Scotty was flattered that he even asked. He had asked Sam repeatedly if he could record instrumentals in his studio, and Sam always stalled or made excuses. Scotty jumped at Sherrill's offer. "I'd like to take the credit for having the idea," said Sherrill "I think Scotty was too shy back then to want to be the star of his own album. I had always admired Scotty's style. I think he had the most unique style of any guitar player in the world. He did it before anyone else did it— those rock 'n' roll licks. I wanted to capitalize on the fact that he was the man who played the guitar that changed the world."

The Guitar That Changed the World was one of Sherrill's first projects as a producer, and he went on to become one of the most successful producers in

Scotty Moore, circa 1994. (James L. Dickerson)

Nashville. Scotty was elated to have something of his own in the record stores. This story should have had a happy ending, but it didn't. When Scotty returned to Memphis, he told Sam Phillips about the album, expecting him to be excited, but Sam was not happy at all. He accused Scotty of going behind his back, which Scotty did not understand because he was not under contract to Sam as an artist. A few days later, Scotty was handed a dismissal letter when he reported for work. Sam Phillips was not an easy man to work for, but he was a remarkably easy man from whom to get a termination notice.

Like just about everyone else that Sam fired or ran away, Scotty moved to Nashville, where he found a partner with whom to open his own studio, Music City Recorders. Scotty continued to work on occasional projects with Elvis, but playing music was no longer his focus. Instead, he threw himself into his work as an engineer, working on projects for a variety of artists, including Tracy Nelson (*Make a Joyous Noise*), Ringo Starr (*Beaucoup of Blues*), Dolly Parton, and actress Ann-Margret.

◆ ▲ ◆ ▲ ◆

In many ways, Nashville has always existed in a parallel universe within the Mojo Triangle. White and black. Democrat and Republican. Country music and...well, yes, rhythm & blues. In 1926, one year after National Life and Accident Insurance Company proved that WSM could sell insurance to "under-serviced" whites, Life and Casualty Insurance built a station to sell insurance to under-serviced blacks. The call letters were WLAC (all stations east of the Mississippi River had to begin with W; the LAC represented Life and Casualty). With state-of-the-art studios installed on the fifth floor of the insurance company's building, the station was part-time in the beginning, broadcasting on one thousand watts; but it soon found its voice and went to five thousand watts in 1928, and in 1942, it became one of only sixty-four stations in America licensed to operate with fifty thousand watts on a clear channel, which allowed it to reach five states during the daylight hours and twenty-eight states at night.

Two decades before WDIA in Memphis made history by becoming the first station with an all-black format and all-black personnel, WLAC was broadcasting rhythm & blues to a predominately black audience, but all the announcers at WLAC were white men who sounded like they were black. In 2004, the Country Music Hall of Fame in Nashville released a CD titled *Night Train to Nashville*; it is a compilation of rhythm & blues songs, either recorded in Nashville or recorded elsewhere by Nashville artists. Hall of Fame director Kyle Young explained it this way: "All of this great music was happening alongside the growth in country music. We're showing how all of this was connected." In the liner notes, black music critic Ron Wynn wrote that he had listened to WLAC while growing up in Knoxville in the late 1950s and early 1960s and had considered the radio station his answer to Harlem: "It was a most profound culture shock for me many years later to discover that jocks such as 'Hoss' Allen and 'John R' weren't gray-haired, big bellied African-American jocks, but merely good ol' southern white boys...It didn't seem logical or possible—or, for that matter, conceivable—that white guys could have all that soul."

WLAC contributed to the growth of rhythm & blues in Nashville, just as WSM promoted country music, creating a thriving music community that exists to this day. Today, there are only a few venues that offer country music—the Bluebird Café and Tootsie's Orchid Lounge for example—but there are many venues for rhythm & blues, and rock 'n' roll, and those are the after-hours places that attract the city's country music executives, simply because they are more hip and vibrant than the country venues.

During the late 1950s and 1960s, black Nashville nightclubs such as New Era and Del Morocco attracted the top black artists in the country. B.B. King was a regular visitor, as were Aretha Franklin, Jimi Hendrix, and Etta James, who recorded *Etta James Rocks the House* at the New Era in 1963. In addition to WLAC and a strong nightclub scene, Nashville boasted two local rhythm & blues television shows that predated "Soul Train" (a videotape has survived of a very young Jimi Hendrix making his best effort on one of the shows, "Night Train," while backing a group called Buddy and Stacey).

It is not generally known, but in the 1960s Nashville studios attracted some of the top rhythm & blues artists in the country. Among them was Bobby "Blue" Bland, who was born just outside Memphis in Rosemark, Tennessee, but later moved to Memphis as a child with his mother and grew up singing in churches throughout the city. Five years younger than B.B. King, he worshiped the bluesman as a teen and eagerly accepted a job with King as his touring driver, a position that eventually led to him joining his band.

Bland did some sessions in Memphis with Ike Turner, and one of the songs, "Cried All Night," was released as a single, but he wasn't able to follow up because he was drafted for a two-year stint in the Army. After his discharge, he was signed by a Texas-based label called Duke Records, and put together an orchestra to go on the road to promote his records. Bland has one of the most unique voices in music. One minute he can be ultra-sophisticated, silky smooth, doing sensual things to ballads that are probably illegal in some states, and the next minute he can shout out a high-energy, up-tempo rocker that can raise the roof an inch or two.

By the early 1960s, there was no one who could compete with him on college campuses, where white males became addicted to hits such as "Turn on Your Love Light," "Cry, Cry, Cry," the powerful "St. James Infirmary," and the slow-dance anthem that was the stimulus to many an unwelcome campus pregnancy, "Stormy Monday Blues." In the early to mid-1960s, white college students talked about "Turn on Your Love Light" and "Stormy Monday Blues" the way college students today discuss download-ing tips or Britney's latest outfit. Incredibly, Bland was equally popular with black audiences—with unfaltering grace, he tapped into universal feelings about romance, the vagaries of life, and even death, making life's ultimate experience seem almost soulful.

Bland sometimes recorded in Texas, but many of his most soulful hits were recorded in Nashville. "Turn on Your Love Light," one of the most popular rhythm & blues songs of all time, was recorded at Bradley's Barn, owned by legendary Nashville producer Owen Bradley. "It was kind of a rainy day," Bland later recalled. "It was a good session, up-tempo stuff that I wasn't that familiar with. Up until that time, I was doing ballads and slow blues. I did some up-tempo things before then, [but not many]." Bland laughed, thinking about it twenty years after the fact. "We didn't really think it would do anything, but it turned out to be one of the biggest things we ever did."

The odd thing about Bland's career is not that he recorded in Nashville, but that he didn't record in Memphis, at least not until much later in life. The reasons for that are not hard to understand. He has lived in Memphis for most of his life, yet the city has never embraced him the way it should. Of all the music legends associated with Memphis, only he and Lil Hardin Armstrong were authentic citizens of the city, and it is disgraceful the way that the city has virtually ignored their contributions. Bland was once asked if Memphis had dropped the ball with the blues, in the sense that it had not embraced the music the way it should. "Memphis is sorta' swishy swatchy, in a sense," Bland said, his voice becoming dismissive. "But they will never get rid of the label, 'Home of the Blues,' because W.C. Handy saw to that." Nor—he might have added—will the city be able to escape his own enormous contributions to the blues. They don't call him Bobby "Blue" Bland for nothing.

◆　▲　◆　▲　◆

The country music scene in Nashville during the 1960s and 1970s was in an almost constant state of flux. Once the record labels opened branch offices in the city, the competition for new talent became fierce. Because all of the existing artists—Johnny Cash, Eddy Arnold, Hank Snow, and so on—had record deals, typically with RCA or Columbia, the newer labels had to create a demand for new artists, or perish. The result was a new wave of artists, all signed from the mid-1960s to the mid-1970s: Buck Owens, Merle Haggard, Loretta Lynn, Dolly Parton, Reba McEntire, Tanya Tucker, Tammy Wynette,

Tom T. Hall, Waylon Jennings, and Willie Nelson.

Arriving from Mississippi, by way of Memphis, Tammy Wynette brought a level of sex appeal to country music that had been missing in previous years—and she did it without being terribly obvious about it. No one would have dreamed of marketing her as a She-Elvis, simply because her music was a long way from rock 'n' roll, but she had a personal quality that attracted people at a visceral level, the same Mojo magic that gave Elvis an edge. Perhaps it was because she grew up in the same area as Elvis, seeing the same sights, eating the same food, feeling the same cultural restrictions—or, perhaps it was because she was personally influenced by Elvis at an early age while visiting her mother at the dry cleaners where she worked. Elvis rehearsed there with Scotty and Bill, and when things were slow at the cleaners, Scotty and his brother Carney, and his wife, Auzella, took turns pushing Tammy around the store in a clothes hamper, simply to hear her squeal with delight.

One day, Elvis and the boys were walking down the stairs from the rehearsal room, when Auzella shouted up at them: "My, my, my. Look at the stars!" Twelve-year-old Tammy was star-struck at the sight of Elvis. "Elvis was nothing then," she later recalled, "but he looked at her with that little smile of his and he said, 'Auzella, one of these days I'll wrap you up in hundred-dollar bills.'"

Tammy Wynette on Austin City Limits. (Scott Newton/Photofest)

Tom T. Hall, a former journalism student at Roanoke College in Virginia, also made an impact on Nashville, though for different reasons. He began his career as a songwriter while holding down a job as a disc jockey. When publishers showed interest in his work, he moved to Nashville and signed on as a contract writer at a salary of fifty dollars a week. After he won one songwriting award after another—his song "Harper Valley P.T.A." was a smash hit for Jeannie C. Riley—he was persuaded to try his hand at singing, which he did with phenomenal results, especially with records such as "The Year that Clayton Delaney Died" and "Old Dogs, Children and Watermelon Wine."

What set Hall apart were his lyrics—thoughtful, literary in scope, always on target with imagery that stuck with you long after the song had stopped—and his refusal to bow to the emerging right-wing mania that was taking place during the Vietnam War years of the late 1960s and early 1970s. With songs such as "The Monkey That Became President" and "I Washed My Face in the Morning Dew," he was labeled "liberal," though he was not that so much as he was a democrat in the tradition of Jimmie Rodgers and Hank Williams—artists who stood up for the common man and feared the effect of America's Big-Business class. Nashville of the late 1960s and early 1970s was corporate all the way—a mouthpiece for the moneyed class.

"As you get older, I think you become disillusioned with a lot of things," said Hall, referring to the music industry as a whole. "So you have to keep this romance going for as long as you can, because if you explore it too much, it's like everything else, there is a trick to it. Usually, there's just that one pony and that one trick. So if you're looking for a new trick, you've got to check out a new pony."

With the exception of artists like Tom T. Hall, the music of 1960s and early 1970s didn't depart radically from that of the 1950s—though horns and percussion were used more frequently—but the music was performed by fresh faces, and that held the public's attention, at least until the mid-1970s, when even the fresh faces began to look a little worse for wear. Country music is not fickle in its artistry, but the corporations that control country music are as fickle as the stock market on a bull run, and what they needed more than anything else in the mid-1970s was an edgier product.

The music executives prayed for a savior, and that prayer ultimately was answered by Chips Moman, who left Memphis in 1973 with the 827 Thomas Street Band and moved to Atlanta, where he built a studio in the mistaken belief that music outside the Mojo Triangle was as vibrant as it was within the pyramid. The new studio was a bust because there was very little talent in the city, and no one could be persuaded to travel there to record. Within six months, he and the band had relocated to Nashville, where he built yet another studio and shed his pop and blues sensibilities—well, not entirely, if the truth be known—and got down to the business of producing country artists, a style of music that was not his favorite.

One of his first albums was with B. J. Thomas, with whom he had produced a number of pop hits in Memphis. Thomas had had some rough times since the first sessions, caused by an extravagant life style, so Moman knew that recording a hit with him would not be easy. Moman solved that problem by writing Thomas a hit song himself, a song that reflected his own mixed feelings about country music. "Somebody Done Somebody Wrong Song" was a smash hit and let Nashville know that Chips Moman was in town, ready to do business.

Chips Moman, circa 1960s. (Mississippi Valley Collection, University of Memphis)

What Moman and the 827 Thomas Street band brought to the table was that edgier sound the record labels had been praying for. Moman couldn't help but fuse rhythm & blues and rock influences, because that music was in his blood. Those influences were most evident when he worked with B. J. Thomas and Waylon Jennings on albums such as Waylon's *Ol' Waylon* or Townes Van Zandt's *Flyin' Shoes*.

Beginning in 1975, it became conceivable in Nashville to give country music a gritty aftertaste, a dark inner lining that spawned the so-called Outlaw Movement shepherded by Waylon and Willie Nelson. Waylon and Willie deserve credit for their contributions to the movement, but it would be a mistake to underplay the influence of Moman and the fabulous band he brought from Memphis.

By the early 1980s, Moman was working with Willie Nelson, producing one of his best albums, *Always On My Mind*, which won awards from the Country Music Association for both Single and Album of Year. In 1985, Moman produced a million-selling landmark album with Johnny, Waylon, Willie and Kris Kristofferson titled *Highwayman*. That same year, this author was attending one of Moman's recording sessions with Johnny Cash, when the singer put the differences between Memphis and Nashville in perspective: "The musical minds of Memphis are very, very sophisticated...I really think that Nashville is more locked into itself, you know. It is too into itself." Several days later, Waylon came into the studio to sing one of Cash's songs. Reflecting on the same subject, Waylon said, "I never could quite conform to the rules and do it the way they did things in Nashville. I'm not saying it's not good. It worked for other people. It just didn't work for me. I don't like to do things on an assembly line basis. We do things on impulse. That's the way I have to work."

By the time the *Highwayman* had its run, it was clear that the Outlaw Movement had come and gone, leaving Waylon and the others uncertain about what the Next Big Thing would be, knowing only that there would be a Next Big Thing. "Country music gets rediscovered about every ten years," Waylon explained. "It's its own fault if it doesn't hold its own. They get a little pop exposure and they'll start running toward that and then they get lost in the shuffle. You'll notice that anything that gets some crossover has been something that has been back to the roots of it, the honesty of it. Then they start that 'pop-it is,' as I call it. When you go into sessions, and they say that sounds like a pop smash, and they're trying to cut a country record—they're contradicting themselves. It takes them about ten years to wear something out. I don't really see anything on the scene that is really new, but there will [be]...something will come along."

◆ ▲ ◆ ▲ ◆

As Waylon was predicting the future, something new already was taking shape in studios all over town, out of sight and out of mind of those not intimately involved. The music boom initiated by mojo producers such as Moman, Sherrill, and Clement had provided Nashville with ten years of excitement, but by the mid-1980s it had run its course, leaving the industry in a slump, and record executives were giddy over the Next Big Thing. New faces. New sounds. Same old audience.

In the mid-1980s, the Next Big Thing consisted of artists such as Vince Gill, Marty Stuart, Sweethearts of the Rodeo, T. Graham Brown, Patty Loveless, George Strait, the Judds, Kathy Mattea, Randy Travis, Mary Chapin Carpenter, Rosanne Cash, K. T. Oslin, and Garth Brooks. "There's a clear signal coming back from the marketplace, from the fans, that simply says, 'I like country music as well as I did five years ago, but give me something new, fresh, and exciting. I'm tired of the sameness," CBS Records/Nashville head Rick Blackburn said in a 1987 interview. "That's a clear signal. If you ignore the signal, you will have serious problems. The fan base is now responding to a sound first and the artist second. It used to be they were extremely loyal. Whatever Conway Twitty or George Jones put out was fine, because it was George and Conway. They still love George and Conway, don't get me wrong, but they will hear a T. Graham Brown on the radio or the Sweethearts of the Rodeo, or the O'Kanes, and like that and purchase the music and know little about the artist...We used to have extreme artist loyalty, but the emphasis has shifted to a sound."

RCA Records/Nashville chief Joe Galante was not entirely comfortable with that philosophy, but he went along with it anyway. Galante had irritated the country music establishment when he first moved to Nashville in the 1960s, but had become a pillar of that establishment by the mid-1980s. "I'd say the life of the roster would be between five and ten years," he said in a 1988 interview. "In some cases, the ten years will be offset by the twenty percent that would be one or two years. If you come onto the roster and you're not doing anything within two years, well, it's nothing personal, it's just that there's someone else out there ready to do it. If we've given you two years, and I mean two years with records, and you haven't made it, something is wrong and I'm not about to go down the aisle with you."

Tough words in a tough industry, but universally believed at every label in Nashville. For the older artists, it was a depressing mindset that made them worry about their old age. The country music industry had changed greatly since the 1950s, when artists who became stars figured that they had it made for life. Why would country music fans want new stars, they asked themselves, when so many of the old faces were still around, still making great music?

Of course, the Next Big Thing didn't see it that way. They figured there was always room at the top. It never occurred to them that if they defied all the odds and made it to the top that they would replace one of their heroes. The Next Big Thing dreamed of someday standing beside, not above, country artists such as Johnny Cash, George Jones, Willie Nelson, and Waylon Jennings. "I don't know if we will be like Willie and Waylon in that we start our own community, but there is a handful of us that all enjoy the same food, the same lifestyles," Vince Gill said of his contemporaries. "Everyone helps everyone out how they can."

No one was more gung-ho about being a member of the Next Big Thing than Marty Stuart. Signed to CBS in 1985 by Rick Blackburn, he released his first single, "Arlene," in early 1986, and watched it debut at sixty-eight on the charts, a hopeful sign that it would move up fast enough to put him in the Top 10. "You have a real traditional line here in Nashville—Ricky Skaggs, Reba McIntire, that set of folks," Marty said shortly after the release of "Arlene." "Then there is a group of young mavericks who have had a lot of stuff bottled up inside them for years. They are dying to turn it loose. I'm afraid I qualify for that group. I still love playing my mandolin, but I also like turning up my guitar real loud and playing that way, too."

"Arlene" didn't make the Top 10, but it aligned Marty with the stars, and all the insiders—the people who write the columns and predict the future— said they saw a raw talent, a passion, in Marty that would take him far in country music. Marty's problem was that he had a conscience. He meant what he said when he spoke of "stuff bottled up inside," but he was too new to the business to understand that whatever his record label gave to him had to be taken away from someone else, reflecting the country adage that you can only cut so many slices from the same pie. He learned quickly enough when word spread that Rick Blackburn had dropped Johnny Cash from the roster, severing a thirty-year relationship with the Man in Black. Marty was devastated, because he knew that Johnny was devastated. It seemed like a cruel, heartless thing to do to a man who had done so much for country music. "When Blackburn dropped Cash, I went into his office, being the arrogant punk that I was, and spilled it out all over the place about what I thought he was," Marty recalled. "Then I went downstairs and the promotions man said, 'I don't know what you just did, but congratulations, you just killed your career around here.' My second single was getting ready to go, and they were putting a bunch of money into it. It was a tune called 'Crime of Passion.' And they pulled it and they gave the song to Ricky Van Shelton to start his career with." Marty paused in the telling of it, thinking back, shaking his head, and then he added, "There's always been a price to pay for speaking your mind, and a lot of time it's worth it."

Heartbroken, not just over Johnny's loss, but his over own loss as well, Marty got in his car and drove to Memphis, a place that had always inspired him. "One of the greatest moments of my life was a personal moment—and when I get to Heaven, I want to thank God for it," Marty explained. "Usually, when I go to Memphis I get lost. This time, I somehow wound up on the wrong street. Anyway, I went across the bridge into Arkansas. It was a day about like this, gray and overcast, and there was a lot of fog. I went across that river bridge to that first exit and got off to turn around and go back. I looked, and a train track was peeking out of the fog. It was a pretty sight and there was nobody out in the country. I was just looking at the fog when I heard a train coming. All of a sudden, out of the fog came the train. I happened to have 'Mystery Train' in the car, and I put it into the CD player. It was one of the highlights of my life. That song carries a whole lot of depth to me. It don't say much, but it says a whole lot—the feel of it. Scotty Moore is one of the most eloquent guitar players that ever picked up a guitar. Scotty is the personification of soul in guitar playing. It's timeless."

Marty wasn't the only person who felt the pull of Memphis. At the end of his "ten year cycle"—and sensing that Nashville was about to turn its back on mojo music in general—Chips Moman packed up his wife and young son and moved back to Memphis, leaving behind the 827 Thomas Street Band, who had individually created successful careers in Nashville as session players and songwriters. However, the band promised to travel to Memphis for sessions whenever Moman needed them.

Moman's first project was a massive undertaking: To assemble the major Sun Records survivors for a reunion album to be titled *Class of '55*. Answering his call were Johnny Cash, Carl Perkins, Jerry Lee Lewis, Roy Orbison—all survivors of the 1950s, all legends, all in need of record deals. Explained Moman, "To me, one of the most important things in music history was to have these four guys—and it was a shame we couldn't have Elvis—brought back to that studio and recorded together and to have it documented." First, Moman conducted several days of sessions at the former Memphis Recording Service, where all the legends had gotten their start; then, he moved everyone over to the old American studio, where he had recorded Elvis in the late 1960s. The highlight of the session was a jam on John Fogerty's "Big Train (from Memphis)," with Fogerty flying in to sing background, along with Rick Nelson, the Judds, producer Dave Edmunds, Ace Cannon, June Carter Cash, Marty Stuart, and the man who had started it all, Sam Phillips, who told the author, "Invariably, everyone here I have talked to feels the same way. You can feel it in the air. It's not just, 'Oh, boy, we have us a hit record.' They see a future in a city they know started it all, and believe me this cycle is going to make itself known again."

When the session ended, the studio cleared remarkably fast. With everyone gone, Moman allowed tears to streak down his cheeks. "I can't believe this happened," he said, his eyes sparkling with excitement. "I never thought I'd ever seen anything like this."

In the weeks that followed, Memphis was abuzz over the session, confident that Big Time music had returned to the city, after an absence of nearly twenty years. Unfortunately, when the album was mixed and submitted to the major record labels, it was turned down by executives who didn't buy Moman's pitch that the Next Big Thing was the Old Things that had breathed life into rock 'n' roll. Undeterred, Moman raised money from Memphis investors to start up a label and release the album as an independent, with PolyGram as the distributor. Each artist received about a quarter-million-dollars, as advance against royalties, but the album never sold enough copies to pay royalties or to recoup the investment.

Moman tried to rebound with a session with Ringo Starr, but it fell apart after the local newspaper printed a column in which the writer made derogatory comments about the ex-Beatle. Despite vocals that people said were the best that Starr had ever delivered, the album never came out, and Moman and Starr ended up suing each other in federal court in Atlanta. Frustrated, Moman returned to Nashville with his wife and son, only to see his marriage fall apart. After about five years in Nashville, he moved on to Georgia, where he built a studio in the rural area where he grew up.

Memphis went into a deep depression, musically speaking, but Nashville didn't seem to notice because it was knee-deep into the Next Big Thing.

◆　▲　◆　▲　◆

As the 1980s drew to an end and the new decade began, it became apparent that the Next Big Thing was Garth Brooks, an Oklahoma transplant whose vision of country music was initially somewhat mysterious to everyone except his co-managers, Pam Lewis and Bob Doyle, and, of course, his mother, Colleen, who had encouraged him from an early age. Within days after Brooks released his debut album, *Garth Brooks*, this author interviewed him for a syndicated radio program called Pulsebeat—Voice of the Heartland. At that point, no one knew what to think of Brooks, least of all his record label. For that interview, one of the singer's first, Brooks was unusually relaxed— more so than most veterans. He talked about each of the songs on his album, explaining why they were important to him, but his eyes didn't really sparkle until he talked about his mother, "one of the most talented women singers I've ever heard in my life."

"She's so happy about the album, more happy than I am," Brooks explained. "She calls me up every now and then, and I can hear that she's been crying when she's heard her boy on the radio. When she got the album, her and dad made the mistake of listening to it on a friend's CD player. So, mom called me and said, 'Well I bought the CD.' I said, 'Really?' She said,

'Yeah—it cost me eight hundred dollars.' I said, 'What do you mean, Mom?' She said, 'Well, you know we don't have a CD player—or we didn't used to have one.' They went out and bought a whole new stereo system for this album, so I was pretty tickled."

So that was the Next Big Thing! The sensitive male country singer, whose non-threatening, mama's-boy looks and souped-up traditional country music stood in stark contrast to the Outlaw years that Johnny and Willie and Waylon had ridden day and night, stopping only long enough to change horses.

"Everybody passed on him," said manager Pam Lewis. "I had people I thought I could count on, and they didn't see it right away. They really saw him as sort of a Clint Black clone...Bob [Doyle] and I were going on a wing and a prayer. One time, Bob looked at me and said, 'You know, what I feel like?' 'What?' 'I feel like I'm Mickey Rooney and you're Judy Garland, and it's like, "Let's do a play."' We were like so stupid that God smiled on us. I'm not saying we were dumb people, but there was a part of us that was so green. It was like, us against the world."

Garth Brooks peaked at Number Thirteen on the Top 200 charts and at Number Two on the country charts, and spawned four hit singles, which, except for one, were written or co-written by Brooks. His second album, *No Fences*, also provided four Number One singles. "Friends in Low Places" and "The Thunder Rolls" generated sales of more than ten million copies—and all that happened before 1990 concluded. From that point on, it was all Garth, sparking sales for all country music artists. The Country Music Association gave him credit for the jump in country music sales that occurred between 1990 and 1992: A leap, in dollar amounts, from $6.6 million to $1.4 billion.

Vince Gill benefited from this unthreatening-male trend in country music, and he ended up a star in his own right. Others, such as Allan Jackson, also benefited. Jackson was doubtful at first, because he was threatening enough in appearance to belong to a previous generation, but when he opened his mouth, with his deep Georgia drawl and his polite "aw shucks" attitude, he countered the fears that anyone might have had based on the way he looked.

Garth Brooks and his band of non-threatening males (if that seems negative, it's not meant to be, only a description of what was happening) seemed indestructible, up until the mid 1990s, when the Next Big Thing blew into Nashville on a cold wind from Canada. Shania Twain went from being the music industry joke—another cutie who would be better off in the kitchen—to becoming the best-selling female country singer of all time. Her arrival coincided with a trend in pop music that would change everything.

The Next Big Thing was a natural extension of the non-threatening male: Women with sex appeal and feminist attitudes, and singers and song-writers that could deliver what female record buyers wanted even more than they wanted a sensitive male—self-respect and a voice that would "tell it like it is" from a woman's perspective. In 1996, for the first time in history, female recording artists in country and pop out-charted their male counterparts. It was a historic year that made a superstar out of Shania Twain, and opened the door for Faith Hill and the Dixie Chicks.

Nashville was turned on its head, but it didn't surrender without a fight. As an industry, it fought the women's movement every step of the way, proclaiming that it was just a passing fad and had nothing to do with *real* country music, which, as everyone in Nashville knew, was a guy thing at its core—always had been, always would be. Well, they were wrong, as they soon learned. Beginning in the mid-1990s, women redefined country music, taking it to new heights, setting new sales records. It is somehow fitting that a mojo woman, Faith Hill, was one of the big three who revolutionized country music, because the women's movement was a rejec-tion of the anti-mojo phase exem-plified by Garth Brooks, and Nashville's musical readjustment required a return to basics. The women's movement in country music was strong through 2003, then started slowing down in 2004 as it approached the end of its ten-year cycle, leaving pundits wondering about the Next Big Thing—or the ultimate nightmare, No Next Big Thing.

The deaths of Johnny Cash and his wife, June Carter Cash, in 2003, left a hole not just in country

Faith Hill at an outdoor concert in Jackson, Mississippi. (James L. Dickerson)

music, but in the fabric that binds the Mojo Triangle, for it was Cash who best captured the spirit of all the divergent elements: Old Natchez, the Natchez Trace, Memphis, the Mississippi Delta, Muscle Shoals, New Orleans, and Nashville, the city that at first welcomed him as a savior and then cast him out as a musical leper.

"I think that when he was right, he was one of the greatest communicators of our time," observed Marty Stuart. "His unique gift was going inside subcultures, seeing the truth, inspiring the subculture with his presence, and then coming back out and merging into the mainstream. Sometimes he made a difference. Sometimes it fell on deaf ears. Waylon had a great line. He said, 'Nashville is rough on the living, but it sure speaks well of the dead.' If you go back through the history of it all, Hank Williams looked like an archangel, but in truth when he died he was cast out of the city. Patsy Cline wasn't exactly the queen of the ball around here—now you would think she was. Where's Nashville been on Johnny's behalf for the past twenty years? There's been no relationship, basically—other than a couple of labels dropping him and not knowing what to do with him. Today, they are trying to set him up as a saint, and I don't think he would want that. He was very proud of being Johnny Cash."

POSTSCRIPT

If you've reached this point of the book, you've been on quite a journey: Back through time to an ancient culture, through floods, earthquakes, epidemics; through slavery, war, and reconstruction; through the Great Depression and nightriders, through the building of a nation, and the creation of a musical culture that is second to none. The inescapable truth is that, while America's popular music has thrived in almost every state, its creation has been confined within the borders of the Mojo Triangle.

It may be that America has given the world all that it can in the way of music. If the story ended here, with the death of Johnny Cash, it would not be a tragedy, for jazz, blues, rock 'n' roll, and country music are an eternal gift that the world can never repay. But, if by chance, a new music is to emerge in America in the future—if the mojo is made to rise again—it is a stone-cold certainty that it will be born out of the magical pyramid anchored by

New Orleans, Memphis, and Nashville. That prediction is not made with a sense of misplaced hubris, but rather with the knowledge that the America that exists outside the Triangle has never created an original genre of music, unless you count hip-hop, and that assertion would be open to spirited debate, not only on historical grounds, but on artistic grounds as well.

There is no mystery attached to the rich legacy of music and literature that has come from the Mojo Triangle: It is a product of the land, a spiritual re-creation of all that has taken place on the land, whether caused by God, bad luck, or man himself. Mojo dwellers are not made of mere flesh; they are of the ancient earth, products of everything that has ever happened on the land. If you cannot understand that one critical point, then you will never understand the music. If New York, or California, or Illinois had undergone the same cultural and historical baptism of fire experienced by the Triangle, then rock 'n' roll, the blues, jazz, and country music would all have different mailing addresses.

There are hundreds of fine musicians and recording artists who did not grow up in the Triangle, but none of them can claim to be the originator of any major genre of music. They are imitators—people who have taken mojo and put their on spin on it. It requires talent to be a great imitator, but it takes genius to be an innovator, and that is the main difference between the Mojo Triangle and other regions of the country.

Marty Stuart was speaking about Mississippi when he said the following, but it would apply to the whole of the Triangle: "I take it that the modern-day soul and spirit of Mississippi is actually a ghost in wandering, looking for a way out. Very few people in the state acknowledge and see its importance, but I see it as a musical citizen. We are absolutely world royalty. God put something real special in that area there—it's immeasurable."

ENDNOTES

Chapter One

Christian Schultz's impressions of Natchez in 1808 can be found in his book *Travels on an Inland Voyage*. Several libraries, including Louisiana State University's, have pages of the book available on line.

Information about early Mississippi River Valley history came from a variety of sources, including Patricia Galloway's *Choctaw Genesis: 1500-1700*; H. B. Cushman's *History of the Choctaw, Chickasaw, and Natchez Indians*; William C. Davis' *A Way Through the Wilderness*; William R. Sanford's *The Natchez Trace: Historic Trail in American History*; the journals of Governor Winthrop Sargent and Governor William Charles Cole Claiborne as published in *The Mississippi Territorial Archives*; and Jim Barnett's "The Natchez Indians," published in the Mississippi Department Archives and History Popular Report.

Information about Indian music came from a variety of sources, including James H. Howard and Victoria Lindsay Levine's *Choctaw Music and Dance*; the quarterly magazine *Nanih Waiya*, published in Philadelphia, Mississippi; various sources in the Choctaw National Archives near Philadelphia, Mississippi, including a paper titled "Religion of the Primitive Choctaw" by Glenn Myers; and Gilbert Chase's *American Music: From the Pilgrims to the Present*.

The lyrics sung in the Choctaw myth about "cannibal" and the ducks came from George E. Lankford's *Native American Legends*. The book discusses a number of myths from the Choctaw, Natchez, Chickasaw, and other tribes.

Information about early Natchez history came from a variety of sources, including Steven Brooke's *The Majesty of Natchez*, Hugh Howard's *Natchez: The Houses and History of the Jewel of the Mississippi*, Noel Polk's *Natchez: Before 1830*, and the *Mississippi Official and Statistical Register (1976-1980)*.

Richard Wright's comment can be found in *Conversations with Richard Wright*, edited by Keneth Kinnamon and Michel Fabre.

Chapter Two

The information about Meriwether Lewis was obtained from many sources, including interviews, books and magazine articles. The comments from James Starrs are from an author's interview, obtained while camping out at the grave site with Starrs and other researchers and media representatives.

Information about yellow fever epidemics came from many years of collecting data from various books, journals, and newspapers, the most useful academic sources being Jo Ann Carrigan's *The Saffron Scourge*, Margaret Humphreys' *Yellow Fever and the South*, John E. Harkins' *Metropolis of the American Nile*, and *Rhodes History of the United States*.

The William Faulkner quote regarding good and evil came from Jean Stein's interview with him, published in the Spring 1965 issue of the *Paris Review*.

Information about the Civil War and Reconstruction came from Annie Harper's *Annie Harper's Journal: A Southern Mother's Legacy*, J. G. Randall and David Donald's *The*

Civil War and Reconstruction, Ralph Newman and E.B. Long's The Civil War (volume II), Ralph Newman and Otto Eisenschiml's The Civil War (volume I), Shelby Foote's The Civil War: Red River to Appomattox, and R. H. Henry's Editors I Have Known.

In addition to his own research, the author is indebted to the authors of two fine books on the Mississippi River flood of 1927: Pete Daniel, author of Deep'n As It Come, and John M. Barry, author of Rising Tide: The Great Mississippi Flood of 1927 and How it Changed America. Fred Chaney's comments about the flood are from his memoir, "A Refugee's Story," located at the Mississippi Department of Archives and History. William Faulkner's comments about Light in August can be found in Faulkner in the University, a collection of class conferences held at the University of Virginia.

Information about the Mississippi Sovereignty Commission and civil rights activity in the Triangle came from numerous sources, including FBI files, Commission records, and interviews. FBI agent Joe Sullivan's comment is from an author interview. The subject is covered in more detail in the author's book, Dixie's Dirty Secret.

Chapter Three

For the section about Jimmie Rodgers, the author is indebted to Mike Paris and Chris Comber's excellent biography Jimmie the Kid: The Life of Jimmie Rodgers, Carrie Rodgers' biography of her husband, Jimmie Rodgers' Life Story, Irwin Stambler and Grelun Landon's Country Music: The Encyclopedia, and Robert K. Krishef's Jimmie Rodgers, a youth-market biography that nonetheless offers a good

overview of the singer's life.

Information about William Faulkner came from a variety of sources, including magazine and newspaper interviews, and books such as Joseph L. Blotner and Frederick L. Gwynn's Faulkner in the University, Elizabeth M. Kerr's Yoknapatawpha: Faulkner's 'Little Postage Stamp' of Native Soil, Joseph Blotner's Faulkner: A Biography, and Robert Coughlan's The Private World of William Faulkner. The William Faulkner quote regarding time came from Jean Stein's interview with him, published in the Spring 1965 issue of the Paris Review.

Information about Tennessee Williams came from newspaper and magazine articles, and two books, the playwright's autobiography, Memoirs, and Gilbert Maxwell's biography Tennessee Williams and Friends.

Marty Stuart's comments are from author interviews.

The Bo Diddley quotations came from George R. White's Bo Diddley: Living Legend.

Belinda Rimes' comments about LeAnn winning the dance contest were given to Larry Holden for Country Weekly magazine.

Information about Tammy Wynette came from her autobiography, Stand By Your Man, and from an author interview.

Information about Faith Hill came from interviews done by the author for a biography he wrote on the singer titled Faith Hill: Piece of My Heart.

Chapter Four

Information about the Winterville Mounds can be found at the Mississippi Department of Archives and History. Some of that information is accessible online.

The B.B. King quotes are from author interviews.

The Jimmy Reed quotes are from Jim O'Neal's interviews, first published in *Living Blues magazine*, and then compiled in his book *The Voice of the Blues*.

All Mose Allison quotes not otherwise attributed are from author interviews.

The Pinetop Perkins information comes from an author interview.

The Bobbie Gentry information comes from an author interview.

The Sam Chatmon quote is from Margaret McKee's and Fred Chisenhall's *Beale Black & Blue*.

The Sunshine Sonny Payne quotes and other information about KFFA are from author interviews.

The Willie Morris excerpt is from his book, *Yazoo*.

William Faulkner's quote about August in Mississippi can be found in *Faulkner in the University*, edited by Frederick L. Gwynn and Joseph L. Blotner. The author is also indebted to *William Faulkner: Essays Speeches and Public Letters*, edited by James B. Meriwether; *The Private World of William Faulkner* by Robert Coughlan; *William Faulkner: A Critical Study* by Irving Howe; *Yoknapatawpha: Faulkner's Little Postage Stamp of Native Soil* by Elizabeth M. Kerr; *The Selected Letters of William Faulkner*, edited by Joseph Blotner.

Anyone interested in comparing Robert Johnson's music to Choctaw music can examine the transcriptions in Woody Mann's *The Complete Robert Johnson* and in James H. Howard and Victoria Lindsay Levine's *Choctaw: Music and Dance*.

William Alexander Percy's memoir is titled *Lanterns on the Levee*; Hodding Carter wrote about his early experiences in Greenville in *Southern Legacy*.

Shelby Foote's comments about the KKK can be found in William C. Carter's *Conversations with Shelby Foote*.

Chapter Five

All quotes from Chips Moman that are not otherwise attributed are from author interviews.

Johnny Shines' comment about Memphis Minnie was made to Paul and Beth Garon in *Woman With Guitar: Memphis Minnie's Blues*.

The information about Lil Hardin Armstrong is distilled from research the author did for his biography of Armstrong, *Just for a Thrill*.

The Bonnie Raitt quote is from an author interview.

All B.B. King quotes are from author interviews; the account of the Michigan concert at which King was approached by a young woman was reported in Jerry Hopkins' *Festival!*

The Scotty Moore quotes are from author interviews, most of which can be found in Moore's autobiography, *That's Alright, Elvis*, which was co-written by the author.

The Rufus Thomas comment was made to the author.

The Carl Perkins quotes are from author interviews.

The Johnny Cash quotes are from author interviews.

The Jack Clement quotes are from author interviews.

The Jerry Lee Lewis quotes are from author interviews.

The Willie Mitchell quotes are from

author interviews.

The John Evans quotes are from author interviews.

The Don Nix quotes are from author interviews.

The Estelle Axton quotes are from author interviews.

The Rita Coolidge quotes are from author interviews.

The Booker T. Jones quotes are from author interviews.

The Steve Cropper quotes are from author interviews.

The Dave Edmunds quotes are from author interviews.

The Jimmie Vaughan quotes are from author interviews.

The John Hampton quotes are from author interviews.

The John Fry quotes are from author interviews.

The Stevie Ray Vaughan quotes are from author interviews.

The Bobby Womack quotes are from author interviews.

The Kim Wilson quotes are from author interviews.

Chapter Six

The quotations from Jelly Roll Morton about the origins of jazz came from Laurence Bergren's *Louis Armstrong: An Extravagent Life*, and Geoffrey C. Ward and Ken Burns' *Jazz: A History of America's Music*.

Louis Armstrong's comments about awakening to find his wife holding a knife to his throat were taken from James Chilton's book *Louis*.

Lil Hardin Armstrong's comments about

the importance of their music was taken from an interview released on an audio CD by Riverside Records. Other information about Lil Armstrong and her relationship with Louis was distilled from research done for the author's biography of Lil Hardin Armstrong, *Just For a Thrill*. Particularly helpful was *Louis Armstrong: In His Own Words*, selected writings edited by Thomas Brothers.

Information about Dr. John came mostly from author interviews, but some background information came from a variety of magazines and newspapers.

All non-attributed quotations from Lisa Angelle came from author interviews, and the author's story published in the February 23, 1986 issue of *Mid-South* magazine.

The Wynton Marsalis comments are from an interview for Ken Burns' *Jazz: A History of America's Music*.

Chapter Seven

Information about George Colbert and early area history can be found in William C. Davis' *A Way Through the Wilderness*, and in publications made available by the U. S. Park Service.

All Jimmy Johnson comments are from an author interview.

All David Hood comments are from an author interview.

All Don Nix comments are from author interviews. His memoir is titled *Road Stories and Recipes*.

Walt Aldridge's comments about Muscle Shoals were made to Dawn Baldwin, who wrote a profile on The Shooters for the March/April 1987 issue of the author's magazine, *Nine-O-One*. T. Graham Brown's comments about his experiences in Muscle Shoals were made to Baldwin for a subsequent issue.

Lacy J. Dalton's comments are from an author interview.

B.B. King's comments about working at WDIA were made to the author. He also provided background information on the radio station. Additional information about WDIA can be found in Bert Ferguson's article in *Memphis: 1948-1958*, a paperback published by Memphis Brooks Museum of Art. It is an excellent source of information about Memphis during that period.

Jerry Wexler's comments can be found in Joe Smith's *Off the Record: An Oral History of Popular Music.*

Peter Guralnick has an excellent chapter on Muscle Shoals music in *Sweet Soul Music.*

Bobby "Blue" Bland's comments are from an author interview.

Tom T. Hall's comments are from an author interview.

Billy Sherrill's comments are from an author interview.

Jack Clement's comments are from an author interview.

Scotty Moore's comments are from author interviews.

Tammy Wynette's comments are from an author interview.

Chapter Eight

Marty Stuart's comments are from author interviews.

Johnny Cash's comments are from author interviews.

Waylon Jennings' comments are from author interviews.

Chips Moman's comments are from author interviews.

Rick Blackburn's comments are from an author interview.

Vince Gill's comments are from an author interview.

Garth Brooks' comments are from an author interview.

Pam Lewis' comments are from an author interview.

Joe Galante's comments are from an author interview.

Sam Phillips' comments are from an author interview.

BIBLIOGRAPHY

Books

Armstrong, Louis. *Louis Armstrong: In His Own Words.* New York: Oxford University Press, 1999.

Barry, John M. *Rising Tide: The Great Mississippi Flood of 1927 and How It Changed America.* New York: Simon & Schuster, 1997.

Bergreen, Laurence. *Louis Armstrong: An Extravagant Life.* New York: Broadway Books, 1997.

Booth, Stanley. *The True Adventures of the Rolling Stones.* New York: Vintage Books, 1985.

Bronson, Fred. *The Billboard Book of Number One Hits.* New York: Billboard, 1985.

Broven, John. *Rhythm & Blues In New Orleans.* Gretna, Louisiana: Pelican Publishing, 1978.

Carrigan, Jo Ann. *The Saffron Scourge: A History of Yellow Fever in Louisiana, 1796-1905.* Lafayette, Louisiana: Center for Louisiana Studies, 1994.

Carter, Hodding. *Southern Legacy.* Baton Rouge: Louisiana State University Press, 1966.

Carter, William C. *Conversations with Shelby Foote.* Jackson, Mississippi: University Press of Mississippi, 1989.

Chase, Gilbert. *America's Music: From the Pilgrims to the Present.* New York: McGraw-Hill, 1955.

Coughlan, Robert. *The Private World of William Faulkner.* New York: Cooper Square Publishers, 1972.

Cushman, H. B. *History of the Choctaw, Chickasaw and Natchez Indians.* Norman, Oklahoma: University of Oklahoma Press, 1999.

Daniel, Pete. *Deep'n As It Come: The 1927 Mississippi River Flood.* New York: Oxford University Press, 1977.

Davis, William C. *A Way Through the Wilderness.* New York: HarperCollins, 1995.

Dickerson, James L. *Just For a Thrill: Lil Hardin Armstrong, First Lady of Jazz.* New York: Cooper Square Press, 2002.

Dickerson, James L. *Colonel Tom Parker: The Curious Life of Elvis Presley's Eccentric Manager.* New York: Cooper Square Press, 2001.

Dickerson, James L. *Faith Hill: Piece of My Heart.* New York: St. Martin's Griffin, 2001.

Eisenschiml, Otto and Ralph Newman. *The Civil War (Volume I).* New York: Grosset & Dunlap, 1956.

Escott, Colin. *Tattooed on Their Tongues.* New York: Schirmer Books, 1996.

Faulkner, William. Edited by Joseph Blotner. *Uncollected Stories of William Faulkner.* New York: Random House, 1931-1979.

Foote, Shelby. *The Civil War: Red River to Appomattox.* New York: Vintage Books, 1974.

Galloway, Patricia. *Choctaw Genesis: 1500-1700.* Lincoln, Nebraska: University of Nebraska Press,

Garon, Paul and Beth. *Woman With Guitar: Memphis Minnie's Blues.* New York: Da Capo Press, 1992.

Gruber, J. Richard. *Memphis: 1948-1958.* Memphis, Tennessee: Memphis Brooks Museum of Art, 1986.

Guralnick, Peter. *Sweet Soul Music: Rhythm and Blues and the Southern Dream of*

Freedom. New York: Harper & Row, 1986.

Guralnick, Peter. *Last Train to Memphis: The Rise of Elvis Presley.* Boston: Little Brown, 1994.

Gwynn, Frederick and Joseph L. Blotner. *Faulkner in the University.* New York: Vintage Books, 1959.

Handy, W.C. *Father of the Blues.* New York: Da Capo, 1941.

Harper, Annie. *Annie Harper's Journal: A Southern Mother's Legacy.* Denton, Mississippi: Flower Mound Writing Company, 1983.

Harkins, John E. *Metropolis of the American Nile.* Oxford, Mississippi: Guild Bindery Press, 1991.

Henry, R. H. *Editors I Have Known Since the Civil War.* Jackson, Mississippi: Clarion-Ledger, 1922.

Hoffman, Frederick J. and Olga W. Vickery. *William Faulkner: Three Decades of Criticism.* New York: Harcourt, Brace & World, 1960.

Hopkins, Jerry, and Jim Marshall, Baron Wolman. *Festival: The Book of American Music Celebrations.* New York: Collier Books, 1970.

Howard, Hugh. *Natchez: The Houses and History of the Jewel of the Mississippi.* New York: Rizzoli, 2003.

Howard, James H. *Choctaw Music and Dance.* Norman, Oklahoma: University of Oklahoma Press, 1990.

Howe, Irving. *William Faulkner: A Critical Study.* New York: Vintage Books, 1951.

Humphreys, Margaret. *Yellow Fever and the South.* Baltimore: Johns Hopkins University Press, 1992.

Kerr, Elizabeth M. *Yoknapatawpha: Faulkner's Little Postage Stamp of Native Soil.* New York: Fordham University Press, 1969.

Krishef, Robert. K. *Jimmie Rodgers.* Minneapolis, Minn. Lerner Publications, 1978.

Lankford, George E. *Native American Legends: Tales from the Natchez, Caddo, Biloxi, Chickasaw, and Other Nations.* Little Rock, Arkansas: August House, 1987.

Lee, George W. *Beale Street: Where the Blues Began.* New York: Robert O. Ballou, 1934.

Mann, Woody. *The Complete Robert Johnson.* New York: Oak Publications, 1991.

Meriwether, James B. *William Faulkner: Essays, Speeches and Public Letters.* New York: Random House, 1965.

Moore, Scotty. *That's Alright, Elvis: The Untold Story of Elvis's First Guitarist and Manager, Scotty Moore.* New York: Schirmer Books, 1997.

Morris, Willie. *My Mississippi.* Jackson, Mississippi: University Press of Mississippi, 2000.

Willie Morris. *Yazoo: Integration in a Deep-Southern Town.* New York: Harper's Magazine Press, 1971.

Maxwell, Gilbert. *Tennessee Williams and Friends: An Informal Biography.* Cleveland, Ohio: World Publishing, 1965.

Muirhead, Bert. *The Record Producers File: A Directory of Rock Album Producers 1962-1984.* London: Blandford Press, 1984.

McKee, Margaret, and Fred Chisenhall. *Beale, Black & Blue.* Baton Rouge: Louisiana State University Press, 1981.

Newman, Ralph and E. B. Long. *The Civil War (volume II).* New York: Grosset & Dunlap, 1956.

Nix, Don. *Road Stories and Recipes.* New York: Schirmer Books, 1997.

O'Neal, Jim, and Amy Van Singel. *The Voice of the Blues: Classic Interviews from Living*

Blues Magazine. New York: Routledge, 2002.

Paris, Mike and Chris Comber. *Jimmie the Kid: The Life of Jimmie Rodgers.* New York: Da Capo, 1977.

Penick, Jr., James Lal. *The New Madrid Earthquakes.* Columbia, Missouri: University of Missouri Press, 1981.

Percy, William Alexander. *Lanterns on the Levee.* Baton Rouge, 1941.

Polk, Noel. *Natchez Before 1830.* Jackson, Mississippi: University Press of Mississippi, 1989.

Randall, J. G. and David Donald. *The Civil War and Reconstruction.* Lexington, Massachusetts: D. C. Heath and Company, 1969.

Rodgers, Mrs. Jimmie. *Jimmie Rodgers' Life Story.* Nashville: Ernest Tubb Publications, 1953.

Rowland, Dunbar. *The Official and Statistical Register of the State of Mississippi (1924-1928).* New York: J. J. Little and Ives Company, (no copyright date).

Rowland, Dunbar. *The Mississippi Territorial Archives (1798-1803).* Nashville: Press of Brandon, 1905.

Sanford, William R. *The Natchez Trace: Historic Trail in American History.* Berkeley Heights, New Jersey: Enslow Publishers, 2001.

Schultz, Christian. *Travels on an Inland Voyage.* New York: Isaac Riley, 1810.

Sims, Patsy. *The Klan.* New York: Stein and Day, 1978.

Smith, Joe. *Off the Record: An Oral History of Popular Music.* New York: Warner Books, 1988.

Sokolow, Fred, transcribed by *Jimmy Reed: Master Bluesman.* New York: Hal Leonard, 1996.

Stambler, Irwin, and Grelun Landon. *Country Music: The Encyclopedia.* New York: St. Martin's Griffin, 1969-1997.

Stokes, W. Royal. *The Jazz Scene: An Informal History from New Orleans to 1990* New York: Oxford University Press, 1991.

Trynka, Paul. *Portrait of the Blues.* New York: Da Capo Press, 1997.

Welty, Eudora. *A Curtain of Green.* New York: Harcourt, Brace & World, 1936-1941.

Author unknown. *One Writer's Beginnings.* Cambridge, Mass.: Harvard University Press, 1983.

Whitburn, Joel. *Billboard: Top 1000 Singles (1955-1992).* New York: Hal Leonard Publishing, 1993.

White, George R. *Bo Diddley: Living Legend.* United Kingdom: Castle Communications, 1995.

Williams, Tennessee. *Memoirs.* New York: Bantam Books, 1975.

Wright, Richard. *Native Son.* New York: HarperCollins, 1940 and 1991.

Newspapers and Magazines

Baldwin, Dawn. "Delivering the Goods." *Nine-O-One,* Jan./Feb. 1987.

Baldwin, Dawn "The Shooters: Muscle Shoals Group Guns for Hip Sound." *Nine-O-One,* March/April 1987.

Clemons, Walter. "Meeting Miss Welty." *The New York Times,* April 12, 1970.

Dickerson, James L. "Lacy J. Dalton." *Nine-O-One,* Nov./Dec. 1986.

Dickerson, James L. "Chips Moman: Coming Home." *Mid-South Magazine,* May 5, 1985.

Dickerson, James L. "Marty Stuart & Friends/Nashville's New Hopes." *Mid-South Magazine,* February 23, 1986.

Dickerson, James L. "Waylon At Ease." *Playbook (The Commercial Appeal),* July 19, 1985.

Gerome, John. "Nashville's Lost History." *Associated Press,* March 7, 2004.

Palmer, Robert. "Sam Phillips." *Memphis Magazine,* December 1978.

Pareles, Jon. "Blues Guitarist John Lee Hooker Dies at 83." *The New York Times,* June 22, 2001.

Pugh, Ronnie. "Country Music is Here to Stay." *Journal of Country Music,* Volume: 19-01.

Riley, Michael. "Tales From the Crypt." *Time,* September 14, 1992.

Stein, Jean. "William Faulkner: An Interview." *The Paris Review,* Spring 1956.

Thomas, William. "Willie Morris, Home Again." *Mid-South Magazine,* March 2, 1980.

Unknown author. "Wynton Marsalis Interview. *Academy of Achievement,* January 8, 1991.

Author unknown. "Record Producer Sam Phillips Dead at 80." *Associated Press,* July 31, 2003.

1   The word "mojo" is often used inter-changeably with voodoo; more specifically, mojo is the vehicle through which voodoo is delivered. A mojo can be used for both evil and beneficial purposes; the earliest folk blues songs made frequent references to mojo, such as this line from a classic anonymous blues song: "Going down to Louisiana, get me a mojo hand / Gonna show all you womens how to love a good man." (In this instance, a mojo hand is the bag that voodoo doctors put together to deliver a curse or blessing.)

INDEX

#1 Record (album), 153
827 Thomas Street Band, 146–47, 148, 150, 152, 221–22, 226
3614 Jackson Highway (album), 200

Acuff, Roy, 73
Adena Indians, 5
African Americans
enslavement of, 3–4, 8–9, 12, 17, 78
interaction with Indians, 10–12, 118
in Memphis, 34–35
as professional musicians, 40, 57–61, 87–88, 117–21, 158–69
yodeling style of, 54
Aldridge, Walt, 204–5
Alexander, Jason Allen, 179
Allen, "Hoss," 217
Allison, Mose, 108, 110–12
Allman, Duane, 197
Always On My Mind (album), 222
A&M Records, 138
"American Bandstand" (TV show), 151
American Recording Studio, 138, 143, 146–52, 193, 226
Ames, Boogaloo, 100
Angelle, Lisa, 170–72, *172*
Animals, the, 78, 99
Ann-Margret, 216
"Any Day Now," 151
ARC records, 90
Ardent Recording Studio, 152–56
"Arlene," 224–25
Armstrong, Lil Hardin, 56, 122, 164–66, 172, 219
Armstrong, Louis, 56, 100, 108, 160–66, *163,* 172, 179
Arnold, Eddy, 211, 219
Atkins, Chet, 110, 135, 212–13, 215
Atlanta, Georgia, 221
Atlantic Records, 141, 148, 193–94, 199–200
Austin, Patti, 77
Autry, Gene, 188
"Away out of the Mountain," 55
Axton, Estelle, 139–46, *140*
Axton, Packy, 142

"Baby, Please Don't Go," 95
"Baby, What You Want Me to Do," 99
Baby One More Time (album), 178
"Back in the Saddle Again," 188
Baker, Gary, 204
"Bald Head," 167
Ballard, Glen, 76–77
banjar, 9
banjos and banjo players, 53, 55, 87
Barnett, Ross, 72
Barry, John M., 42
Bartholomew, Dave, 167
Bass, Lance, 77
Bate, Dr. Humphrey, 209
"Battle of Manassas," 40
"Bay Area Blues," 204
"Be Bop Baby," 189

"Beale Street Blues, The," 120, 172
Beatles, the, 78
Beaucoup of Blues (album), 216
Beavis, Fred, 197
Beckett, Barry, 197–98, *199,* 205
Beckwith, Byron De La, 47–48
"Behave Yourself," 143
Bell, William, 142–43
"Ben Dewberry's Final Run," 55
Berry, Chuck, 189, 194
"Bette Davis Eyes," 138
"Big Boss Man," 99, 108
Big Star, 153
"Big Train (from Memphis)", 226
"Bill Bailey," 53
Bill Black Combo, the, 136, 147
Billings, Barry, 205
Black, Bill, 129–30, *130,* 136, 150, 212–13, 220
"Black Pearl," 151
Black Swan Troubadours, 165
Blackburn, Rick, 204–5, 223, 224–25
"Black-eyed Blues," 202
Blakey, Art, 174
Bland, Bobby "Blue," 122, 205, 206, 218–19
Blind Tom, 40
Blood in the Fields (album), 174
"Blue," 80–81
"Blue Bayou," 134
Blue Light Til' Dawn (album), 76
Blue Moon Boys, the, 212
"Blue Moon of Kentucky," 131, 212
"Blue Suede Shoes," 132–33
"Blue Yodel," 55, 56
"Blue Yodel #9," 56
"Blueberry Hill," 167, 168
blues, 76, 218–19
"Chicago-style," 78
Delta, 87, 89–101, 111–12, 113–14
Handy's publications, 119–21
New Orleans, 159–60, 162
Blues in the Night (film), 58
Blues Jumpers, the, 167
"bluesman," 60
Bo Diddley (Ellas Bates), 77–79, 189
Bolden, Charles "Buddy," 158
Bonnie and Delaney, 138
Bono, Sonny, 199, *199*
boogie-woogie, 90, 93, 99
Booker T. and the MGs, 143–44, 191
"Boom, Boom," 113
Booth, Stanley, 200, 201
"Born a Woman," 147
Bourbon Street (album), 173
Box Tops, the, 148–49
Bradbury, John, 27–28
Bradley, Owen, 219
Bradley's Barn, 219
"Bright Lights, Big City," 99
"Bring Back Love," 171
"Bring It on Home," 93
Brooks, Garth, 223, 227–28
Brooks, Jared, 28
brothels and prostitution

in Memphis, 117, 123–24
in Natchez, 18
in New Orleans, 157–58, 159, 161
Brothers' Keeper (album), 176
Brown, James, 202
Brown, Larry, 79
Brown, T. Graham, 205, 223
"Brown Sugar," 201, 202
Bryan, Eliza, 28
Bryant, Don, 137
Bryant, Roy, 47
Buffett, Jimmy, 77
Bullet Records, 127
"Bumble Bee," 124
Burnett, Chester Arthur. *See* Howlin' Wolf
Burns, Rebecca, 186
Burton, James, 189
"Bye Bye Blackbird," 43

Cain, Jonathan, 204
"Call Me," 202
"Candida," 151
Canned Heat, 202
Cannon, Ace, 226
Cantrell, Bill, 136
Capitol Records, 106–7, 197–98
Carnes, Kim, 202
Carpenter, Mary Chapin, 223
Carter, Clarence, 197
Carter, Hodding, 103–4
Carter, Hodding, III, 104
Carter, Philip, 104
Carter Sisters & Mother Maybelle, The, 211
Cash, Johnny, 74, 132, *133,* 133–34, 214–15, 219, 222, 224, 225, 226, 229–30
Cash, June Carter, 226, 229–30
Cash, Rosanne, 223
"Cause I Love You," 141
CBS Records, 174, 204–5, 223, 224–25. *See also* Columbia Records
"Chain of Fools," 148
Chaney, Fred, 42
Chaney, James, 48, 70
Charles, Ray, 194, 212
Chase, Gilbert, 12
Chatmon, Bo, 88
Chatmon, Ezell, 88
Chatmon, Lonnie, 88
Chatmon, Sam, 88–89, 123
"Cheatin' On Me," 58
Cher, 198–200, *199*
Cherokee Indians, 10, 198
Chess Records, 93, 95
Chet Atkins' Gallopin' Guitar (album), 212
Chicago, Illinois
blues in, 78, 95, 113, 122, 123
jazz in, 163–66
recording in, 93, 99
Chicago Coliseum, 165
"Chickasaw County Child," 108
Chickasaw Indians, 5, 9, 10, 14, 16, 23, 115, 181–82
earthquake knowledge of, 27, 28–29
Muddy Waters and, 94

removal of, 16, 36, 66
Chickasaw Syncopators, 57–58
Chilton, Alex, 148, 153, *153*
Chisenhall, Fred, 89
Choctaw Indians, 3, 5, 9–16, 157
earthquake knowledge of, 27
Muddy Waters and, 94
music of, 11–12, 20, 78, 90, 118
removal of, 16, 36, 66
Stuart and, 71–72
yodeling of, 54
cholera, 34
Chrisman, Gene, 147
church music, 67, 69, 72, 74, 78, 96
civil rights movement, 47–49, 70–71, 103–4
Civil War, 36–40, 65, 116, 157–58, 207
Claiborne, William C. C., 15–16
Clapton, Eric, 91, 112
clarinetists, 172–73
Clark, Petula, 149
Clarksdale, Mississippi, 64, 96, 99, 108, 112–14, 117–19
Class of '55 (album), 226
Claunch, Quinton, 136
claves, 11
Clay, Otis, 138
Clement, Jack, 134–35, 214–15, *215*
Clemons, Walter, 63
Cline, Patsy, 80, 211, 230
Cocker, Joe, 202
Cogbill, Tommy, 147
Colbert, George, 181–82, 185
Cole, Howard, 72
Collins, Tom, 170–71
Columbia Records, 177, 214–15. *See also* CBS Records
Columbus, Mississippi, 64
Comber, Chris, 53
Communique (album), 202
Conley, Arthur, 197
Connick, Harry, Jr., 176–77
Cooke, Sam, 113
Coolidge, Rita, 138, *138*
Copycat (film), 177
"Cornet Chop Suey," 165
cornets, 184
Costello, Elvis, 112
"Cotton Candy," 173
Cotton Club (New York), 58
Couch, Tommy, 191, 205–6
country music, 72, 76, 109–10, 176
early, 54–57, 60, 88, 91
Muscle Shoals recordings, 204–5
Nashville recordings, 170–72, 209–16, 219–30
Outlaw Movement in, 222–23, 228
women's movement in, 228–29
country-western music, 188, 211
Craig, Edwin W., 208–9
"Crawling Kingsnake Blues," 113
"Crazy," 211
"Crazy Arms," 135
Creek Indians, 10
Creole Jazz Band, 164
Creoles, 77–78, 157, 159
"Cried All Night," 218

"Crime of Passion," 225
Cropper, Steve, 142, 143–44, 199
Crudup, Arthur "Big Boy," 130
Crump, E. H., 119–20
"Cry, Cry, Cry," 218
"Cry Like a Baby," 149
"Cryin'", 134
"Crying in My Sleep," 202
Cunningham, Bill, 148
Cuoghi, Joe, 136
Curb Records, 80
Cushman, Horatio Bardwell, *History of the Choctaw, Chickasaw and Natchez Indians,* 11

Dalton, Lacy J., 204
Davis, Chalmers, 205
Davis, Jefferson, 37
Davis, Jimmie, 170
Davis, Miles, 173
Decatur, Alabama, 186
Decca Records, 58
Dee, Kiki, 76
Dees, Rick, 146
Del Rays, the, 190–92, 195
Delta Democrat-Times (newspaper), 104
Delta Sweetie, The (album), 108
Diamond, Neil, 149
Dickinson, Jim, 153, *153,* 154, 200, 201
Diddley, Bo. *See* Bo Diddley
Dillon, Mike, 205
Dire Straits, 202
"Disco Duck," 146
"Dixie," 40
Dixie Chicks, the, 229
Dixie Echoes, the, 72
Dixieland groups, 158, 164, 172–73
Dixon, Willie, 76, 111
"Do Right Woman, Do Right Man," 148, 199
Dodds, Baby, 163
Dodds, Johnny, 163
Domino, Antoine "Fats," 166–68, *168*
Domino, Fats, 77
"Don't Know Much," 176
"Don't Start Me Talking," 93
"Don't Throw Your Love on Me So Strong," 100
"Don't Turn Your Back on Me," 137
Dorsey, Jimmy, 173
Dorsey, Tommy, 173
Double Trouble, 154
Douglas, Ellen, 79
Dowd, Tom, *199*
"Down South Jukin'", 202
Doyle, Bob, 227–28
Dr. Hook, 202
Dr. John, 168–69, *169*
DreamWorks Records, 171
drums, 40
Native American, 11, 19, 78, 87
Duke Records, 218
Dukes of Dixieland, the, 172
Dundy, Elaine, *Elvis and Gladys,* 68
Dunn, Donald "Duck," 142, 143, 145, 202
"Dust My Broom," 93

Dylan, Bob, 199
Dynamic Clarence Carter, The (album), 197
Dynamics, the, 191

earthquakes, 27–31, 115
Edmunds, Dave, 154, 226
Ellington, Duke, 166
EMI-America, 171
Emmons, Bobby, 147
Entertainment Weekly, 178
Epic Records, 216
Ertegun, Ahmet, 200
Esquires, the, 191, 192
Estes, Sleepy John, 123
Etta James Rocks the House (album), 218
Evans, John, 148
Evers, Medgar, 47–48, 63, 70
"Every Night About This Time," 167
"Everybody Wants to Go to Heaven," 204
"Eyes of a New York Woman," 149
"Eyesight to the Blind," 111

Fabulous Johnny Cash, The (album), 73
Fabulous Thunderbirds, the, 154–55
fairs, 67–68, 70, 72–73
Fame Studio, 148, 190–01, 196–98, 204–5
Family Groove (album), 176
Family Style (album), 155
"Fancy," 108
Farragut, David G., 158
"Fat Man, The," 167
Faulkner, William, 36, 39, 61–62, *62,* 64, 65–67, 114, 125, 174
Faulkner, William Clark, 65–66
Ferguson, Bert, 186–87
Fernwood Records, 215
fiddles and fiddling, 12, 19–20, 40, 78, 88
Fisk University (Nashville), 57, 58, 208
Flatt, Lester, 71, 73–74, 211
Flatt and Scruggs band, 71, 73–74, 211
Flatt and Scruggs Greatest Hits (album), 73
floods, 40–43, 84
Florence, Alabama, 181–85, 188–90
flutes, 40
Native American, 11, 19
"Fly Me to the Moon," 149, 150
Flyin' Shoes (album), 222
Fogerty, John, 226
Fontana, D. J., 150
Foote, Shelby, 103, 104–5, 122
"For Dancers Only," 58
Forrest, Nathan Bedford, 44–45, 46, 59, 65
Foster, George "Pops," 162
Fountain, Pete, 172–73
Franklin, Aretha, 121, 148, 196–97, 199, 202, 218
Freeman, Morgan, 85–87, 100, 113
French culture, in Natchez, 3–4, 10
French horns, 12
"Friends in Low Places," 228
Fritts, Donnie, 192
Fry, John, 152–56

Galante, Joe, 224

Garfunkel, Art, 202
Garon, Paul and Beth, 124
Garth Brooks (album), 227–28
"Gee Whiz," 141
"Gentle on My Mind," 151
Gentry, Bobbie, 106–8, *107*
Gentrys, the, 147, 149
Getz, Stan, 111
Ghosts of Mississippi (film), 48
Gibson, John, 104
Gill, Vince, 223, 224, 228
Gilley, Mickey, 76
Glendora, Mississippi, 91
Goin' to Memphis (album), 149
Gold, Andrew, 171
Gooch, Jacqueline, 100
Goodman, Andrew, 48, 70
Goodman, Benny, 58, 166, 173
"Goodnight Sweet Dreams," 149
Gordon, Kelly, 106, 107
Gorgas, William, 35
gospel music, 72
Granberry, Jackie, 80
Grand Ole Opry (Nashville), 73
"Grand Ole Opry" (radio show), 209–11
Grand Tour, The (album), 176
Grant, Ulysses S., 38, 208
"Great Balls of Fire," 135
Greatest Horn (album), 173
Green, Al, 137–39
Green (album), 154
"Green Onions," 143
Greene, Marlin, 192, 193
Greenville, Mississippi, 84–87, 100–101
  flooding in, 41–43
  Native American cultures around, 83
  writers from, 102–6
Greenville Delta Star (newspaper), 103–4
Greenwood, Mississippi, 47, 90, 100, 106–8
Greeves, R. B., 200
Gris-Gris (album), 169
Grisham, John, 79
"Groovy Kind of Love, A," 151
Ground Zero (club), 113
Guitar That Changed the World, The (album), 216
guitars and guitarists, 18, 53–57, 60–61, 68–74, 77–79, 87, 88, 97–101, 123–24, 168, 183–84, 189–90
"Gut Bucket Blues," 165

Haggard, Merle, 219
Hall, Rick, 190, 191–94, 196–98, 199, 204–5
Hall, Tom T., 220–21
Hampton, John, 155
Handy, Charles B., 183–84
Handy, W. C., 87, 117–21, *121*, 122, 159–60, 162, 172, 182–84
Handy, William Wise, 183
hangings, 46
Hannah, Barry, 79
Hardin, Lil. *See* Armstrong, Lil Hardin
harmonica players, 99
Harper, Annie, 37–38, 46
"Harper Valley P.T.A.", 220

Harrah, Bill, 108
Harris, Ray, 136
Hawkins, Roger, 190, 193, 197–98, *199,* 205
Hay, George D., 208–9, 210, 213
Hayes, Isaac, 144, 145, 146, 152
Hazelhurst, Mississippi, 89
"Healing Chant," 176
"Heartbreak Hotel," 213
"Heebie Jeebies," 165
Heidt, Horace, 173
Helena, Arkansas, 91–94
Hemingway, Ernest, 174
Henderson, Fletcher, 165
Hendrix, Jimi, 218
Henley, Beth, 79
Henry, R. H., 45–46
Henson, Jim, 105–6
He's the King (album), 173
"Hey! Bo Diddley," 78
"Hey Jude," 197
Hi Records, 136–39, 152–53
Hideaway Club (New Orleans), 167
"High Time We Went," 202
Highway 61 Blues (album), 100
Highway Diner (album), 204
Highwayman (album), 222
Hill, Faith, 74–76, 80, 229, *229*
"hillbilly" music, 55–56, 210–11
Hinton, Eddie, 197
Hirt, Al, 173–74
"Hold on, I'm Coming," 144
"Hold on to What You've Got," 149
"Hold What You've Got," 192
Hollandale, Mississippi, 88–89
"Holly Holy," 149
"Honey Bee," 95
"Honky Tonk Woman," 203
Hood, David, 195–98, 199, *199,* 205, 206
"Hooked on a Feeling," 149
Hooker, John Lee, 113
Hope Floats (film), 177
Hopewell culture, 5, 9
Horton, Walter, 126
Hot Fives, the, 165
Hot Number (album), 154
House, Son, 89, 121
"How Far Is Heaven," 69
Howlin' Wolf (C.A. Burnett), 59–61, *60,* 126, 127, 132, 188
Hughes, Jimmy, 192
Hunter, Jimmy Ray, 190
"Hurts So Good," 202
Husky, Ferlin, 190

"I Believe I'll Dust My Broom," 90
"I Can't Stand the Rain," 138, 139
"I Die a Little Each Day," 138
"I Fall to Pieces," 176, 211
"I Got a Thing About You, Babe," 152
"I Never Loved a Man," 148
"I Saw the Light," 171
"I Walk the Line," 133
"I Want to Walk You Home," 167

"I Was the One," 212
"I Washed My Face in the Morning Dew," 221
"I Wear Your Love," 171–72
"If I'm a Fool for Loving You," 147
Ike and Tina Turner Revue, 138
"Iko Iko," 169
"I'll Take You There," 146
"I'm a Man," 78
"I'm Counting on You," 212–13
"I'm in the Mood," 113
"I'm Still in Love With You," 138
"I'm Talking About You," 124
In Step (album), 155
"In the Ghetto," 151
In the Zone (album), 179
Indian Removal Law of 1830, 16
Indianola, Mississippi, 95–97, 100, 128
Ingram, James, 76–77
interracial musical groups, 143–44
Intimacy Calling (album), 174
"It Had to Be You," 177
"It Wasn't God Who Made Honky Tonk Angels," 211
"It's Only Make Believe," 109
"I've Been Loving You Too Long (To Stop Now)", 144
"I've Got a Woman," 212
Ivy, Quin, 192–94

Jack Laine's Ragtime Band, 158
Jackson, Al, 137, 143, 202
Jackson, Allan, 228
Jackson, Andrew, 10, 116, 181, 207–8
Jackson, Michael, 77
Jackson, Millie, 202
Jackson, Mississippi, 62, 74–75
Evers murder in, 47–48
Jackson, Wayne, 142, 145
Jackson Clarion-Ledger (newspaper), 46
Jagger, Mick, 200–201, *201*
James, Elmore, 93
James, Etta, 218
Japanese American internment camps, 104
"Java," 169, 173
jazz, 76, 110–12, 158–66, 172–75
Jazz Messenger, 174
Jefferson, Thomas, 14, 16, 21–22, 25
Notes on Virginia, 9
"Jelly Roll Blues," 159
Jennings, Waylon, 215, 220, 222–23, 224, 230
Jimmie Lunceford Orchestra, 58–59
Jimmie Rodgers Entertainers, 55
Jive Records, 178
"Joe Turner Blues," 120
John, Elton, 76
"John R.," 217
"Johnny B. Goode," 189
Johnny Wright and the Harmony Girls, 211
Johnson, Dexter, 189–90
Johnson, Jimmy, 188–94, 195, 197–98, *199,* 200, 201, 205, 206
Johnson, Paul, 72
Johnson, Robert, *89,* 89–91, 121
Johnson, Sly, 138
Johnson, Terry, 142

Johnson Brothers, 188
Johnston, Arch, 30–31
Joiner, James, 190
Jones, Booker T., 143
Jones, Brian, 201
Jones, George, 71, 224
Jones, Quincy, 76
Jordan, Louis, 100
Jubilee Singers, 57, 208
Judds, the, 223, 226
juke joints, 60, 62, 91
jukeboxes, 136
"Just Between You and Me," 110
"Just Enough to Keep Me Hangin' On," 199
Justis, Bill, 136, 214–15

Karnofsky, Morris, 161
"Keep On Dancing," 147
Keisker, Marion, 125–26, 128–29, 134
"Kentucky Rain," 151
Kentwood, Louisiana, 177
Keppard, Freddie, 159–60, 161
KFFA (Helena radio station), 92–94, 95–96, 108
Kid Ory's Band, 162
"Kind Hearted Woman," 90
King, Albert, 100, 144, 202–4
King, B. B., *95,* 95–97, 126–28, *127,* 187, 188
King, John, 153
King, Martin Luther, Jr., 145–46
"King Biscuit Time" (radio show), 92–93, 95–96, 97, 98
"King Porter Stomp," 159
Kiva, 155
Knoxville, Tennessee, 208
Kosciusko, Mississippi, 79
Kristofferson, Kris, 222
Ku Klux Klan, 44–49, 99, 102, 105, 182
KWEM (West Memphis radio station), 127

La Salle, René-Robert de, 3
"Lady Soul," 202
Lady's Not for Sale, The (album), 138
Laine, Jack "Papa," 158
"Land of 1,000 Dances," 197
"Land of a Thousand Dances," 149
"Last Night," 142
"Lay Lady Lay," 199
Le Moyne, Jean Baptiste, 157
Lee, Brenda, 190
Lee, Robert E., 40
Leech, Mike, 147
Leland, Mississippi, 96, 97–98, 100, 105
"Let's Stay Together," 137, 139
"Letter, The," 148–49
Lewis, Furry, 100, *100,* 123
Lewis, Jerry Lee, 76, 132, 134–35, *135,* 214, 215, 226
Lewis, Meriwether, 21–26, 115, 146
Lewis, Pam, 227–28
"Like a Road Leading Home," 204
Lincoln, Abraham, 40
Lindstrom, Carl, 117–18
Little Milton, 101
"Little Queen of Spades," 90
Lockwood, Robert Junior, 93

Lomax, Alan, 94
London, Julie, 191
"Lonely Blue Boy," 109
"Look What You Done for Me," 138
"Lorena," 40
"Lost That Lovin' Feelin'," 149
Louis, Joe Hill, 126
Louisiana Purchase, 16, 157
Louisiana Territory, 21–22
Louisville, Kentucky, 33
Louvin Brothers, the, 211
"L-O-V-E," 138
Love, Andrew, 145
"Love—It's the Pitts," 171
Lovejoy (album), 204
Loveless, Patty, 223
"Loves Me Like a Rock," 202
Lowe, Junior, 193, 195, 197
loyalists, 4, 37
Lunceford, Jimmie, 57–59
Lynn, Loretta, 219
Lynyrd Skynyrd, 202

Mack, Bill, 80
Madison, James, 15, 22, 23
Maffei, Vigello, 119
Make a Joyous Noise (album), 216
Mala Records, 148–49
Malaco Records, 205–6
Mann, Herbie, 149
Manning, Terry, 153, 154
Marable, Fate, 162
"Mardi Gras in New Orleans," 168
"Margie," 58
Mar-Keys, the, 142, 202
Marsalis, Branford, 174
Marsalis, Delfeo, 174
Marsalis, Ellis, 174, 177
Marsalis, Wynton, 174–75
Martin, Max, 178
Mattea, Kathy, 171, 223
"Maybellene," 194
MCA Records, 176
McCoy, Joe, 124
McDaniel, Gussie, 77–78
McDowell, Mississippi Fred, 205
McEntire, Reba, 108, 219
McGraw, Tim, 170
McKee, Margaret, 89
McKinley, Ray, 173
McMurry, Lillian, 93
McVoy, Carl, 136
Me and Mr. Johnson (album), 91
"Mean Woman Blues," 134
Meigs, R. J., 181
Memphis, Tennessee, 57–58, 70, 115–56, 208
Beale Street, 117, 119, 122, 123–24, 124, 126
blues musicians in, 122–24, 219
Civil War in, 37, 38
history of, 115–17
Lewis in, 100
Presley in, 68–69
race riots in, 46

recording in, 100, 125–56, 186–88, 212, 222, 225–27
yellow fever in, 34–35, 116
Memphis Belle (film), 177
"Memphis Blues, The," 87, 120
Memphis Horns, the, 145, 154, 194, 196
Memphis Minnie (Lizzie Douglas), 122–24
Memphis Recording Service, 125–26, 128–31, 186
Memphis Slim (Peter Chatman), 123
Memphis Underground (album), 149
Mercury Records, 109
Meridian, Mississippi, 52–54
"Mickey Mouse Club, The" (TV show), 178
"Midnight Mover," 150
Milam, J. W., 47
Miller, Glenn, 58
minstrel shows, 53, 55, 158
Mississippi Delta, 83–114
ethnic diversity of, 84
flooding in, 41–43
literary tradition, 102–6
location of, 83
musical development of, 87–88
"Mississippi Delta," 106, 108
"Mississippi Delta Blues," 56
Mississippi Sheiks, the, 88
Mississippi State Penitentiary, 112–13
Mississippi Valley Indian cultures, 5–8
"Mister Crump," 119–20
Mitchell, Willie, 136–39
Mobile, Alabama, 33
Moman, Lincoln "Chips," 140–41, 142, 143, 146–52, 197, 199, 221–23, 222, 226–27
"Money, Honey," 212
"Monkey That Became President, The," 221
Monroe, Bill, 131, 211
Monroe, Charlie, 211
Moore, Carney, 70
Moore, Max, 92
Moore, Scotty, 128–32, 130, 136, 150, 212–13, 215–16, 216, 220, 225–26
More Sweet Soul (album), 197
Morissette, Alanis, 77
Morris, Willie, 84–85, 101–2
Morton, Ferdinand "Jelly Roll," 158–60
Mose Allison Sings (album), 111
"Mother Was a Lady," 55
Motown Records, 100
"Mr. Pitiful," 144
"Mr. Sandman," 212
Muddy Waters (McKinley Morganfield), 78, 94–95
Muscle Shoals, Alabama, 148, 171, 181–206, 216
Muscle Shoals Rhythm Section, 198
Muscle Shoals Sound, 198–206
Music City Recorders, 216
"Muskrat Ramble," 172
"Mustang Sally," 197
"My Blue Heaven," 58
"My Heart," 165
"My Heart Will Always Lead Me Back to You," 165
"My Kind of Carryin' On," 128
"Mystery Train," 225
Mystics, the, 195

Nance, Jack, 109
Nash, Francis, 207
Nashville, Tennessee, 207–30
Civil War in, 37, 38, 207
history of, 207–8
nightclubs in, 218
recording in, 110, 170–72, 206, 212–16, 221–30
rhythm & blues in, 217–19
Natchez, Mississippi
antebellum, 17–20
Civil War in, 37–38
European settlement of, 1–3, 10–20
Native American culture around, 1, 3–17
New Madrid earthquake and, 30
as state capital, 16
yellow fever in, 34
Natchez Indians, 3–9, 157
music of, 7–8, 78
yodeling of, 54
Natchez Trace, 24–26, 51–81, 181, 207
described, 51–52
Natchez Under the Hill, 18–20
"National Barn Dance" (radio program), 208–9
Native American cultures, 1–17, 26–27. *See also specific groups*
African American music influenced by, 78
in Mississippi Delta, 83
syncopation in, 57
yodeling in, 54
"Natural Woman," 148
Neely, John, 23–24, 25
Nelson, Rick, 226
Nelson, Ricky, 189
Nelson, Tracy, 216
Nelson, Walter, 168
Nelson, Willie, 220, 222, 224
Neville, Art and Aaron, 169
Neville Brothers, 176
New Albany, Mississippi, 65
New Madrid earthquake, 27–28, 30–31, 115
New Orleans, Louisiana, 157–79
Civil War in, 37, 38
French Quarter, 157, 173–74, 177
history of, 157–58
Storyville, 159, 161
yellow fever in, 31–33, 35
Night Moves (album), 202
Night Train to Nashville (album), 217
nightriders, 44–49, 84
Nix, Don, 142, 145, 202–4
No Fences (album), 228
Nordan, Lewis, 79
Norwood, Brandy, 77
N'Sync, 77

"Ode to Billie Joe," 106–8
Oertle, Ernie, 90
"Oh, Pretty Woman," 134
Okeh Records, 165
Ol' Waylon (album), 222
"Old Dogs, Children and Watermelon Wine," 220
"Old Man River," 3
"Old Time Rock and Roll," 202
"Old Zip Coon," 19

Oldham, Spooner, 191–94, 197
Oliver, Joe "King," 159–60, 162, 163–65
Olympia Orchestra, 159
One More River to Cross (album), 202
O'Neal, Jim, 98, 99
"Ooby Dooby," 134
Oops!...I Did It Again (album), 178
Orbison, Roy, 132, 134, 190, 215, 226
"Organ Grinder's Swing," 58
Ory, Kid, 172
Oslin, K. T., 223
"Over You," 176
Overton, John, 116
Owens, Buck, 219
Owens, Jesse, 103–4
Oxford, Mississippi, 38, 65–66, 191, 195

Paine, Silas, 185
Palmer, Robert, 185
"Papa, Won't You Take Me to Town With You," 108
"Parchman Farm," 108, 111–12
Paris, Mike, 53
Parker, Colonel Tom, 150
Parker, Daisy, 162–63
Parton, Dolly, 216, 219
Patrick Gilmore Band, 117
Patton, Charley (or Charlie), 60, 88, 89, 121
Paul Revere and the Raiders, 149
Payne, "Sunshine" Sonny, 92, 94
Peebles, Ann, 137, 138, 139
Penn, Dan, 148, 191, 197, 199
"People," 202
Pepper, John, 186–87
Percy, Alexander William, 42–43
Percy, Charles, 84, 102
Percy, Walker, 105
Percy, William Alexander, 102–3, 104, 105
Perkins, Carl, 132–33, *133,* 215, 226
Perkins, Pinetop, 93, 114
Philadelphia, Mississippi, 48, 70–73
Phillips, Dewey, 187–88
Phillips, Sam, 125–35, *126,* 136, 184–88, 212, 213, 214–16, 226
Phillips Country Ramblers, 108
pianists, 93, 114, 159–60, 166–69
Pickering, Timothy, 13
Pickett, Wilson, 149–50, 197
Pierce, Webb, 211
"Pink Pedal Pushers," 133
Pittman, Bob, 79
Platinum and Gold (album), 202
"Please Don't Tell Me," 199
Plotkin, Chuck, 204
Pollard, Jesse, 42
PolyGram, 227
pop music, 176–79, 198–202
Popular Tunes, 136
Porter, David, 144
Portman, Natalie, 177–78
Posey, Sandy, 147
Powerful Stuff (album), 154
Presley, Elvis, 67–69, 74–75, 108, 129–32, *130, 131,* 150–51, 152, 167–68, 179, 188, 212–14, 216

Presley, Lisa Marie, 150
Presley, Vernon and Gladys, 67–69
Prestige Records, 111
"Pretty Thing," 78
Price, Cecil, 48
Pride, Charley, 108, 109–10, 215
Private Dancer (album), 139
Professor Longhair, 166–67, 168
Pryor, Richard, 144
Pugh, William Hollis, 69
Pushmataha, Choctaw chief, 14
Putnam, Norbert, 190, 192

Quinivy Studio, 192–94, 195

racial violence, 44–49, 145–46
Radio City (album), 153
ragtime, 60, 88, 158
Rainey, Lawrence, 48
Raitt, Bonnie, 112, 124
"Ramblin' on My Mind," 91
"Raunchy," 136
RCA Records, 110, 133, 173, 211, 212–13, 224
Reconstruction, 38–39, 182
Ku Klux Klan and, 44–46
Redding, Otis, 71, 144, *144,* 197, 199
Reed, Jimmy, 97–100, 108, 189
Reed, Jimmy, Jr., 100
Reed, Mama, 99
Reiner, Rob, 48, 177
Reliance Brass Band, 158
R.E.M., 154
Replacements, the, 154
Resolution of Romance, The (album), 174
"Respect," 144, 148
"Respect Yourself," 202
rhythm & blues, 72, 93, 130, 137–39, 167, 169, 176,
205–6, 217–19
Rhythm Country & Blues (album), 176
Richards, James, 191
Richards, Keith, 200–201
Riley, Billy Lee, 152
Riley, Jeannie C., 220
Rimes, Belinda, 80
Rimes, LeAnn, 80–81
"Ring My Bell," 205
Roadrunners, the, 191
"Rock and Roll Waltz," 139
"Rock House," 134
rock 'n' roll, 72, 75, 78, 109, 131, 142, 167–68, 189–90,
195
"Rocket 88," 131
Rodgers, Aaron, 52–53
Rodgers, Carrie Williamson, 54–55
Rodgers, Jimmie, 52–57, *55,* 81, 88, 91, 108, 109, 111,
209, 211, 221
Rodgers, Lottie Mae, 53
Rogers, Will, 56
"Rolling Stone," 95
Rolling Stone magazine, 178, 179
Rolling Stones, the, 78, 99, 200–202
Ronstadt, Linda, 176
Roseland Ballroom (New York), 165

Ross, Doctor, 126
Royal Recording, 136–38
Royal Spades, the, 142
Russell, Gilbert, 21
Russell, Leon, 204
Ruthless (play), 177
Ryman Auditorium (Nashville), 209

Sailin' (album), 202
"Sally Let Your Hands Hang Down," 69
Sam and Dave, 144
Sam Phillips' Recording Service, 215–16
Sargent, Winthrop, 12–16
Satellite Productions, 140–42
Scanlan, T. M., 45–46
Schuller, Gunther, 58
Schultz, Christian, 1–3, 9
Schwerner, Michael, 48, 70
Scruggs, Earl, 71, 73–74, 211
Seger, Bob, 202
segregation, 86
"Sesame Street" (TV show), 106
"Seventh Son, The," 111
"Sex Jag," 171
"Shame, Shame, Shame," 99
sharecroppers, 84
"Sharing the Night Together," 202
Shawnee Indians, 207
"She Even Woke Me up to Say Goodbye," 135
Sheffield, Alabama, 181, 188, 195, 197–202
Sheppard, T. G., 204
Sherman, William Tecumseh, 52
Sherrill, Billy, 190, 216
Shines, Johnny, 124
Sholes, Steve, 212
Shooters, the, 205
"Silver Bell," 212
Simon, George, 58
Simon, Paul, 202
Sims, Zoot, 111
"Singing Brakeman, The" (film), 56
Singleton, Shelby, 215
"(Sittin' On) The Dock of the Bay," 144, 199
"Sitting on Top of the World," 88–89
"Skid-Dat-De-Dat," 165
slapback echo, 213
slavery
Civil War and, 37
Indian ownership of, 8–9
Memphis market, 116
Muscle Shoals area, 182
Natchez area, 3–4, 9, 10, 11–12, 17, 18–20, 46
New Orleans market, 157
Sledge, Percy, 191, 192–94, 196
"Sleep, Baby, Sleep," 55
"Slip Away," 197, 205
smallpox, 34
Smith, Connie, 73
Smith, Fred, 153
Smith, Joe, 194
Smith, Rex, 72
Smith, Smoochie, 142
"Smokie," 136

Smythe, Danny, 148
"Snakes Crawl at Night," 110
snare drums, 11
Snow, Hank, 56, 211, 212, 219
"So Doggone Lonesome," 133
"Soldier's Sweetheart, The," 55
"Somebody Done Somebody Wrong Song," 222
"Son of a Preacher Man," 149
Sonny and Cher, 169
Soto, Hernando de, 3
Soul Gestures in Southern Blue (album), 174
"Soul Man," 144
"Soul Serenade," 137
sovereignty commissions, 47–48
Spanish culture
in Memphis, 115
in Natchez, 4
Spar Music, 190
Spears, Britney, 177–79, 178
Spector, Phil, 169
Speir, H. C., 88, 90
Spencer Davis Group, the, 99
Springfield, Dusty, 149
"St. James Infirmary," 218
"St. Louis Blues, The," 120, 122
Stackhouse, Houston, 93
Stafford, Jim, 108
Stafford, Tom, 190
"Stage Show" (TV show), 213
Staple Singers, the, 146, 202
Star, Mississippi, 75
"Star Search" (TV show), 80
Starlite Wranglers, the, 128, 129
Starr, Kay, 139
Starr, Ringo, 216, 227
Starrs, James, 25–26
Stax Records, 100, 142–46, 148, 152, 193, 196, 202
Stax Studios, 152
"Steal Away," 192
"Steamboat Bill," 53
Stein, Jean, 61
Steinberg, Lewis, 137, 143
Stewart, Jim, 139–46, 148, 203
Stewart, Rod, 202
Sticky Fingers (album), 201–2
"Stop and Listen," 88
"Stormy Monday Blues," 218
Strait, George, 77, 223
Street Survivors (album), 202
Strokers, the, 191
"Struttin' With Some Barbecue," 165
Stuart, Marty, 70–74, 74, 223, 224–26, 230, 231
Sullivan, Joe, 48
Sun Records, 126–35, 187, 214, 215, 226
Supremes, the, 100
"Suspicious Minds," 151
Swaggart, Jimmy, 76
Swan, Jimmy, 72
"Sweet and Easy to Love," 134
"Sweet Caroline," 149
"Sweet Home Chicago," 90
sweet soul, 144–46, 206
Sweethearts of the Rodeo, 223

swing, 58, 165
syncopation, 57

"T for Texas," 55
"Take Me to the River," 138
"Take Time to Know Her," 196
Talley, Gary, 148
Taylor, Eddie, 99
Taylor, Mick, 201
Taylor, Zachary, 21, 115
"Tell It Like It Is," 176
Tex, Joe, 149, 192
That Nigger's Crazy (comedy album), 144
"That's All Right," 111
"That's All Right, Mama," 130, 131
"Theme from Shaft," 144, 146
"There You Go," 133
"These Arms of Mine," 144
"Think," 202
Third, The (album), 153
Thomas, B. J., 149, 221–22
Thomas, Carla, 141, 141–42
Thomas, Irma, 169
Thomas, James "Son," 100, 100
Thomas, Joe, 59
Thomas, Rufus, 126, 127, 132, 141, 141–42, 144, 187, 188, 191
Thomas, William, 101
Thompson, Uncle Jimmy, 209
"Three O'Clock Blues," 127
"Thunder Rolls, The," 228
Till, Emmett, 47
Timberlake, Justin, 77, 121, 178
Tippo, Mississippi, 110
"Tired of Being Alone," 137
To Sir with Love (film), 151
"Tonight's the Night," 202
"Too Weak to Fight," 205
Toussaint, Allen, 169
"Tragedy," 215
Travis, Randy, 223
Trumpet Records, 93
trumpets and trumpet players, 40, 164–66
"Try a Little Tenderness," 71
Tucker, Tanya, 171, 219
Tupelo, Mississippi, 57, 67–68, 69
"Turkey in the Straw," 19–20
"Turn on Your Love Light," 218
Turner, Ike, 113–14, 126, 130, 139, 218
Turner, Tina, 114, 138–39, 139
Tuscumbia, Alabama, 182
Twain, Shania, 228–29
Twisted (album), 171–72
Twitty, Conway, 92, 108–9

Van Shelton, Ricky, 225
Van Zandt, Townes, 222
Vaughan, Jimmie, 154, 155
Vaughan, Stevie Ray, 154–55
Vee-Jay Records, 99
Ventures, the, 189
Verrett, Harrison, 167
Vicksburg, Mississippi, 43

Civil War in, 37, 38
yellow fever in, 34
Victor Records, 55–56
Vincson, Walter, 88
Vollers, Maryanne, *Ghosts of Mississippi,* 48

Walden, Phil, 197
"Walk Away," 137
"Walkin' to New Orleans," 167
"Walking the Dog," 144
Walls, Mississippi, 123
Ward, Anita, 205
"Warm and Tender Love," 196
Warm Your Heart (album), 176
Warwick, Dionne, 149
Washington, George, 12
Waters, Muddy. *See* Muddy Waters
Wayne, Thomas, 215
WDIA (Memphis radio station), 127, 186–87, 217
Weiss, Donna, 138
Welk, Lawrence, 173
Wells, Kitty, 69, 211
Welty, Eudora, 61–64, *64,* 174
West Point, Mississippi, 59
Wexler, Jerry, 141, 148, 149, 193–94, 196, 197, *199,* 199–200
"What Made Milwaukee Famous," 135
"When a Man Loves a Woman," 193
When Harry Met Sally (film), 177
"When Johnny Comes Marching Home Again," 40
"When the Saint Comes Marching In," 172
"When You're in Love With a Beautiful Woman," 202
"Whipped Cream," 169
White, Bukka (Booker T. Washington), 111–12, 123, 126
White, George R., 78–79
White, Ted, 196
Who, the, 112
WHOC (Philadelphia radio station), 72
"Whole Lot of Shakin' Going On," 135
Wilcox, Ed, 59
"Wild Horses," 201
"Wildwood Flower," 135
Williams, Hank, 109, 211, 221, 230
Williams, Hank, Jr., 170
Williams, Tennessee, 61–62, 64–65, *65,* 101, 174
Williamson, Sonny Boy, 91–94, 98, 101, 111, 127, 188
Wills, Bob, 188
Wilson, Cassandra, 76
Wilson, Kim, 154
Wilson, Mary, 100
Winchester, James, 115
Winchester, Jesse, 115
Winchester, Marcus B., 115–16
Wine, Toni, 151–52
Winfrey, Oprah, 79–80
Winterville Mounds, 83
WLAC (Nashville radio station), 186, 217–18
WLAY (Muscle Shoals radio station), 186
"Wolverine Blues, The," 159
Womack, Bobby, 149–50
Wood, Bobby, 147
Works Progress Administration (W.P.A.), 63, 67
WREC (Memphis radio station), 125–26, 186–88

Wright, Johnny, 211
Wright, Richard, *Native Son,* 20
writers, 61–67, 79–81, 101–6, 114
WROX (Clarksdale radio station), 114
WSIX (Nashville radio station), 211
WSM (Nashville radio station), 208–10, 212, 217
Wynette, Tammy, 69–70, 76, 219, 220, *220*
Wynn, Ron, 217
Wynonna, 171

Yardbirds, the, 99
Yazoo City, Mississippi, 101
"Year that Clayton Delaney Died, The," 220
Yearwood, Trisha, 171, 176
yellow fever, 31–36, 116
Yellow Moon (album), 176
yodeling, 54, 81, 109
"You Are My Sunshine," 136, 170
"You Don't Have to Do," 99
"You Don't Miss Your Water," 142–43
"You Ought to be with Me," 138
Young, Faron, 170
Young, Kyle, 217
Young, Reggie, 136, 147
"Your True Love," 133

ZZ Top, 153–54, 206